THE WAR ON THE WEST

THE WAR ON THE WEST

ALSO BY
DOUGLAS MURRAY

The Strange Death of Europe: Immigration, Identity, Islam
The Madness of Crowds: Gender, Race, and Identity

THE
WAR
ON THE
WEST

DOUGLAS MURRAY

HarperCollins*Publishers*

HarperCollins*Publishers*
1 London Bridge Street
London SE1 9GF

www.harpercollins.co.uk

HarperCollins*Publishers*
1st Floor, Watermarque Building, Ringsend Road
Dublin 4, Ireland

First published by HarperCollins*Publishers* 2022

1 3 5 7 9 10 8 6 4 2

A catalogue record of this book is
available from the British Library

HB ISBN 978-0-00-849249-6
PB ISBN 978-0-00-849279-3

Printed and bound in the UK using 100% renewable
electricity at CPI Group (UK) Ltd

MIX
Paper from
responsible sources
FSC
www.fsc.org   **FSC™ C007454**

This book is produced from independently certified FSC™ paper
to ensure responsible forest management.

For more information visit: www.harpercollins.co.uk/green

For my godchildren

CONTENTS

Introduction 1

CHAPTER 1 **RACE** 13

INTERLUDE: CHINA *65*

CHAPTER 2 **HISTORY** 83

INTERLUDE: REPARATIONS *135*

CHAPTER 3 **RELIGION** 153

INTERLUDE: GRATITUDE *203*

CHAPTER 4 **CULTURE** 213

Conclusion 255
Acknowledgments 275
Notes 277
Index 295

THE WAR ON THE WEST

INTRODUCTION

In recent years it has become clear that there is a war going on: a war on the West. This is not like earlier wars, where armies clash and victors are declared. It is a cultural war, and it is being waged remorselessly against all the roots of the Western tradition and against everything good that the Western tradition has produced.

At first, this was hard to discern. Many of us sensed that something was wrong. We wondered why one-sided arguments kept being made and why unfair claims kept being leveled. But we did not realize the full scale of what was being attempted. Not least because even the language of ideas was corrupted. Words no longer meant what they had until recently meant.

People began to talk of "equality," but they did not seem to care about equal rights. They talked of "anti-racism," but they sounded deeply racist. They spoke of "justice," but they seemed to mean "revenge."

It is only in recent years, when the fruits of this movement have come into plain sight, that its scale has become clear. There is an assault going on against everything to do with the Western world—its past, present, and future. Part of that process is that we have become locked in a cycle of unending punishment. With no serious effort at (or even consideration for) its alleviation.

In the last decade, I grappled my own way toward understanding this. In 2017, with *The Strange Death of Europe*, I addressed one aspect of it, which was the changes brought about in the West by mass migration. It had seemed to me in the years when I covered the immigration question that something deeper was going on. As I stood on the shores of the Greek and Italian islands, watching the boats come in and mingling in the migrant camps that sprang up in major cities, I saw up close the consequences of the developing world moving into the developed world. I never blamed any migrant for wanting to make that journey. I had been to many of the countries from which the migrants were fleeing. Whether the migrants were fleeing war or (as in the majority of cases) economic deprivation, they were doing something that was very understandable. What I had a problem with was why the Europeans were allowing this to happen and why they were expected to abolish themselves in order to survive. People talked of Europe's having a historic debt that legitimized this movement. But even those who argued this failed to address where the limit to this movement was.

Would there ever be a moment when this Western "debt" would be repaid? Because it seemed that every year the debt was not being paid down but was increasing.

I also began to notice that the same story was playing out across every country that counted as Western. In each of them, the justifications given for allowing this movement of people were the same, despite their very different geographical positions. The United States has for years had its own migration challenge, principally at its southern border. As I traveled throughout America, I heard the same arguments there as I heard back home in Britain and in Europe. A similar type of politician and other public figures kept explaining to the American people why their borders should be lax or entirely porous. As in Europe, there were powerful individuals and entities claiming that the only countries that were civilized were those that let the world in. It was the same in Canada. And it was the same on the other side of the world in Australia. Everywhere, societies that counted as "Western" (that is, European countries or countries descended from European civilization) experienced the same pattern of arguments. Nowhere that wasn't Western got any such treatment.

Only the Western countries, spread across three continents, were told constantly that in order to have any legitimacy at all—to be even considered decent—they should swiftly and fundamentally alter their demographic makeup. The vision of the twenty-first century appeared to be that China would be allowed to remain China, the various countries of the Far and Middle East and Africa should be allowed—indeed expected—to remain as they were, or even return to something they may have once been. But the countries identifiable as the countries of "The West" were expected to become something else or lose all legitimacy. Of course, countries and states have the right to change. Over time a certain amount of change is inevitable. But there seemed something loaded in what was going on: something unbalanced and off-kilter. The arguments were being made not out of love for the countries in question but out of a barely disguised loathing for them. In the eyes of many people, not least within their own populations, these countries appeared to have done something wrong. Something for which they must atone. The West was the problem. The dissolving of the West was a solution.

There were other signs that something was amiss. In 2019, I tackled some of these in *The Madness of Crowds*. I addressed the challenge raised by "identity politics"—specifically the attempt to break down Western societies along lines of sex, sexuality, and race. After the twentieth century, national identity had become a shameful form of belonging, and all these other forms of belonging suddenly appeared in its place. Now people were being told to consider themselves as members of other specific groupings. They were gay or straight, men or women, black or white. These forms of belonging were also loaded to lean in an anti-Western direction. Gays were celebrated so long as they were "queer" and wanted to pull down all existing institutions. Gays who just wanted to get on with life or actually liked the Western world were sidelined. Likewise, so long as feminists were attacking "male structures," Western capitalism, and much more, they were useful.

Feminists who didn't toe that line or thought they were comparatively well off in the West were treated as sellouts at best, enemies at worst.

The discourse on race grew even worse. Racial minorities who had integrated well in the West, contributed to the West, and were even admiring of the West were increasingly treated as though they were race traitors. As though another allegiance were expected of them. Radicals who wanted to tear everything down were venerated. Black Americans and others who wanted to celebrate the West and add to it were talked to and about as though they were apostates. Increasingly, they were the ones called all the worst names. Love of the society they were in was treated as a point against them.

At the same time, it had become unacceptable to talk about any other society in a remotely similar way. In spite of all the unimaginable abuses perpetrated in our own time by the Communist Party of China, almost nobody speaks of China with an iota of the rage and disgust poured out daily against the West from inside the West. Western consumers still buy their clothes cheap from China. There is no widespread attempt at a boycott. "Made in China" is not a badge of shame. Terrible things go on in that country right now, and still it is treated as normal. Authors who refuse to allow their books to be translated into Hebrew are thrilled to see them appear in China. While Chic-fil-A gets more heat for making its sandwiches at home than Nike does for making its sneakers in Chinese sweatshops.

Because in the developed West some different standard applies. With regard to women's rights and sexual-minority rights, and, of course, in particular when it came to the issue of racism, everything was presented as though it had never been worse at the point at which it had never been better. Nobody could deny the scourge of racism—a scourge that is to be found in some form throughout recorded history. In-group–out-group trends are exceptionally strong in our species. We are not as developed as we might like to imagine we are. Yet, in recent decades, the situation in Western countries in regard to racial equality has been better than ever. Our societies have made an effort to get "beyond race," led by the example of some remarkable men and women of every racial background, but most notably by some extraordinary black Americans. It was not inevitable that Western societies would develop, or even aspire to, the tradition of racial tolerance that we have.

It was not inevitable that we would end up living in societies that justly regard racism as among the most abhorrent sins. It happened because many brave men and women made the case, fought for that situation, and claimed their rights.

In recent years, it has come to sound as though that fight never happened. As though it was a mirage. In recent years, I have come to think of racial issues in the West as being like a pendulum that has swung past the point of correction and into overcorrection. As though if the pendulum stays in a slight overcorrection for long enough, then equality can be more firmly established. By now, it is clear that however well intentioned such a belief may have been, it was wildly misguided. Race is now an issue in all Western countries in a way it has not been for decades. In the place of color blindness, we have been pushed into racial ultra-awareness. A deeply warped picture has now been painted.

Like all societies in history, all Western nations have racism in their histories. But that is not the only history of our countries. Racism is not the sole lens through which our societies can be understood, and yet it is increasingly the only lens used. Everything in the past is seen as racist, and so everything in the past is tainted.

Though, once again, only in the Western past, thanks to the radical racial lenses that have been laid over everything. Terrible racism exists at present across Africa, expressed by black Africans against other black Africans. The Middle East and the Indian subcontinent are rife with racism. Travel anywhere in the Middle East—even to the "progressive" Gulf States—and you will see a modern caste system at work. There are the "higher class" racial groups who run these societies and benefit from them. And then there are the unprotected foreign workers flown in to work for them as an imported labor class. These people are looked down upon, mistreated, and even disposed of as though their lives were worthless. And in the world's second most populated country, as anyone who has traveled through India will know, a caste system remains in vivid and appalling operation. This still goes all the way to regarding certain groups of people as "untouchable" for no reason but an accident of birth. It is a sickening system of prejudice, and it is very much alive.

Yet we hear very little about this. Instead, the world gets only a daily report on how the countries in the world that by any measure have the least racism, and where racism is most abhorred, are the homes of racism. This warped claim even has a final extension, which is that if other countries do have any racism, it must be because the West exported the vice to them. As though the non-Western world is always made up of Edenic innocents.

Here again, it is clear that some unfair ledger has been created. A ledger in which the West is treated by one set of standards and the rest of the world by another. A ledger in which it seems that the West can do no right and the rest of the world can do no wrong. Or do wrong only because we in the West made them do it.

These are just some of the symptoms that can be discerned in our time. Symptoms that I have tried to take one by one in recent years. But the more I have considered them and the further across our world that I have traveled, the clearer it has become that this era is defined by one thing above all—a civilizational shift that has been underway throughout our lifetimes. A shift that has been rocking the deep underpinnings of our societies because it is a war on everything in those societies.

A war on everything that has marked our societies out as unusual— even remarkable. A war on everything that the people who live in the West had, until very recently, taken for granted. If this war is to prove unsuccessful, then it will need to be exposed and pushed back against.

The War on the West is a book about what happens when one side in a cold war—the side of democracy, reason, rights, and universal principles—prematurely surrenders. Too often, we frame this fight all wrong. We allow it to be called temporary or on the fringe or merely dismiss it as a culture war. We misinterpret the aims of the participants or downplay the role it will have in the lives of future generations. Yet the stakes here are as high as any fight in the twentieth century, with many of the same principles involved—even with many of the same bad actors.

We have gone from appreciating and weighing up what is good about Western culture to saying that every part of it must be dismantled.

It is now over thirty years since the Reverend Jesse Jackson led a crowd of protestors at Stanford University with the chant "Hey hey, ho ho, Western Civ has got to go." Back then, Rev. Jackson and his followers were protesting against Stanford University's introductory program "Western Culture." They proposed that there was something wrong with teaching the Western canon and the Western tradition. But it was what happened next that was so striking. The university swiftly gave in, replacing the study of "Western culture" with the study of many cultures. What happened at Stanford in 1987 was a sign of everything to come.

In the decades that followed, nearly all of academia in the Western world followed Stanford's lead. The history of Western thought, art, philosophy, and culture became an ever less communicable subject. Indeed, it became something of an embarrassment: the product of a bunch of "dead white males," to use just one of the charming monikers that entered the language.

Since then, every effort to keep alive, let alone revive, the teaching of Western civilization has met with sustained hostility, ridicule, and even violence. Academics who have sought to study Western nations in a neutral light have been prevented from doing their work and subjected to intimidation and defamation, including from colleagues. In Australia, the Ramsay Centre for Western Civilisation, whose board is chaired by former prime minister John Howard, has tried to find universities to partner with so that students can study Western civilization. They have had great trouble finding any universities willing to work with them. And that tells us something about the speed of this great shift. Just a couple of decades ago, a course in the history of Western civilization was commonplace. Today it is so disreputable that you can't pay universities to do it.

In 1969, the BBC ran Sir Kenneth Clark's extraordinary thirteen-part documentary series *Civilisation*. It aimed to give a unified history of Western civilization, and it did so, informing the understanding of millions of viewers around the world. Almost fifty years later, in 2018, the BBC tried to follow this up. *Civilisations* (with an emphasis on the *s*) was a hodgepodge creation of three different historians, trying desperately to make sure that they didn't sound as if they were saying the West was better than anywhere else and giving a sort of world history that made nothing very clear.

In a few short decades, the Western tradition has moved from being celebrated to being embarrassing and anachronistic and, finally, to being something shameful. It turned from a story meant to inspire people and nurture them in their lives into a story meant to shame people. And it wasn't just the term "Western" that critics objected to. It was everything connected with it. Even "civilization" itself. As one of the gurus of modern racist "anti-racism," Ibram X. Kendi, put it, "'Civilization' itself is often a polite euphemism for cultural racism."[1]

Of course, some swing of the pendulum is inevitable and may even be desirable. There certainly have been times in the past when the history of the West has been taught as though it is a story of unabashed good. Historical criticism and rethinking are never a bad idea. However, the hunt for visible, tangible problems shouldn't become a hunt for invisible, intangible problems. Especially not if they are carried out by dishonest people with the most extreme answers. If we allow malicious critics to misrepresent and hijack our past, then the future they plan off the back of this will not be harmonious. It will be hell.

Over the course of the book, I'm going to be exploring two key ideas. The first is that critics of Western civilization do provide alternatives. They venerate every culture so long as it is not Western. For instance, all native thought and cultural expression are to be celebrated, just so long as that native culture is not Western. This is the comparison they want us to make, so we will make it.

Two major problems come from celebrating all non-Western cultures. The first is that non-Western countries are able to get away with contemporary crimes as monstrous as anything that has happened in the Western past. A habit that some foreign powers encourage. After all, if the West is so preoccupied with denigrating itself, what time could it find to look at the rest of the world? But the other major problem is that it leads to a form of parochial internationalism, where Westerners mistakenly presume that aspects of the Western inheritance are common aspirations across the rest of the globe.

From Australia to Canada and America and throughout Europe, a new generation has imbibed the idea that aspects of the Western tradition (such as "human rights") are a historical and global norm that have been rolled out everywhere. In time, it has come to seem that the Western tradition that evolved these norms has uniquely failed to live up to them and that non-Western "Indigenous" cultures are (among much else) purer and more enlightened than Western culture can ever be. These are not fringe views; nor are they new. They stretch back to the eighteenth century, at least. Today they permeate the work of best-selling authors such as Naomi Klein and Noam Chomsky. These views are taught in universities and schools across the Western world. And their results can be seen in almost every major cultural and political institution. They crop up in the most surprising places.

For instance, the "National Trust" in Britain is meant to exist to keep open many of the country's most beautiful and expensive country houses. The Trust's 5.6 million members tend to enjoy wandering around a stately mansion and then having a spot of afternoon tea. But in recent years, the Trust has decided it has another job: to educate its visitors about the horrors of the past. And not just connections to empire and the slave trade, homophobia, and the crimes of primogeniture. It has recently chosen to push the idea that the English countryside itself is racist and is (as the Trust's program director calls it) a "Green Unpleasant Land."

I select that one example, but you can select almost any area of life and find that it has been similarly denounced. Everything from art, mathematics, and music to gardening, sport, and food has been put through the same spin cycle. There are many curiosities in all this. Not the least of them is that while the West is assaulted for everything it has done wrong, it now gets no credit for having got anything right. In fact, these things—including the development of individual rights, religious liberty, and pluralism—are held against it.

This leads us to a second, deeper puzzle. Why open everything in the West to assault?

The culture that gave the world lifesaving advances in science, medicine, and a free market that has raised billions of people around the world out of poverty and offered the greatest flowering of thought anywhere in the world is interrogated through a lens of the deepest hostility and simplicity. The culture that produced Michelangelo, Leonardo, Bernini, and Bach is portrayed as if it has nothing relevant to say. New generations are taught this ignorant view of history. They are offered a story of the West's failings without spending anything like a corresponding time on its glories.

Every schoolchild now knows about slavery. How many can describe without irony, cringing, or caveat the great gifts that the Western tradition has given to the world?

All aspects of the Western tradition now suffer the same attack. The Judeo-Christian tradition that formed a cornerstone of the Western tradition finds itself under particular assault and denigration. But so does the tradition of secularism and the Enlightenment, which produced a flourishing in politics, sciences, and the arts. And this has consequences. A new generation does not appear to understand even the most basic principles of free thought and free expression. Indeed, these are themselves portrayed as products of European Enlightenment and attacked by people who don't understand how or why the West came to the settlements that it did over religion. Nor how the prioritizing of the scientific method allowed people around the world untold improvements in their lives. Instead, these inheritances are criticized as examples of Western arrogance, elitism, and undeserved superiority. As a result, everything connected with the Western tradition is being jettisoned. At education colleges in America, aspiring teachers have been given training seminars where they are taught that even the term "diversity of opinion" is "white supremacist bullshit."[2]

This is not a history of the West and does not aim to be. Such a work would have to be many times this length. Nor do I wish to shut down the considerable debate that is going on at the moment. I enjoy that debate and think it helpful. But to date, it has been riotously one-sided. As we will see, it has involved politicians, academics, historians, and activists getting away with saying things that are not simply incorrect or injudicious but flat-out false. They have got away with it for far too long.

There are many facets to this war on the West. It is carried out across the media and airwaves, throughout the education system, from as early as preschool. It is rife within the wider culture, where all major cultural institutions are either coming under pressure or actually volunteering to distance themselves from their own past. And it now exists at the very top of the American government, where one of the first acts of the new administration was to issue an executive order calling for "equity" and the dismantling of what it called "systemic racism."[3] We appear to be in the process of killing the goose that has laid some very golden eggs.

CHAPTER 1

RACE

There is an obvious, observable truth about people in the West. Historically the citizens of Europe and their offspring societies in the
Americas and Australasia have been white. Not absolutely everybody
has been. But the majority have. The definition is tautological—white
means mostly having ancestors from Europe. Just as the majority of
people in Africa have been black and the majority of people in the
Indian subcontinent have been brown. If for some reason you wished
to level an assault on everything to do with Africa, you might well
at some point decide to target people for being black. If you wanted
to delegitimize everything about Indians, you might at some stage
decide to attack its people for the color of their skin. Both would be
inhumane and would today be easily identified as such. But in the
war on the West, white people are one of the first subjects of attack.
A fact that has been steadily normalized and made into the only acceptable form of racism in the societies in which it happens.

To delegitimize the West, it appears to be necessary first to demonize the people who still make up the racial majority in the West.
It is necessary to demonize white people.

Sometimes the results of this play out in front of everybody's eyes.
In August 2021, the results of the US census that had been carried out

the previous year were released. One of the headline facts was that the number of white people in America had declined. On his *Tonight Show*, Jimmy Fallon mentioned this in his lead monologue. "The results of the 2020 census just came out," he told his studio audience and viewers at home. "And for the first time in American history, the number of white people went down."[1] In response to this, the studio audience whooped and cheered uproariously. For them, it was not just funny news, but good news. Not that the percentage of whites went down but that the actual number of white people alive went down. And though this might come as a surprise to some people, for many of us, this ugly movement had been growing for years.

In February 2016, I was in a large hall in London speaking as a "second" alongside John Allen, the American four-star General and former Commander of NATO forces in Afghanistan. We were taking part in a debate over what to do with the Islamist group ISIS. In addition to rampaging across the Middle East, the group had already carried out attacks in Europe. Foremost on all of our minds that night were the multiple suicide bombings and Kalashnikov attacks that had taken place across Paris a short while earlier, taking the lives of 130 people. Although ISIS bombers had not yet hit the United Kingdom, I used my speech to warn the audience that if ISIS weren't stopped, then some evening soon, perhaps in a hall like the one we were in, perhaps aimed at a younger audience, perhaps targeting a pop concert, ISIS would strike. And when they did, we would wonder what the hell we had been doing, ignoring them as they built up their forces in Syria and Iraq.

General Allen used his remarks to give a deeply measured summary of how to defeat ISIS. His speech was technical, impressive, slightly dull but careful to stress his respect for Arab allies on the ground and across the region. Our opponents that night appeared to have listened, but it was something that one of them said at the opening of her speech that stuck with us. After we had both spoken, one of our opponents—a Palestinian activist and writer called Rula Jebreal—opened by explaining why the audience should not bother listening to what either General Allen or I had to say. "We're again lectured—with all due respect," she said (which in this context always means "none"), "by two white men." I had heard it before, but I noticed the General wince slightly.

The comment was clearly still playing on his mind afterward at dinner because he picked up on it again. "Have you had that before?" he asked me. I said that regrettably I had and was only shocked that he had not. "I never had that," he said. He had spent his life serving in the US military, risking his life, living among the people of Afghanistan, on deployment for years on end. And he seemed genuinely surprised that this and all the rest of his life and experience should be summed up and dismissed through the fact that he happened to be a white man. And lumped in with me, to boot. "Well, I'd get used to it," I told him breezily, little realizing how fast we all would.

That was only a few years ago, but still then, outside of academic circles and racist organizations, it was deemed discourteous to lump people together and dismiss them simply because of the color of their skin. An earlier generation had come to the sensible conclusion that dismissing people, vilifying them, or generalizing about them simply because of the color of their skin was the definition of racism. And racism had become viewed as among the ugliest of human evils. Fail to take people into account as individuals, and we knew where it could lead: to the horrors of the mid-twentieth century, to the nightmares of Rwanda and Bosnia at the end of that century. Closer to home, it led to the racial segregation and occasional racial violence that had scarred America's past, as it had the past of so many other countries.

The lesson had seemed clear: treat people as individuals, and reject those who would try to reduce them to membership of a group they belonged to solely by accident of birth. The message of Dr. Martin Luther King Jr. seemed to have triumphed. The future was meant to be one in which racial categories mattered less and less. Society and the people in it would aspire to be color-blind, just as they also aspired to be sex-blind and blind to differences in an individual's sexual orientation. The aim of society seemed clear and, with some skirmishes still remaining round the edges, was agreed upon across the political spectrum. People should be able to fulfill their potential unhampered by the chance of group characteristics. Anyone who wanted to play with racist rhetoric or find people willing to excuse racism had to mingle with the residue of white supremacists in their increasingly small enclaves or find a home among equally fringe groups, such as Louis Farrakhan's Nation of Islam, with their black supremacy. Such groups were far from the political or social center or mainstream, and the center seemed to want to keep it that way.

Then, in the early years of the present century, this began to change. A vogue began for referring to race more than anyone had in years. Specifically, it led to an upsurge of descriptions of white people in terms that would be used about no other group in society. Commonly it was people who were white themselves who did most of the running, or rather pleading. But it broke out in an extraordinarily wide range of venues. As usual with bad ideas, they originated in the universities.

CRITICAL RACE THEORY

Despite the waning number of overtly racist laws and the power of overt racists in the United States, the disparate results between whites and blacks eroded very slowly. Academics began looking for hidden mechanisms of racism to account for this.

Critical race theory (CRT) emerged over decades in academic seminars, papers, and publications. From the 1970s onward, academics such as bell hooks (the pretentious lower cases are intended), Derrick Bell (at Harvard and Stanford), and Kimberlé Crenshaw (UCLA and Columbia) worked to create a movement of activists within academia who would interpret almost everything in the world through the lens of race. In some ways, their obsession was understandable. Bell, for instance, had grown up during the very last years of segregation. During his time at Harvard, there were only a handful of black faculty members. Instead of taking the incrementalist approach favored by others, those who formed the bases for CRT first asserted that race was the most significant factor in hiring decisions at Ivy League universities, and then that it was the single most important lens through which to understand wider society. Meaning that at the very moment that things were improving, and more black faculty members were coming through, everything in the academy and everything in the academy's understanding of wider society was racialized, or rather racialized anew.

Of course, there were obvious and clear counters to this. The Civil Rights Act had been passed and working for years. Antidiscrimination laws were already on the statute books and growing in number. Yet followers of CRT saw nearly all progress in American race relations as an illusion. That is how Bell himself referred to it in 1987, when he wrote that "progress in American race relations is largely a mirage obscuring the fact that whites continue, consciously or unconsciously, to do all in their power to ensure their dominion and maintain their control."[2] When Harvard failed to give tenure to two followers of CRT in 1986, Bell and others staged a sit-in at the university. Like any revolutionary sect, the followers of CRT knew how to make themselves felt and heard and knew how to change the intellectual weather in a corner of society not known for its heroism.

The more places scholars could see invisible racism, the more popular they became.

Naturally, it was the case that very few people who this ideology was coming for knew what was coming for them. Even if they had known, they would have found it hard to oppose. Because one of the distinguishing marks of CRT was that its assertions were based not on evidence, as it might previously have been understood, but essentially on interpretations and attitudes. This marked a significant shift in the manner in which people were expected to prove assertions. While rarely announcing the fact, the rules of CRT had no need for normal standards of evidence. If a person's "lived experience" could be attested to, then the question of "evidence" or "data" had to find a place further back in the queue, if at all. The intersectionalists who grew up at the same time comfortably overlapped with CRT. These people, who built a theory from the assertion that all oppressions "intersect" and must be simultaneously "solved," made this leap possible. Suddenly academic papers were able to be produced (most famously by Peggy McIntosh at Wellesley) that consisted of nothing more than lists of assertions. All made from a standpoint which was neither provable nor disprovable. It was simply asserted.

Whether leveling claims against colleagues or against wider society, it became sufficient to fall back simply on the evidence of one's own perceptions. If one person pointed to evidence that proved America had become less racist, another person could say that he knew this not to be the case. Why? His own "lived experience" (as though there is any other kind). In many ways, it was a clever move to make. For it is true that no individual's personal experience can ever be fully comprehended. But neither can it be always and wholly believed. Certainly, assertions about entire societies and groups of people should come with some evidence attached? Well, not now. At its best, the shift from evidence to "me" allowed a stalemate: You have your views and reality. I have mine. At its worst, it left any exchange of ideas vulnerable to being taken over by bad-faith actors who simply insisted that things are as they say they are. And that is precisely what happened.

One of the distinguishing marks of CRT is that from the outset, its advocates and adherents have been remarkably clear about what they want and how they intend to get it. CRT's progenitors, followers, and admirers laid out their stall early and often. For instance, the claim that CRT is not a school of thought or set of propositions but a "movement" is something that is admitted to by its own apostles. In their 2001 work *Critical Race Theory: An Introduction*, the authors Richard Delgado and Jean Stefancic admiringly described CRT as a "movement" consisting of "a collection of activists and scholars interested in studying and transforming the relationship among race, racism and power. The movement considers many of the same issues that conventional civil rights and ethnic studies discourses take up, but places them in a broader perspective that includes economics, history, context, group and self-interest, and even feelings and the unconscious. Unlike traditional civil rights, which embraces incrementalism and step-by-step progress, critical race theory questions the very foundations of the liberal order, including equality theory, legal reasoning, Enlightenment rationalism, and neutral principles of constitutional law."

That is quite the list of things to question. The principles of the Enlightenment, the law, neutralism, rationalism, and the very foundations of the liberal order. Had this been written about CRT by an enemy, that would be one thing. But this was written by its adherents about themselves.

What is more, as Delgado and Stefancic boasted, although CRT started in the realm of the law, "it has rapidly spread beyond that discipline" throughout all fields of education.

"Today, many in the field of education consider themselves critical race theorists who use CRT's ideas to understand issues of school discipline and hierarchy, tracking, controversies over curriculum and history, and IQ achievement testing . . . Unlike some academic disciplines, critical race theory contains an activist dimension. It not only tries to understand our social situation, but to change it; it sets out not only to ascertain how society organizes itself along racial lines and hierarchies, but to transform it for the better."[3]

This is an unusual language for academics to write in: to boast that a particular collection of academics and teachers are, in fact, academics "with an activist dimension." And as for the admission that CRT seeks not just to understand society but to "transform it"? This is the language of revolutionary politics, not a language traditionally used in academia. But revolutionary activists were exactly what those involved in CRT turned out to be.

The hallmarks were there from the beginning. An absolute obsession with race as the primary means to understand the world and all injustice. The claim is that white people are in their totality guilty of prejudice, specifically racism, from birth. That racism is interwoven so deeply into white-majority societies that the white people in those societies do not even realize that they live in racist societies. Asking for proof was proof of racism. And, finally, there is also the insistence that none of the answers Western societies have come up with to address racism are remotely adequate or capable of dealing with the task at hand. The work of Eduardo Bonilla-Silva and others insisted that even the concept of aspiring to be "color-blind" when it comes to issues of race is itself deeply racist.[4]

But what was racism by this new and assertive definition? It was, it was repeatedly asserted, "prejudice plus power." Partly thanks to the influence of Michel Foucault, these academics had become obsessed with the issue of power.[5] They saw it both as the central issue of a free society and as being wielded negatively by all state institutions. As a result, the priority was to wrestle power out of these hands and wield it elsewhere. Attributing power, or taking power, on the basis of skin color was enormously advantageous to these academics, even if their thinking on the matter remained wildly confused. For instance, they maintained that someone could not be guilty of racism if they had no power—even if they were prejudiced. And in the power structure that devotees of CRT remorselessly laid out, it was axiomatic that only white people had power. Therefore, only white people could be racist. Black people either could not be racist or, if they were racist, were racist only because they had "internalized whiteness."

Of course, while all of this was taking place in universities across America, most Americans were able to remain blissfully ignorant of it. And while it is certainly possible to underestimate what a group of activist scholars might be able to accomplish, it is also possible to overestimate their impact. For most Americans, the work of Crenshaw, Bell, and others need not have touched their lives at all. But out in the wider world, in the realm of popular entertainment, some of these habits started to catch on. Attitudes that had been marginal shifted to the mainstream. Claims that would only recently have been regarded as esoteric took on a life of their own.

For example, in 2001, the opinion-documentary maker Michael Moore cranked out a number-one best-selling book called *Stupid White Men*. Its chapters included one titled "Kill Whitey." During its course, Moore reeled off a list of the crimes he blamed on white people. They included, though were not limited to, the black plague, warfare, chemicals, the internal combustion engine, the Holocaust, slavery, the genocide of Native Americans, and job layoffs in corporate America. As Moore concluded, "You name the problem, the disease, the human suffering, or the abject misery visited upon millions, and I'll bet you ten bucks I can put a white face on it."[6] Perhaps Moore had never heard of the problems of Rwanda, Sierra Leone, or Myanmar, to name just a few places. Here and throughout his accompanying tours, speeches, and documentaries, Moore made himself rich and famous by asserting that white people—or "whitey" as he persisted—were responsible for everything bad. Everyone else was just a victim.

Naturally, many people disliked this sort of talk. They recognized the truth of Thomas Sowell's 2012 observation that if racism in America is not dead, then it is certainly "on life support." They knew the claims starting to be hurled out against their societies to be false, unfair, and much more. But they failed to take into account Sowell's follow-on observation that racism was now being kept alive "by politicians, race hustlers, and people who get a sense of superiority by denouncing others as 'racists.'"[7]

These exact figures were the ones who now gave racism a new lease on life. They did so by two means in particular. The first was by declaring a change of rules. The second was in announcing themselves to be the referees. In doing so, among much else, they identified and cut off all the paths that a normal person would have to avoid being accused of being a racist. If you were unable to see it everywhere, it was only because your racism prevented you from really looking.

In 2018, an obscure academic called Robin DiAngelo, who also happened to be white, published a book which brought together a number of her recent writings under the title *White Fragility*. It became DiAngelo's contention not only that white people were all racist but that white people who disliked being told that they were racist, or objected to being called racist, were simply providing further evidence of their racism. This logical trap is the same one favored by witch-dunkers in the Middle Ages: if the woman drowns, she is innocent; if she floats, she is a witch and can be burned. In DiAngelo's logic, the person who denies that they are racist is racist, and so is the person who says they are racist. Meaning that the best thing to do in any given situation is for a person to save time and confess to being a racist.

That suited the man who wrote the foreword to her book. There, Michael Eric Dyson actually declared that "Robin DiAngelo is the new racial sheriff in town." He went on, "She is bringing a different law and order to bear upon the racial proceedings."[8] This new law and order included the naming of guilty parties. Describing racism as "America's Original sin," Dyson insisted: "We cannot possibly name the nemeses of democracy or truth or justice or equality if we cannot name the identities to which they have been attached. For most of our history, straight white men have been involved in a witness protection program that guards their identities and absolves them of their crimes while offering them a future free of past encumbrances and sins."[9]

Describing DiAngelo's tortuous work as "beautiful," he added that it is "a bracing call to white folk everywhere to see their whiteness for what it is and to seize the opportunity to make things better now. Robin DiAngelo kicks all the crutches to the side and demands that white folk finally mature and face the world they've made while seeking to help remake it for those who have neither their privilege nor their protection."[10]

It is a list of assertions that is worth pausing over. The idea that white people are all immature, for instance, might easily slide by, coming as it does alongside the claim that straight white men are all racist criminals. Yet none of these assertions seemed far-fetched given the assertions made inside the book Dyson was writing about. In her very first line, DiAngelo wrote: "The United States was founded on the principle that all people are created equal. Yet the nation began with the attempted genocide of Indigenous people and the theft of their land. American wealth was built on the labor of kidnapped and enslaved Africans and their descendants."[11] And then she went on, like Dyson, to list the things that all white people think, believe, and do—such as to claim that "Anti-blackness is foundational to our very identities as white people."[12] If DiAngelo knew that what she was doing was in some way bad, she didn't seem to mind it. In fact, she happily admitted to it, writing, "I am breaking a cardinal rule of individualism— *I am generalizing*" [italics hers].[13] Until this point, "generalizing" about people had indeed been deemed to be a low tactic.

To say "all Chinese people think this" or "all black people behave like that" had been thought to be rude as well as ignorant. But Robin DiAngelo positively reveled in the naughtiness of doing it and getting away with doing it because she was doing it against white people.

In the same way, it had been thought until the fairly recent past to be at the very least rude to condemn people for traits over which they had no say and claim that these traits were in fact without any merits at all. But DiAngelo enjoyed breaking that ethic too. "There are many positive approaches to antiracist work," she wrote. "One of them is to try to develop a positive white identity . . . However, a positive white identity is an impossible goal. White identity is inherently racist; white people do not exist outside the system of white supremacy." And yet DiAngelo says that white people should not stop identifying as being white, for to do so would be to deny racism and constitute "color-blind racism." What is her positive suggestion for her readers? They should "strive to be 'less white'" is her answer, adding for the sake of clarity that "to be less white is to be less racially oppressive."[14]

If it was true that white Americans were inextricably racist, yet also fragile about that fact, it did not stop them from buying DiAngelo's big book of generalizations. In fact, they bought it in great piles. DiAngelo's book sold over three-quarters of a million copies. And perhaps it was because of the acclaim and commercial success that DiAngelo was emboldened to make more extreme claims in her later interviews. In an interview on *Amanpour and Company* in 2018, she claimed that white people find racism "exciting" and enjoy "indulging" in it. DiAngelo's interviewer on this occasion, Michel Martin (who happens to be black), tried to pin her guest down on such claims.

"Why do you say that though?" Martin asked. "You're a scholar. Where's your data? What makes you say that?"

DiAngelo may or may not be a scholar, but she had no evidence to back up her claims. Instead, she simply made another (unrelated) assertion: "There is a kind of glee in the White collective when Black bodies are punished."[15]

That interview was broadcast again two years after its first showing because two years later, everything had changed again. George Floyd had been killed by the policeman Derek Chauvin, and footage of the death had been broadcast around the world. Protests broke out worldwide, and DiAngelo's book was one of those that benefited from the spike of interest in antiracism. In just a month after Floyd's death, *White Fragility* sold almost half a million copies.

There is something in that moment that is worth confronting right away. Because there are those for whom the killing of George Floyd was not just something that happened in America but something that was emblematic of America. And this perspective, that what happened that day was not the behavior of a rogue cop who was subsequently arrested, tried, convicted, and imprisoned for his crime but rather a pulling back of the curtain and a revealing of something in the heart of all white Americans, was an interpretation that DiAngelo, the critical race theorists, and others had primed Americans for. And primed college-aged Americans for in particular. Polls showed that positive views on the state of race relations in America peaked at the time of President Obama's inauguration in 2009. At that time, a CBS/

New York Times poll found that 66 percent of Americans thought that race relations were generally good.[16] But as it tracked the polls over the following years, the Associated Press noted that views on race "started to sour" in 2014.[17] One interpretation of this is that America became more racist over the two terms of its first black president. Another is that the media attention on certain incidents—whether justifiable or not—helped to alter America's view of itself.

What made this worse was that a generation of students brought up with elements of CRT had been persuaded that race relations in their country were wildly worse than they were. People in the American academy had invented and popularized a whole set of concepts and terms to help this along. Just as their colleagues in the intersectional arena insisted on the idea that everyone lived in a "cis-heteronormative patriarchy," so the professors of CRT introduced a set of racialized terms into the academic language and from there into the nation's language. They argued, for instance, that America was not merely a white-dominated society, or that America had a white-majority population, but a "white-supremacist" society. They claimed that all white people benefited from allowing white-supremacist rule. They claimed that when confronted by their racism, white people deliberately changed the subject or made themselves into the victims. They claimed that there was a specific phenomenon known as "white tears" (and a subcategory within that, "white women's tears").

They also claimed that whiteness was contagious. For how else to deal with the fact that many black people were not in 100 percent agreement with the new racial theorists and did not all agree with the new ideas being foisted upon everyone? One answer was to claim that black people who were not in agreement that America was an intrinsically racist society were enacting "whiteness," or otherwise imbibing it, like some terrible disease.[18] After the 2020 US presidential election, the *Washington Post* even introduced its readers to the concept of "multiracial whiteness" as a way to explain how ethnic minorities might have voted for the Republican candidate.[19] In these settings, in which you could get black-white people, though not white-black people, it becomes clear that "black" and "white" had simply become synonyms for "good" and "bad."

Advocates of this theory claimed that race was not just one lens through which to view society. They insisted that it was the most important, in fact, the only, lens through which to view society. And much of the venom and fury that exists today in America, and in the West as a whole, now comes down to this one specific problem: that people have been shown a version of their society that is exaggerated at best and wildly off at worst. Take just one, perhaps the most famous "racist" event of recent years—the storm that blew CRT and its theories across the whole Western world: the murder of George Floyd in Minneapolis in May 2020.

In the days, weeks, and months after that terrible event, there was barely an organ or an individual in America or the wider world that did not interpret the appalling video of that death through a single lens. That a white policeman was caught on camera killing a black man and that this was a racist killing. Not content with that explanation, everything about this interpretation was then extrapolated outward. This was not just an individual racist killing. It was a racist killing that told us about the nature of racist policing in America. From there, it went out again. We learned that this racist policing was just one aspect of a wider racist society. And from there that not just America but all white-dominated societies (and societies in which white people simply had a presence) were somehow revealed in that moment. The interpretation that was popularized across the globe was that what happened to George Floyd told us about a routine injustice. It claimed that black lives were able to be stolen with impunity in modern America and that this was because America, and the wider West, was institutionally racist, white supremacist, and otherwise guilty of a no-longer-avoidable bigotry.

Actual public understanding of the issue turned out to be wildly, provably, out of sync with reality. For instance, when US citizens were polled and asked how many unarmed black Americans they believed had been shot by police in 2019, the numbers were off by several orders of magnitude.

Twenty-two percent of people who identified as "very liberal" said they thought the police shot at least ten thousand unarmed black men in a year. Among self-identified liberals, fully 40 percent thought the figure was between one thousand and ten thousand. The actual figure was somewhere around ten.[20]

By proportion of the population, unarmed black Americans were slightly more likely to be shot by the police than unarmed white Americans. But as figures compiled by the *Washington Post* Police Shootings database confirm, in the years before the death of George Floyd, more police officers were killed by black Americans than unarmed black Americans were killed by the police.[21]

Almost none of this cut through. But the polls seemed to suggest that increased reporting on this issue in the 2010s may have had the inadvertent effect of causing Americans to imagine that the problem of deadly interactions between unarmed black men and the police was exponentially worse than before. Whatever the realities of race in America, a group of divisive activists were ready for this moment, with their pre-prepared theories, phrases, claims, and demands about eradicated hidden racism. And they got very busy indeed.

That was why sporting teams across the world began to "take the knee" before every match. They were inveigled into thinking they had to do so to demonstrate that they were against racist killing, that black people were freely killed by policemen, and that they should not be. That is why politicians across the West took the knee and gave speeches against racism. It is why Nancy Pelosi, Chuck Schumer, and the rest of the leadership of the Democratic Party wore African kente cloth scarves and kneeled for eight minutes forty-six seconds before being winched back up again by their attendants. It is why the idea of "educating yourself" if you were white suddenly entered the popular lexicon. It is why CEOs such as the editor in chief of *National Geographic* started to put under their name and title as a sign-off "Race Card: White, privileged, with much to learn."[22]

It was a moment when silence in the face of "racism" was deemed to be violence. A moment when actual violence was excused as a form of legitimate political speech. A moment an academic could blithely declare that "the state of black America as a whole is probably worse than it was fifty years ago."[23] It was at this moment, in the days after Floyd's death, that concepts such as "white privilege" spilt out from the fringes of academia, where they had been incubated, and flooded through every part of society.

So it is worth pointing out a potentially unpopular but nevertheless crucial fact about this origin story. Which is that there is still no evidence that the killing of George Floyd was a racist murder. At the trial of Derek Chauvin, no evidence was produced to suggest that it was a racist murder. If there had been any such evidence—that Chauvin harbored deep animus against black Americans and set out that May morning hoping to murder a black person—then the prosecution chose to make no such evidence available at Chauvin's trial. In fact, there is good evidence to suggest that no racial element existed at all. How can we say that? One reason is that four years before Floyd's death, on August 10, 2016, another man was killed in almost the exact same horrific circumstances as was Floyd.

Thirty-two-year-old Tony Timpa was killed in Dallas while being detained by five police officers. He himself called 911 from a parking lot, saying that he was afraid and needed assistance. He told the services that he suffered from depression and schizophrenia and had failed to take his medication. He was reportedly off his mental-health medication, though he had, like Floyd, taken other drugs. The detention and death of Tony Timpa, like those of George Floyd, was caught on camera—this time in police bodycam footage. Like Floyd, Timpa was unarmed, and like Floyd, his death was horribly, brutally protracted. Like Floyd, the policeman detaining Timpa could hardly have come across as more callous, entitled, or flippant in dealing with the life of a man. Timpa can be heard in the footage wailing and pleading with police as he is handcuffed and pinned to the ground by his shoulders, knees, and neck. Just as George Floyd yelled that he couldn't breathe, Tony Timpa could repeatedly be heard screaming, "You're going to kill me! You're going to kill me." He pleaded for help more than thirty times. He was held in exactly the same knee-hold position that Floyd was held in. But Timpa was held in this position for a full thirteen minutes before finally losing consciousness. As he lay there, the police officers laughed and joked about him. When the first responders arrived, they waited for four minutes before beginning CPR. While the last gasps of life left Tony Timpa's body, the detaining officers joked that they could hear him snoring.

So much for the similarities. What is more noteworthy are the differences between the two cases. In the case of George Floyd, the footage of the killing emerged immediately. Whereas it took the *Dallas Morning News* three years of legal fights to acquire the police body-cam footage of the Timpa killing. And whereas the facts surrounding Floyd's death emerged swiftly, the facts about Timpa took years to come out. The police reports of the Timpa killing turned out to be seriously contradictory in themselves, and even more seriously so when the tape of the killing was finally released. One of the Dallas police department records reported that Timpa had been combative with officers. The footage that was eventually released showed that this was not true. He was already handcuffed and restrained by private security guards by the time the Dallas police arrived. At least one of the Dallas officers who detained Timpa was black. But there is another major difference between the cases as well. Within under a year of the death of George Floyd, Derek Chauvin was tried and convicted on all counts. Whereas four years after the death of Tony Timpa, in July 2020, a federal judge threw out a suit brought against the five officers who caused the death of Tony Timpa. The putative charge was that they had used excessive force. No officer was ever charged. One of the officers involved has now retired, but four of the five officers remain on active duty.

The reason that I mention this is not to diminish what happened to Floyd, any more than it is to diminish what happened to Timpa. The reason is to point out that these two cases are very similar and that in neither case was a racial motive proved. Nor is it to say that there never has been any racism in America or that there is no residual racism anywhere in the Western world. But it is to point out that the killing of George Floyd has been interpreted as commonplace in American society when it is by any measure an anomaly in America. Still, it is insisted that in this anomaly, the true nature of America can be discerned. It is an extension of the old left-wing idea that if you only provoked the police a little, they would reveal the true face of the democratic state and that its face would be fascist. Today there is a widespread belief that if you pull back the mask of the American state, you have a state that is not just racist but white supremacist and that its agents and representatives, as well as the citizenry as a whole, are dedicated to the casual murder of black people.

That is why even more than a year since the death of George Floyd, athletes continue to take the knee before sporting games. It is why football teams around the world continue to think it worth risking the growing irritation of their fans by kneeling before games. It is because Floyd's death is believed to have revealed something. But if the killing is to be interpreted in this way, then we would need to be absolutely certain of the truth of the interpretation. We would need to be absolutely certain that this fons et origo—the foundational story—that we are telling ourselves about American society and the West as a whole is accurate.

And it is not. What is proved is that by 2020 America was ready and primed for a certain interpretation of itself to burst out. That interpretation had been prepared in the academy. It had been popularized in the media. And in record time, it had been given into by corporate entities, civil society organizations, and nowhere so much as in the campuses of the United States. We know this because long before 2020, American campuses had been undergoing a set of moral panics that future historians will look on with deep puzzlement. American students had been primed for a white-supremacist, racist interpretation of their own society to grip them. How do we know?

Because for a decade or more, they had been seeing ghouls and monsters that were not there.

MORAL PANICS

In April 2016, an extraordinary panic kicked off at the University of Indiana. It was at around nine o'clock in the evening that somebody reported that a member of the Ku Klux Klan (KKK) had been spotted on the campus at Bloomington. Social media lit up. "Students be careful," one student wrote, "there's someone walking around in KKK gear with a whip." Others immediately criticized the college authorities. One student wrote, "There's a man walking around campus in a KKK hood carrying a whip, and there's NOTHING you can do to make students feel safe?" Students and their supervisors spread messages of support. "Please PLEASE PLEASE be careful out there tonight," said one. "Always be with someone and if you have no dire reason to be out of the building I would recommend staying indoors if you're alone." The panic only subsided when it was discovered that the suspected member of the KKK was, in fact, a Dominican monk, wearing the traditional white robes of his order. The "whip" he was said to have been carrying in his hands turned out to be a rosary. Despite these facts becoming clear, not all of the students stood down graciously. "OK seriously," asked one. "Why the fuck was a priest walking around campus at night?"[24]

It might be easy to laugh off this panic at the University of Indiana if it had been the only such incident. But it was not. Over the last decade, multiple universities across the United States had similar panics. For example, one morning in 2013, there was a sighting of a person in a Klansman outfit at Oberlin College in Ohio. The panic at this liberal arts college led to the cancellation of all classes for the rest of the day. The police were called to chase the Klansman off the premises. But when the police arrived to investigate the sighting, they found no members of the KKK. It transpired that the sighting was most likely caused by either a homeless pedestrian wrapped in a blanket or a woman who was seen the same morning carrying a blanket across the campus.[25]

In November 2015, a queer black activist who was also a former student-body president caused a virtual stampede at the University of Missouri when he claimed that the KKK had been spotted on campus. "Students take precaution," he warned on social media. "Stay away from the windows in residence halls. The KKK has been confirmed to be sighted on campus. I'm working with the MUPD [campus security], the state trooper and the national guard." In fact, the only force he was working with was his own imagination. Nobody needed to keep away from any windows. The student eventually apologized for sharing "misinformation."[26] Other panics followed a similar trend. In June 2017, the University of Maryland's police department was called after an alleged "noose" was spotted under a tree on campus. The police inspecting the scene discovered that the "noose" was nothing but a knotted piece of white plastic lying on the floor. Though they looked into any possible "hate crime bias," the police concluded that the material was of the kind used "to contain and protect loose items during transport." Still, many students at the university were dissatisfied with the conclusion and posted images of the piece of white plastic on social media inviting their fellow students to "make their own conclusions." One complained that "they [the police] didn't even try to entertain me and my friend by acknowledging the possibility that this was a symbol of hate. They were very adamant."[27] As well they might have been in the circumstances, being called out to investigate a refuse sack tie.

A few months later, in October, it was the turn of Michigan State University to have a noose sighting. There a student claimed to have come out of her dorm room and been confronted by a hanging noose. Condemnations for this hate incident came swiftly from everyone on campus from fellow students all the way up to the university's president. Their condemnations and commiserations continued until it transpired that the "noose" was one half of a pair of shoe-laces that had been lost and hung up by the person who found them so that they could be reclaimed by their owner.[28]

In March 2018, it was the turn of Vincennes University, where a student claimed that he had been approached by a man in a white head covering who was brandishing a gun and hurling racial slurs. The campus authorities swiftly sent out a warning to the whole Vincennes community. The dean of students issued a statement saying, "Vincennes University is totally dedicated to respect, diversity, and inclusion. We take such reports very seriously and the ongoing investigation is of the highest priority." The subsequent police investigation used CCTV to discover that the incident never happened.[29]

If these sorts of panics had been confined to campuses in the United States, then they might have been easily dismissed as a problem of overprivileged, overcredentialed youth. But in recent years, they began to happen among adults too, including among adults with some of the highest visibility of anyone in the country.

In February 2017, the comedian Sarah Silverman went out for her morning coffee. She was shocked to find signs on the pavement of what looked like an *S* with a line through the middle. Silverman promptly snapped a photo of the pavement and sent it out to her many millions of Twitter followers. "Is this an attempt at swastikas?" she asked. "Do neo-Nazis not have Google?"[30] But it turned out that illiterate neo-Nazis had not taken to the town's pavements to ineptly try to paint swastikas overnight. The signs on the ground were chalk markings made by construction workers identifying the areas in which they needed to do their job.

In September 2019, the restaurant of a former NFL player, Edawn Louis Coughman, was vandalized with racist graffiti and swastikas. Coughman called his insurance company to report the incident, but when the police caught up with him they arrested and charged him, alleging that the black paint they found him with had been used to carry out the "racist attack" on himself.[31] And then, of course, there were the freezing hours of a January night in 2019 when the actor

Jussie Smollett claimed that he had been set upon outside a branch of Subway by two white men shouting racist and homophobic slurs. He claimed that they physically attacked him, put a noose around his neck, and covered him in an unknown substance, an incident throughout which he allegedly held on to his Subway sandwich. Reaction from the highest quarters in the country was swift and credulous. Senator Kamala Harris, who turned out to know Smollett, was among those who described what had happened as "an attempted modern day lynching."[32] Smollett stuck to his story in the days afterward, occasionally adding extras. At a singing performance a week later, he told his sympathetic and supportive audience that he had fought back against his attackers and would not allow them to win because he, Jussie Smollett, stood for love. But as the story fell apart, so did much of the public support for him. Nothing about the story stood up. And as the CCTV footage started to be scanned, police got the opportunity to catch up with the white supremacists who had carried out the attack. They were Abimbola Osundairo and Olabinjo Osundairo, two large weight-lifting brothers from Nigeria, who turned out to be known to Smollett. It became apparent that Smollett believed that a successful claim of a hate crime against himself would give him leverage to negotiate a pay raise on the show *Empire*, in which he felt he was undervalued. So the Osundairo brothers were drafted in to beat him around a bit.

The question of what was, or was not, going through Smollett's mind at this time is certainly interesting. But what is far more interesting is the eagerness with which his story was believed. It wasn't just Harris but dozens and dozens of prominent Americans, from Nancy Pelosi to Stephen Colbert, who took Smollett's story at face value. Indeed, on his next evening show, Colbert invited a sandpaper-voiced actress called Ellen Page on to sermonize about the Smollett incident and what it meant. This was when some doubt had already been cast over Smollett's story, and this was unforgivable in Page's eyes. "We have a media that's saying it's a debate whether or not what just happened to Jussie Smollett is a hate crime," she said. "It's absurd," she added, thumping one fist into the other for emphasis. "There [bleep] isn't a debate." At which the studio audience whooped and shouted, "Yeah!" "Sorry I'm like I'm like really fired up tonight," she said, as if she was apologetic. "Not at all," agreed Colbert: "You have to be fired up. You have to be fired up." "It feels impossible to not feel this way right now," Page added to more whoops and applause.[33]

None of this is to say that racism does not occur and that racial violence is unheard of in America or anywhere else. Yet these cases, and many others that could be cited, do not suggest a population with a healthy perspective on the risk and likelihood of racist incidents. There seems, in fact, to be a perception—honestly held or otherwise—of a type of racism that if it still exists, does so at the furthest margins of society. Americans over the last decade have not lived in a country where Klansmen prowl the land—always interestingly alone. And they certainly have not lived in a country in which members of the KKK can routinely be found strolling around the nation's campuses. They do not live in a country in which lynchings are a feature of everyday life. They actually live in one in which there is such a dearth of white supremacists that weight-lifting Nigerians occasionally need to be flown in to take on the role. What appears to have happened is that a picture of America has formed in the heads of certain Americans. A picture set and stuck at some time around the early part of the last century. An America in which the KKK roamed the land and Hollywood actresses deserved applause for daring to stand up to "attempted lynchings."

HOW DID THIS HAPPEN?

How did this happen? One possibility is to see that the state of race relations in the United States resembles the effect created by a projecting device. The details of the image being projected matter enormously—indeed, matter more than anything else. One explanation for America's savage but intense dissection of every killing of a black American at the hands of the police, for example, is that America needs to fight over the precise nature of these details. Breonna Taylor, Michael Brown, and other cases ring in the public mind because the most minute details are being wrestled over. At one end, there are people who would like to claim that these and other deaths of black people at police hands are a demonstration of the true face of a white-supremacist, institutionally racist nation. At various other ends are people pleading that these are the sort of incidents that are inevitable when a heavily armed citizenry and a heavily armed police force try to negotiate their way through millions of annual interactions. The details are worth fighting over, bitterly if need be. Because if Michael Brown was shot with his hands in the air and posed no threat to the arresting officers, then that could well point to a very serious problem in a nation. But if he was not shot with his hands in the air and the riots that resulted from his death were whipped up for no reason, then some dishonest actors have a lot of accounting for their own actions to do.

The details are fought over because America is the world's most powerful nation, the world's most influential nation, and the nation whose sins and errors are likely to be exported just as much as are its virtues and attainments. And just as America watches what is projected on the wall, so the world watches too, with less attention to the details, but with just as great an interest in what ends up being projected on the wall of the world. The size of the protests in Berlin, London, Brussels, Stockholm, and many other major cities in the days after George Floyd's death suggested one thing in particular. That people felt they had to come out because they had to voice their outrage at the world's most powerful and influential country deeming the lives of its black citizens so cheaply that it allows its police officers to strangle them with impunity in broad daylight. Protestors around the world responded to an image that they see projected of America. A picture in which a whole catalog of subtle mistakes, manipulations, and extortions had been infinitely magnified. But the distortion comes from America and is projected from America, by America.

RACIST BABIES

Even in such a relatively genteel world as the world of books, this marked radicalization could be witnessed in the last decade. In the 2010s, during the Obama presidency, mainstream publishers started to pump out books that seemed intent on radicalizing people from the cradle upward. At the time, some of it seemed so preposterous as to be funny. Innosanto Nagara's work *A is for Activist* (2012) was a children's alphabet picture book intended to produce the next generation of activists. As well as being anticapitalist, it was also naturally on board with all the latest identity politics. *L* is for "LGBT," and of course *T* is for "Trans" before it is for "Trains." But the main point of the book is to tell children that they should grow up to protest and fight for "equality," "diversity," and more. Which is why *X* is for Malcolm X, *I* is for "indigenous" and "immigrant," *Y* is for "Your truth," and the *A–Z* finishes with *Z* is for Zapatista.

From the age they could begin to read, children were being taught through popular literature that the best way to live your life is as a revolutionary, manning the barricades to fight against capitalism, "cis-heteronormativity," and of course racism. Whole industries seemed intent on reprogramming people to make them view the world through a completely clear lens in which there were obvious good guys and obvious bad guys. Intelligent adults began to speak in the same language. In 2019, Adam Rutherford (author of *How to Argue with a Racist*) finished a lecture to a room full of adults with the statement, "If you are a racist then you are my enemy."[34] As though lecture theaters are routinely filled with Klansmen. He then quoted the American political activist Angela Davis: "In a racist society, it is not enough to be non-racist. We must be anti-racist." Even before the death of George Floyd, it seemed to have become so commonly stated as to be generally agreed upon that people in Western societies lived in racist societies and that the answer to this peculiar Western problem must be a peculiarly Western answer: to become devout, active antiracists. This, too, had to be taught from the cradle upward, and no start was too early.

This was why the American writer Ibram X. Kendi would produce a book called *Antiracist Baby*, published to great fanfare and covered on its release by most of the main networks in the United States. It explains that "Antiracist baby" is bred, not born, and must strive "to make equity a reality." If explaining the concept of equity to a three-year-old seems difficult, the illustrator and Kendi try as hard as possible to make it easy. The nine-step program for babies includes the suggestions that antiracist baby should "use your words to talk about race," "point at policies as the problem, not people," "knock down the stack of cultural blocks," and "confess when being racist."[35] So when your two-year-old knocks down his or her play blocks, you can ask if this is a metaphorical observation on the lived reality of racial violence.

The book is designed for children still needing pictures, rather than words, to explain things. And there are lots of jolly illustrations to help them along, showing happy antiracist babies, caterpillars turning into butterflies, and the like. But what is the imperative to indoctrinate children in this way? One explanation is again that Americans in prominent positions have suggested that even American babies need reprogramming from the racist society they have been born into. As no less an authority than the Arizona Department of Education recently declared, babies are able to become racist by the age of three months old. And, according to the "equity toolkit" published by the department, which made this claim, it is white babies that are the problem. The toolkit claims that "expressions of racial prejudice often peak at ages 4 and 5" but that while "Black and Latinx children" at the age of five show "no preference towards their own groups," "white children at this age remain strongly biased in favor of whiteness."[36] A reminder that from even before the moment they are able to speak or walk, it is white children who are the problem. And white children who must be worked on to achieve the change that everybody seems to have agreed is needed.

ANTIRACISM

As it happens, *Antiracist Baby* is a children's version of a slightly more grown-up book by Ibram X. Kendi. The author's story is one of quite amazing success—a success that has mirrored that of another black American writer of the same generation—Ta-Nehisi Coates. Like Coates, Kendi appears to believe that his personal story, or a mix of his personal story plus extrapolation of its political meaning, should be a sufficient base from which to reframe race relations in America. Like Coates, he is full of anger. Yet, like Coates, his career has been not just golden but magnificently well oiled at every turn. Like Coates, he has had a youthful book of memoir published to near-unanimous acclaim and turned into a best seller. Like Coates, he has won a National Book Award. Like Coates, he was awarded a MacArthur "Genius Grant." Unlike Coates, Kendi was (at the age of just thirty-eight) awarded the most prestigious tenured chair at Boston University. The only previous holder of the Andrew W. Mellon Professorship in the Humanities was the Holocaust survivor and Nobel Prize–winning author Elie Wiesel.

Yet even more so than Coates, Kendi has a problem in his heroic narrative of fighting his way through a racist, oppressive country: which is that the strongest stories he has are striking in their insignificance. At one point in his book *How to Be an Antiracist* (2019), Kendi writes about an incident in third grade where a white teacher calls on an eager white student in the front of the class rather than a shy black girl who is sitting at the back. All these years later, Kendi gets almost a whole chapter of his book out of it. He can recall every detail of the incident, as he shows the reader. But he stresses that he cannot remember the name of the white teacher. "Forgetting her may have been a coping mechanism," he now says, just one of "many racist White people over the years who interrupted my peace with their sirens."[37]

Some people would say this was an unimportant incident; others might claim that it was at most a racial microaggression. But Kendi would not accept any such claims. He says of this incident, "What other people call racist microaggressions I call racist abuse."[38] Defining or rather redefining terms and words has become a career specialty for Kendi. Indeed, in *How to Be an Antiracist*, every chapter opens with a definition or a set of definitions. They give the work a pseudoscholastic glow, although the definitions are not always as helpful as the author thinks. For example, his first chapter is headed by two definitions: that of a racist ("One who is supporting a racist policy through their actions or inaction or expressing a racist idea") and of an antiracist ("One who is supporting an antiracist policy through their actions or expressing an antiracist idea"). There are several things that diminish the brilliance of these definitions. The first is the realization that like all the other definitions throughout the work, the definitions offered are written by Kendi himself. The second is the fact that they are not very good definitions.

Most people would recognize a racist as someone who regards members of one racial group as inferior to another simply by dint of this one characteristic over which they have no say. But Kendi does not define racism like this. Kendi's definition of a racist is someone who engages in racist actions—a definition that is at best circular, for it uses the thing being defined to define the thing. It also leaves unaddressed the question of what a racist action is and who designates it as such. Though a suspicion lingers. Meantime, Kendi's definition of an antiracist is somewhat simpler. It is, essentially, the invitation to be like Kendi.

Today when Kendi is asked to define racism before audiences, his definition has become something of a party trick. "Racism is a marriage of racist policies and racist ideas that produces and normalizes racial inequities" is one of his standard answers. It has become his version of a crowd-pleaser, often greeted by great laughter and applause. But given the huge influence that Kendi's work now has, and the near complete array of sectors that it has run through, it is worth noting one particular failing. Which is that Kendi is not opposed to racism. He is opposed to certain forms of racism: specifically white on black racism. Other racisms can be, in his own definitions, a positive force. For instance, in his writing on discrimination and inequity, he cannot avoid one particular conclusion beckoning to him: "The only remedy to racist discrimination is antiracist discrimination. The only remedy to past discrimination is present discrimination. The only remedy to present discrimination is future discrimination."[39]

Much depends here on what he means by "racist" and what he means by "antiracist." It appears that by "racist" Kendi means things he does not like. Whereas "antiracist" means things he does like. There are no areas of neutral in Kendi's color chart. There are only white supremacists and white nationalists and then white people who agree with him. Similarly, there are black people who agree with Kendi and black people who do not. Those black people who do not go along with everything proposed by him are also racists. For instance, Kendi does not like the conservative Supreme Court justice Clarence Thomas. Likewise, he does not like the black former Ohio secretary of state Ken Blackwell, who worked for George W. Bush, condemning him with typical understatement for "the most egregious Black on Black racist crime in recent American history." Kendi has no truck with such people. "Remember, we are all either racists or antiracists," he says, before saying that "Black on Black criminals like Blackwell get away with their racism. Black people call them Uncle Toms, sellouts, Oreos, puppets—everything but the right thing: racist. Black people need to do more than revoke their 'Black card,' as we call it. We need to paste the racist card to their foreheads for all the world to see."[40]

In Kendi's world of definitions, it isn't just Clarence Thomas that is racist. A whole pile of other things are as well. And, conveniently enough, they all help to delineate the boundaries of Kendi's own political and other prejudices. For instance, he makes it clear that it is racist to oppose reparations for slavery. It is also racist not to have any opinion on the matter. So you must either share Kendi's specific view on the matter or you are—guess what?—a racist. Everywhere you turn, the other exits are blocked. For instance, referring to a "post-racial society" is also racist. Either you must accept Kendi's definition of the society you live in or you are a racist. This neat trick works with almost everything. Kendi is opposed to voter ID laws. So, can anybody guess what people who support voter ID laws might be? That is right: they, too, are racists. Strangely it is also racist to not agree with what Kendi wants to do in regard to climate change.

Again and again, he divides the world clearly and firmly between just these two camps of people. We are all either racist or antiracist. We are all either striving to be racist or striving to be antiracist. An eminent black justice who does one thing wrong in Kendi's eyes becomes a racist. While if a person does absolutely everything right in Kendi's eyes, agreeing with all his own often contradictory views, then they can in time be granted the badge of "antiracist." About one thing, there can be little doubt: the placing of these boundaries is enormously convenient for Kendi himself. But it is highly inconvenient for any society that follows these rules. After all, there must be some issues—such as voter registration or the environment—that can be discussed without being viewed as either a racist or an antiracist issue. If there are not, then the likelihood of addressing any or all of these issues recedes considerably.

Rather than taking race out of a discussion (the very concept of which Kendi also describes as racist), this worldview goes out of its way to impose race into every discussion. And to do so in the most stark and unforgiving terms. If one portion of your society is racist and another portion antiracist, then normal political settlement becomes impossible. Some people will go along with a policy or position they know to be incorrect simply in order not to be sullied by the label "racist." While others might be genuinely persuaded that the world is this Manichean and that it divides not between a range of people with a variety of wildly different ideas but between racists and antiracists, white supremacists and Ibram X. Kendi.

Perhaps it is inevitable that a whole industry should wish to mirror the commercial success of Kendi's work. Among the spin-offs, there is a work titled *How to Be an Antiracist Family*, consisting of "25 inspiring tales about racism to read with the kids."[41] It seemed as though anything could be published so long as it whipped along the same narrative that white people are oppressors and able to be insulted at every turn. Meanwhile, black people are the oppressed and able to say anything, however insulting, so long as it is said about white people. For instance, there is Ijeoma Oluo's work *Mediocre: The Dangerous Legacy of White Male America* (2020). And the London-born author Otegha Uwagba's work titled *Whites: On Race and Other Falsehoods*.

In Britain, the Americanized tone of the era can be seen: a grand narrative of racism and antiracism all extrapolated out from minute events, spliced together with constant catastrophism. For instance, at one point, Uwagba describes how she is meant to be attending a friend's Christmas party but cancels at the last minute "because I know I'll probably be the only Black person in a room full of white ones." She worries that after some of "the requisite hand-wringing" about racial issues, someone will suggest talking about something "less depressing 'because it's Christmas.'" Uwagba says that she will then "smash a plate against a wall because I don't think there's anything else we should be talking about, don't think it's fair that white people get to change the subject." So instead, she says, "I stay at home and cry."[42]

Uwagba appears to be a difficult friend to have. She complains bitterly when white friends don't ask her how she is. And she then complains bitterly about it when white friends do ask her how she is. After the death of George Floyd, she claims that her email inbox became "a dumping ground for white guilt." Again she tells off friends who ask her how she is and berates those who do not ask. "Everywhere white shame looms large," she writes, "sucking the oxygen out of the room, threatening to obscure the issue at hand. Even at their most penitent, white people have a way of making it hard to breathe."[43]

TAKE IT TO THE STREETS

At the exact moment that racism had never been more discredited or more socially and politically unacceptable, it is portrayed as omnipresent and needing a great pushback.

As I toured the United States in the months after George Floyd's death, I was struck by this fact time and time again. In the cities where Black Lives Matter (BLM) flags and signs were flown, BLM had become something like the national religion. It was there in the bookstores packed with books telling white Americans how they needed to retrain their minds. Everywhere there was a high-resolution projection of a society that was significantly off, though seemingly projected and agreed upon by individuals and corporations alike.

Cities that were once proud and beautiful, such as Seattle, were almost entirely boarded up in their centers. Small and large businesses had been almost completely destroyed by months of riots and COVID-19. And those businesses that did remain were not just asking but begging to be left alone—pleading with any potential mob to pass them by. Shops beside what had briefly been the city's autonomous zone ("CHAZ") included some classic Don't Hurt Me signs in the windows. A hairdresser's salon had not only the compulsory Black Lives Matter sign but a sign stressing that the business in question was "A minority owned, women led, LGBTQIA+ staffed local business." In case anybody mistook it for a white-supremacist hair salon.

At the other end of the corporate scale was the city's remaining Whole Foods shop. Boarded up, like most of the buildings in the city center, it had a vast banner hanging at the front of the remaining storefront. In huge letters, as big as the shop's name, it declared, "Racism has no place here." As though the fruit and nuts aisle of the Whole Foods in Seattle had been a known gathering place for the Klan. In nearby Portland, Uber had taken out a vast banner, unfurled down one entire side of a gigantic office building. "If you tolerate racism, delete Uber," read the banner, adding, "Black people have the right to move without fear." How many visitors disagreed with that idea so vehemently that it needed saying at building-length? How bad must the racial problem be in a country such as America that commercial companies should have to hector the public like this? Exactly what situation do they believe the country to be in?

I went to Portland ahead of the 2020 presidential election to try to find out. This city in the Pacific Northwest has become infamous in recent years for its virulent strand of anarcho-syndicalism that has ended up morphing from a form of student Marxism into a wider Antifa-BLM agenda. For years, self-described "Antifa" activists had held protests and riots in the city. In the aftermath of the death of George Floyd, this movement turned into a nightly protest movement. In time, every federal building in the state was attacked or turned into a fortress. Commercial businesses were attacked, and by the autumn of 2020, almost every government building and business in downtown Portland was either closed, boarded up, or effectively barricaded against the nightly riots. Portland had become a ground zero for a portion of the US culture war. One reason being an asymmetry in the reporting from the city. Whenever reporters did go to cover the protests, they were accused of giving succor to the Far Right. Whenever they ignored it (as they mostly did), people on the right accused them of giving cover to the Far Left. But for an outsider to actually see firsthand the unbelievable oddity of the situation in Portland was eye-opening. As one long-term resident said to me, "This used to be a very civil town." Not anymore.

The ostensible cause of the nightly Antifa-BLM riots is that the participants seem to believe the image projected about their country. Nightly they take to the streets to oppose systemic racism and white supremacy. For a couple of days and nights in Portland, I joined the group, dressed as them, and attended their gatherings, in order to see for myself how a part of this generation really believes what they have been told about America.

Certainly, like everywhere else, the madnesses that already existed in the city had been exacerbated by the coronavirus and the ensuing decision to shutter the economy and lock down the population. But downtown Portland had become a desolate, dangerous place, populated by the vast number of homeless people who had flooded into the area over recent decades, incentivized by local government allowing them to pitch their tents wherever they liked. In the main squares, unattended tables of food and drink were set out for them to pick at, like a twenty-four-hour buffet.

But it wasn't just the virus or the reaction of the authorities that had led to this wasteland. For months, protestors had dragged passing motorists from their cars, assaulted businesses, and hospitalized journalists whose reporting was disobliging to them—all without law enforcement taking any significant interest. The businesses that still operated did so as in a city under siege. I visited one restaurant that had only recently opened. The owner was a proud black American patriot. On the walls of his restaurant, he had erected posters of American heroes: a soldier, a fireman, and other first responders. For this reason, his restaurant had been targeted. Two nights earlier, someone had fired live rounds of ammunition through his restaurant's windows. The boarding was still up over the area where the glass had shattered. What kind of interpretation of the country had somebody come to when they fired live shots through the windows of a black-owned business to object to the heroizing of anyone involved in the American state?

It seemed that Portland had become the epicenter of a confusion that has afflicted activists in Britain and other Western countries as well. That was the taught perception that they live in a patriarchal, unequal, cis-heteronormative, irredeemably racist society. They have been persuaded of this and are reacting in line with that perception: if this is indeed the state of society, then society needs to be acted against. And the authorities had done nothing to challenge this interpretation of their society. Indeed, the city's left-wing mayor had expressly forbidden the police from working with the federal authorities to meaningfully act against the rioters. At his reelection campaign in late 2020, the only candidate running against him was an open supporter of Antifa.

Recent successful operations carried out by that mayoral candidate's favored militia included the pulling down of almost every statue and public monument in the city. All historical figures had been removed by mobs of protestors. The weekend before I was there, it was Abraham Lincoln who had been pulled down, his empty pedestal now scrawled with graffiti and the single word "Landback." On other occasions—in a quasi-pagan ceremony—rioters repeatedly set on fire a monument of an elk, until the authorities removed it. By now, a tour of the sights in Portland consisted of a wide variety of empty plinths.

Over the summer, the president had sent in federal guards against the wishes of the local authorities. These remaining federal agents were now among the few targets Antifa had left. The first night on which I joined them was for a "Fuck Gentrification" march (my first). With no police officers in sight, the activists used their own police force, including outriders on motorcycles, to block off roads and then parade through the streets screaming through megaphones at customers in the remaining bars and at the inhabitants of a residential neighborhood that protestors claimed had once been lived in by black and Indigenous families. Many of the people who lived in these houses came out and put their fists in the air or waved in solidarity. Most had BLM posters in their windows. All were accused of living on "stolen land" by the mostly white marchers. Other chants included "Wake up, motherfucker, wake up."

A night later, we were outside the Immigration and Customs Enforcement facility by the waterfront. This federal facility was boarded up, but Antifa likes to try to burn these buildings down with the occupants inside. The federal authorities were keen to stop this from happening. So a cat-and-mouse game kicked off, one at which both sides were now very practiced. The Antifa activists hurled projectiles at the boarded-up facility and beat on drums to work themselves up into a frenzy. They lit fires in the street and tried to make their way to the doors of the facility. Only after sufficient warning sirens had been given and the rioters got right up to the doors did the agents of law enforcement break out. Tear gas was fired and pepper bullets were used.

And so a running battle saw the protestors chased back for a time, only for the police to retreat under a barrage of "oink" noises from the protestors. One young white woman in a pink onesie jumpsuit kept shouting "Nazis" at the officers through a megaphone, occasionally changing her attack to telling the officers how much their children would grow up to hate them. What can have happened to a society for such behavior to have become normal? One answer is that a set of claims about America and American society were allowed to wash by. People made claims about the state of race in America that were subtly, and sometimes not so subtly, untrue.

Pushing back against these claims needed attention to detail and an obsession with the facts. A monomania as intense as that of the people who created this vision. And so it was just allowed to roll on by. Only now, when the resulting vision can be seen blown up in large, projected onto the wall of the world, can the full consequences of the work that has been put in be perceived. Minute claims of "systemic racism," "institutional whiteness," and much more were ignored. But blown up on the projector system of American culture, they now show a picture that is monstrous. Which is why a middle-class adolescent from one of the luckiest generations in human history, living in one of the freest societies in human history, can be found outside a police facility at night, in a pink jumpsuit, screaming obscenities at any representative of the state.

POPULAR ENTERTAINMENT

Portland may be an extreme. But it is only an extreme manifestation of a misperception that now exists throughout America and the Western world. One consequence of which is that there is not an area of life that cannot now be perceived, or misperceived, through this prism.

In early 2021, the popular television show *The Bachelor* reached its twenty-fifth season, and for the first time, the eligible man for the season was black. The casting of the twenty-eight-year-old black real estate agent from North Carolina, Matt James, could have been a unifying moment for the show. Instead, the predictable thing happened. Race entered the arena and blew the whole show apart. One of the four female contestants chosen for the final round was twenty-four-year-old Rachael Kirkconnell. Once she was on television, her social media accounts were inevitably scoured for evidence of wrongdoing. And it was discovered that three years earlier, in 2018, Kirkconnell had been photographed at an antebellum-themed party. A scandal was created. The show's host, Chris Harrison, called for people to have "a little grace, a little understanding, a little compassion." But then, for "defending" Kirkconnell, Harrison himself became the object of an antiracist stampede. Dozens of former contestants condemned Harrison, and the women of season twenty-five released a joint statement announcing that they wanted to make it clear that "we denounce any defense of racism" and "any defense of racist behavior,"[44] as though Harrison were guilty of either.

Meanwhile, in the real world of the reality TV show itself, Kirkconnell and James actually got together as the final couple, with James telling Kirkconnell that he wanted her to be the mother of his children. But that was before the social-media posts came to light, and at that point, the couple split with James deciding that he "wasn't okay" with it and saying he feared Kirkconnell might not understand "what it means to be black in America."[45] And the scouring did not end there. After nineteen years, Harrison was eventually forced out of his role presenting the show in what was subsequently referred to as a "racism controversy."[46]

That season it was *The Bachelor*. But it could as easily have been any other show. In July 2021 in the UK, a woman who had failed to make it into the final of *Strictly Come Dancing* six years earlier, Anita Rani, gave an interview to the media in which she said that she still wondered about the reason. The television presenter said, "I still find myself wondering whether I would have got into the final if I didn't have a brown face."[47] This claim was then blazoned across the headlines, ignoring the fact that Alesha Dixon, Mark Ramprakash, Louis Smith, and Ore Oduba had all won *Strictly* without being held back by a severely racist Saturday-night audience.

But anything could be subjected to the same remorseless view. In the spring of 2021, it was the turn of the game show *Jeopardy* to have a race meltdown. A middle-aged contestant named Kelly Dono-hue may have already looked suspicious because he was wearing a dark suit with a red tie. At one point, he exacerbated the problem by holding out three fingers to the camera. A number of viewers imme-diately asserted online that this was a well-known white-supremacist sign. The American media picked up the story, Donohue's Facebook page was scoured for evidence. Fan groups for the show claimed that the sign looked as though it could well be a "white power" gesture and admitted that while "we can't know his intent," *Jeopardy* fan sites were "not here to provide safe harbor for white supremacists." Soon 595 former contestants on *Jeopardy* were jointly signing a letter demanding to know why *Jeopardy* had not edited out the nanosec-ond on the show on which the three fingers had been held out. "We cannot stand up for hate," the former contestants said. "We cannot stand next to hate. We cannot stand onstage with something that looks like hate."

After this and much more, Donohue (who works as a bank ex-aminer for the state government in Massachusetts) tried to explain what had actually happened. As the tapes of the previous episodes showed, when he won his first victory, he held one finger against his jacket. On the second victory, he held out two. On the night in question, he had just achieved his third victory, and so he held out three fingers, with his thumb and forefinger tucked in. "That's a three. No more. No less," he wrote. "There wasn't a hidden agenda or any malice behind it."

Not everyone was convinced. Other contestants on the show condemned his attempted self-defense. "Most problematic to us as a contestant community is the fact that Kelly has not publicly apologized for the ramifications of the gesture he made," they wrote in a joint statement. This, in turn, prompted another statement from Donohue in which he felt compelled to state, "I reject and condemn white supremacy." He had not been sending out bat signals to white supremacists, he had been counting to three on his fingers.[48]

It may be easy to laugh at some of the situations in which people see white supremacy everywhere. But in the end, this projection has repercussions that are more monstrous than they are laughable. So it is that in sector after sector, acting on the projection that it believes exists, a movement that started by being academic already has consequences that are disturbingly practical.

PRACTICAL CONSEQUENCES

If you created a movement that sought to demonize "blackness," then that movement would inevitably end up demonizing black people. As it was with the old racism, so it is with the new racism. If you are going to demonize whiteness and being white, then it must at some stage mean that you are going to demonize white people. In almost any other realm of race relations, this would be understood. And so the logical outcome of all the antiwhite rhetoric of recent years can hardly be a surprise. The ideology has been pumped into the Western system in recent years, and it has resulted in a surge of antiwhite activities.

Education

It starts from the earliest possible stage and now runs through every level of education. Twenty years ago, when Delgado and Stefancic talked of the many people "in the field of education" who consider CRT to have "an activist dimension," they meant it. Two decades later, the results of the activism can be seen in the curriculum and at schools across America and the West. You can select almost any school district across the country today and find the same, retributive, game being played.

In Buffalo, public schools have forced children in kindergarten to watch videos of dead black children in order to teach them about "police brutality."[49] In California, children in third grade have been taught that they should rank themselves in order of "power" and "privilege," while a new ethnic studies curriculum in the state calls for "counter-genocide" against white Christians.[50] In Seattle, the public schools have claimed that white teachers in the schooling system are "spirit murdering" black children.[51] And then, of course, there is always New York. There are case studies enough for a conference in that city alone.

At the East Side Community School in New York, white parents have been sent a "tool for action" that tells them that they must become "white traitors" and then advocate for "white abolition." One helpful part of the tool kit for parents identifies the eight different "white identities" they might be suffering from. These range from "white supremacist" to "white abolitionist." It gets there by way of "white voyeurism," "white privilege" (naturally), "white benefit," "white confessional," "white critical," and "white traitor." These last ones, leading up to "white abolitionist," are of course the most positive ones and are said to include the need to "dismantle institutions" and stress the necessity of "dismantling whiteness" plus "not allowing whiteness to reassert itself."[52] Over in the Bronx, a "Disrupt and Dismantle" campaign led to one educator being "grilled" about her ethnic (Jewish) background and being admonished for refusing to perform a "black power" salute.[53]

Of course, not everybody is willing to go along with these racist indoctrination sessions. But where people have spoken out against them, the results have not always helped their careers. In 2021, Grace Church School forced all its students and teachers to participate in "antiracist training." The training in question was done in the name of "increasing equity." But as a math teacher at the public school noted, in reality, it made white students feel that they were "oppressors" while cultivating "dependency, resentment and moral superiority" in those students deemed "oppressed."

One day in early 2021, that math teacher—Paul Rossi—was invited to take part in a mandatory "whites-only" Zoom meeting for students and faculty. During the session, he questioned whether it was really right to label "objectivity," "individualism," and "fear of open conflict," among other traits, as characteristics of "white supremacy." The resulting discussion was reported by some students to have been more productive than they had expected. But someone broke the confidentiality of the forum and reported Rossi for his remarks. The school's head informed Rossi that his challenges at the Zoom meeting had caused "harm" to the students because these were "life and death matters, about people's flesh and blood and bone." He was also told that he had created "dissonance for vulnerable and unformed thinkers" and caused "neurological disturbance in students' beings and systems," and the school's director of studies claimed that Rossi's remarks might even constitute "harassment."

In the following days, the head ordered all the school advisors to read out a public reprimand of Rossi to every student in the school. Rossi himself described the resulting scene. "It was a surreal experience, walking the halls alone and hearing the words emitting from each classroom." Part of the statement read: "At independent schools, with their history of predominantly white populations, racism colludes with other forms of bias (sexism, classism, ableism, and so much more) to undermine our stated ideals, and we must work hard to undo this history." Rossi's ongoing employment at the school was at first made contingent on his working to "heal my relationship with the students of color."[54]

Rossi subsequently spoke with the school's principal, George Davidson, who privately admitted to having some "grave doubts" about "some of the doctrinaire stuff that gets spouted at us in the name of antiracism." The follow-on point that he found it hard to understand, or to admit to understanding, was that this theory must have practical consequences. Rossi asked the principal if he agreed that the materials they were using to teach pupils were in essence "demonizing people." Davidson agreed. Therefore, the school was "demonizing white kids." On this, too, he eventually agreed. They were making white children at the school feel "less than," he admitted, and for "nothing that they are personally responsible for." Yet Davidson did not seem to know what to do about this conundrum. He later denied that he had said any of these things. But Rossi had the good sense to record the conversation with the principal and made the recording publicly available. Rossi was put on leave and eventually made to leave the school he had devoted his teaching years to. But as he said to the principal on his way out, the reason that the principal had not shared the concerns he had about the racist training going on at his school was because "you know exactly what happens to people who do. It is what is happening to me right now."[55]

At other elite private schools, such as the $40,000-a-year Harvard-Westlake School in Los Angeles, parents have struggled to find a way to rebut a similar "antiracist" agenda. That school's aims include explorations of "implicit bias" for seventh graders provided by the unimprovably titled "Pollyanna Racial Literacy Curriculum." There has also been a redesign of the eleventh-grade US history course that is now taught "from a critical race theory perspective,"[56] and students in the tenth grade have been put through Implicit Bias Testing. Meanwhile, at nearby Brentwood ($45,630 per annum), pupils were treated to racially segregated "dialogue" sessions, where the school's reading list had also been put through the usual purge. Out went *The Scarlet Letter*, *Lord of the Flies*, and *To Kill a Mockingbird*. In came such books as Ibram X. Kendi's *Stamped from the Beginning: The Definitive History of Racist Ideas in America*, while the faculty announced a late start for one day for the lower school because of its study of Robin DiAngelo's *White Fragility*.[57]

As though to prove that anything the schooling system can do, the college system can do worse, at least one law professor at an American university has been advocating a ranking system for "whiteness" on American campuses. University of Dayton professor emerita Vernellia Randall has ranked colleges on a chart that records "total whiteness" and "excess whiteness" scores. Among other things, she has demanded that American law schools eliminate "excess whiteness" from their campuses.[58]

Employment

It is easy to imagine that lunacies such as this might be restricted to the education sector and that outside of America's schools and colleges, some other standard of common sense must prevail. But nothing could be further from the truth. In recent years, under the Trump administration as much as in the current administration, the same pattern of thought can be found throughout the public sector.

Agencies from the Justice Department and the Office of the Attorney General to the National Institutes of Health have spent recent years pursuing "antiracism" through employee retraining sessions and more. The explicit goal of the diversity apparatchiks is, as Christopher F. Rufo has noted, that "they want to convert 'everyone in the federal government' to the work of 'anti-racism.'"[59] At these struggle sessions, what occurs is that federal employees are pressured into compelled speech, with professional penalties lying in wait for those who do not comply. These sessions have occurred across a clean sweep of government.

For instance, it has become clear that the FBI has been holding "intersectionality workshops" for its employees.[60] The Department of Homeland Security has been using training documents that tell white employees that they have been "socialized into oppressor roles,"[61] while scientists at the Sandia National Laboratories have been made to attend white male–only reeducation retreats to address their white privilege. At one such session, the employees were told that "white male culture" is the same as the KKK and "white supremacism." The participants were forced to renounce their "white male privilege" and, as part of this exercise, were made to write letters of apology to imagined women of color.[62] How this assists productivity or security, much less equality, at America's nuclear laboratories remains unclear.

The private sector, too, is pouring money into training employees to see white supremacy in every interaction. For example, the services network Ernst & Young has sent out emails to its employees urging them that "It's not enough to be not racist. We need to speak out and take action against racism and discrimination. We must be anti-racist, and at Ernst & Young, our resolve to do and to be just that is stronger than ever." The particular impetus for this call was, as one managing partner said in an email sent out to all employees, the "senseless acts of violence against our Black communities"—on this occasion against Jacob Blake in Kenosha, Wisconsin. Blake subsequently admitted to wielding a knife before police shot him. But Kelly Grier, who sent out the internal email, described the actions of the police as pointing to "The systemic racism that permeates in our country."[63] Why should Ernst & Young be on the side of an accused knife-wielding criminal? Because "antiracist" theory had taught them to draw sweeping morals first and ignore all details later. It was more important to send the right signals than to be right on the facts.

Employees at Cigna, one of America's largest health insurance providers, have likewise been routinely subjected to CRT lessons. These have included them being lectured on "white privilege," "gender privilege," and "religious privilege," and being advised not to consider white men in hiring decisions.[64] And at one of America's most successful companies, Coca-Cola, employees have been made to go through "anti-racism" training that aimed to teach workers how to "be less white."

The mandatory "Confronting Racism" course for employees included a slide instructing employees to be "less white, less arrogant, less certain, less defensive, less ignorant and more humble."

It also told them that "In the US and other Western nations, white people are socialized to feel that they are inherently superior because they are white" and cited "research" that claimed to show that children as young as three years old "understand that it is better to be white."[65] Because Coca-Cola has always paid such attention to helping young children live healthy lives.

If people wonder why more people do not speak out about being force-fed this mental junk food, it is because of the price that can be paid for not toeing the line. A fact that is becoming increasingly clear. In February 2021, the Australian-born chairman of KPMG UK was condemned by colleagues after describing the concept of unconscious bias, during a staff discussion, as "complete crap" and saying that nothing whatsoever had been achieved as a result of forcing people to undergo unconscious-bias training. Junior staff said that the chairman ought to "check his privilege" and reported him to management for his "insensitive comments." After being forced to temporarily step down, "pending investigation" he was eventually forced to resign.[66]

When people wonder why most go along with the whole agenda, it is because it is so often made clear that whether you're a math teacher or a partner in a vast multinational firm, the cost of raising your head above the parapet can lead to your whole career crashing down around you. And it can happen from asking the simplest of questions, asserting a provable truth, or simply acknowledging a belief that everybody held until the day before yesterday.

Very occasionally, things can go in the opposite direction, but only when a huge amount of negative attention is brought upon those people trying to implement policies they presume to be either cost-free or beneficial to their image. For instance, in 2021, Disney told its employees that they should reject "equality" and focus instead on "equity." According to the "What can I do about racism?"

program to which Disney employees were subjected, they must focus on "systemic racism," "white privilege," "white fragility," and more. Their training also included segments on "implicit bias," "microaggressions," and, of course, "becoming an antiracist." In the training module "Allyship for Race Consciousness," employees were told that they should "take ownership" for educating themselves "about structural anti-Black racism." They were told that the USA has a "long history of systemic racism and transphobia" and that white employees at Disney must "work through feelings of guilt, shame, and defensiveness," atone by challenging "colorblind ideologies and rhetoric," and never "question or debate Black colleagues' lived experience." Among the suggestions for white Disney employees was that they work on their racist babies (racist from "3 months old" again) and "donate to anti–white supremacy work such as your local Black Lives Matter Chapter."[67]

Occasionally when such in-house training lessons are made public, the company swiftly removes the lessons, fibs that employees had not been put through them, or pretends that they were optional. Disney removed its training documents from the web and told the *New York Post* they had been "deliberately distorted as reflective of company policy."[68] In nearly every case, these lies get the relevant companies out of a temporarily embarrassing situation. But on not one occasion has there been any sign that a company teaching antiwhite racism to its employees has realized that what it had done is wrong or reversed it for that reason.

Health Care

Such instances of corporate racism may be sinister enough. But infinitely more sinister—because even more practical—have been the inroads of the exact same ideology into the realm of health care. And these have perhaps only come to the fore because, from 2020 onwards, while America was coping with an epidemic of claims of racism produced at home, it was also struggling with a medical epidemic that had spilled out of China.

The two issues overlapped in the question of vulnerability to COVID and access to vaccines. In all the Western countries, starting from America, a debate emerged in which activists asserted that the black and minority ethnic populations were disproportionately suffering from COVID. Even before these facts were asserted, the cause was insisted upon. Before anyone had time to talk about living arrangements, underlying health conditions, or anything else, Afua Hirsch and others had taken to the pages of *The Guardian* and the airwaves. There they managed to suggest that America, Britain, and other Western countries were so racist that they couldn't even import a virus from China without giving it their own special racial spin and using the opportunity to kill as many black people as possible.[69] It is hardly surprising that health authorities everywhere were on high alert to this charge.

Only a short while earlier, it was enough to be "color-blind" in treating the sick. Now, "equity" was the watchword, and it was code for equalizing outcomes even if that meant making things worse for whites instead of better for blacks.

For instance, in December 2020, at the end of the year of COVID and BLM, the Centers for Disease Control and Prevention (CDC) released its initial recommendations on vaccine prioritizations. It identified three competing priority groups (essential workers, the over sixty-fives, and adults with underlying conditions). It then identified three ethical principles to decide who to prioritize among these groups. The three ethical principles included "Promote justice" and "Mitigate health inequities." And here the CDC encountered a serious ethical problem. Because racial and ethnic minority groups were underrepresented among adults over the age of sixty-five.[70]

So, as explained in the *New York Times*, the concluding policy aimed at prioritizing essential workers over the elderly, even though this was expected to cost an extra fifty thousand lives per month. Justifying this shift, Harald Schmidt, an expert in ethics and health policy at the University of Pennsylvania, stated that a perfectly reasonable set of priorities was at play in the new guidance. "Older

populations are whiter," said the expert in ethics. "Society is struc-
tured in a way that enables them to live longer. Instead of giving
additional health benefits to those who already had more of them,
we can start to level the playing field a bit." Of course, "leveling
the playing field a bit" here cannot mean anything other than "let-
ting more white people die."[71] Formal support for this policy also
appeared in the *Journal of the American Medical Association*.[72]

This sort of thing can still cause a certain amount of negative
comment, and it duly followed the accurate reporting on the CDC's
proposals. The CDC backtracked a month later, though not without
loud self-pity from members of the committee who complained that
they had faced "a flood of often vicious accusations" that they had
been "prioritizing other racial groups over white people."[73]

If the CDC guidance had been the only such case, then perhaps
it could have been ignored. But it was not. Since that case, "equitable medicine" has been tried across the land. The state of Vermont
actively sought to give vaccine eligibility to certain groups while ex-
cluding people who identify as white.[74] And at Brigham and Women's
Hospital in Boston, an explicitly racially discriminatory health care
program was put into operation. As two of those involved described
in the *Boston Review*, "colorblind solutions" had "failed to achieve
racial equity in healthcare," and there was a problem with too many
white people being admitted to the cardiology unit, among others.

As a result, a new pilot initiative was begun that would use a "reparations framework" of preferential admissions for "Black and Latinx" heart-failure patients.

This anticipated that "offering preferential care based on race or
ethnicity may elicit legal challenges from our system of colorblind
law" but noted that they nevertheless were encouraged "to proceed
confidently on behalf of equity and racial justice, with backing provided by recent White House executive orders." The executive orders
in question being the recent equity executive orders of the new Biden
administration.[75]

Again, if these were just rogue agencies—a CDC here, a major hospital there—then it could perhaps be understood as some curious anomaly that could be fine-tuned with care. But it is not. Time and again, it is not just the individual agencies or institutions but the presiding institutions that are going along with the same plan, often at the same pace. The American Medical Association (AMA) has released an eighty-six-page "equity plan" that rejects the idea of "equality as a process." Its stated aims are "to dismantle structural racism," to "dismantle white supremacy" and to "acknowledge racism as a public health threat." Furthermore, the AMA criticizes the idea that people from different groups should be treated the same and elevates racist "antiracism" into professional best practice. Naturally, the document quotes, among others, the work of bell hooks.[76]

Of course, there is another danger in all of this. For medicine is one of those areas in which some knowledge of racial background may be not just useful but lifesaving. Different genetic groups carry different vulnerabilities to particular diseases and ailments ranging from cancer to osteoporosis, as well as varying responsiveness to different drugs. And this presents a particular problem. Because it suggests that race is not just a "social construct" but something that affects real areas of our lives, including health. Because this is such an unpalatable truth for the presumptions of the era, whenever the issue arises, it causes a great flare-up of nonmedical concerns. There is, for instance, an ongoing controversy around the accurate determining of kidney function, but "antiracists" have tried to remove the clinical algorithms and treatment guidelines that would help diagnoses, and have done so in the name of combating racism.[77]

Many doctors, including many black doctors, recognize how dangerous this is, and a number took to the pages of the *New England Journal of Medicine* to try to halt it. After several paragraphs of necessary disclaimers, they stressed their point, which was "that genetic differences exist between people belonging to different socially constructed racial categories. We embrace this diversity and acknowledge its clinically meaningful implications."[78] But it is not at all clear that these careful practitioners will be victorious in their attempt to weave around the dogmas of the era. What they are arguing requires an understanding of something other than CRT. It requires a knowledge of certain genealogical and medical facts. But for the time being, an insistence on racism and antiracism as the sole means of looking at any and every problem remains much greater, clearer, and all-encompassing.

That is why, for instance, other medical practitioners from Harvard on down can blame all racial health disparities on whiteness ("anti-racist epidemiology"),[79] claim that systemic racism is to blame for the deaths of pregnant black women,[80] and assert that when white Americans volunteer their DNA for scientific experiments, these white Americans are subtly doing so in order to victimize non-white groups.[81] Overall, the message is that whiteness itself is a pandemic. As one *New York Times* contributing editor recently put it, whiteness is "a virus that, like other viruses, will not die until there are no bodies left for it to infect."[82] And such protogenocidal talk is not uncommon. It has become the norm. To deny it has become unusual. Say anything to the contrary, or even simply express doubt about claims that structural racism is endemic, and not only will you lose your job; those around you will lose theirs.

This is what happened at the *Journal of the American Medical Association* in 2021. The deputy editor said in a discussion that he thought "structural racism" was an unfortunate term and that "many people like myself are offended by the implication that we are somehow racist." For this, not only was the deputy editor the subject of a campaign to get him fired, his editor was forced out of his job through some sort of guilt by association, in what was soon being reported as just one more "racist controversy."[83]

CONCLUSIONS

In this situation, where white people are pathologized and a new mania is invented every month ("white rage" being another recent pseudomedical addition to this lexicon), there remains a question: What exactly are white people supposed to do? The advocates of the new racism are not without suggestions, and there are several possibilities. UCLA law professor and leading critical race theorist Cheryl Harris is one of numerous leading critical race theorists who have argued that the right to private property should be suspended, with land and money seized and then redistributed along racial lines.[84]

Otegha Uwagba, by contrast, has said that because "Black people cannot ourselves abolish whiteness—white people will need to relinquish it." To do this, she says, white people must give up their "racialized privileges." Like what? One suggestion Uwagba has is by boycotting the hairdresser "who gives you an amazing blow-dry but who you know doesn't cut Afro hair." Another idea, she says, is for white people to start to realize that "patronizing Black-owned businesses, reading Black writers, and amplifying our voices . . . is not enough." She says that white people must lose all their privileges, and that this "allyship will cost them the shape of their lives as they know it."[85] It does not seem an especially appealing invitation, even if the situation it denoted were true and the answer it holds out were possible.

Yet compared with other offers, Uwagba's seems positively generous. In April 2021, Aruna Khilanani gave a speech at Yale's Child Study Center titled "The Psychopathic Problem of the White Mind." This first-generation daughter of doctors from the Indian subcontinent had studied critical theory at the University of Chicago and had clearly absorbed all its own psychopathies. Like Kendi, Coates, and others, she had her own origin story. And where Kendi has the tale of the girl with her hand up and Coates has a story of a woman getting into a lift, Khilanani's tale is a terrible story of a fallout with a boss over scheduling vacation time. Building on this traumatic origin story, she used her talk to express visceral and violent racism against white people. For instance, at one stage in her talk, she fantasized about "unloading a revolver into the head of any white person that got in my way, burying their body, and wiping my bloody hands as I walked away relatively guiltless with a bounce in my step. Like I did the world a fucking favor." Which in a lecture ostensibly about psychopaths is a strangely psychopathic way to talk.

Elsewhere Khilanani used her talk to warn of the costs of talking to white people at all. She said that it was "the cost of your own life, as they suck you dry. There are no good apples out there." She described white people as "a demented, violent predator," with "holes in their brain" and said that all white people are "out of their minds, and they have been for a long time." And she declared that talking to white people about race is "useless."[86] Which must be why resorts to violence were so common in her talk.

But Khilanani is not alone. Only a week before she gave her speech at Yale, another psychoanalyst, named Donald Moss, published an academic article titled "On Having Whiteness" based on a set of his seminars. Describing whiteness as a "parasitic-like condition," he also toyed playfully with some sort of permanent cure for the problem. "There is not yet a permanent cure," he warned.[87] Though doubtless, in the years to come, there will be many people eager to pick up the challenge of thinking about one.

INTERLUDE:
CHINA

Most people around the world want to think well of themselves and of the country they are born into. Most do not think it a good idea to wage a remorseless, demoralizing war against everything to do with the majority group in their society. They do not pick up questionable terms invented yesterday and try to roll them out across the entire country, using them to explain each and every problem in the society. These and many more are symptoms of a very Western disease. A disease of self-hatred and self-distrust. And a disease that is, in both senses of the term, a type of self-abuse. One which other powers, outside the West, are more than happy to observe and use for their own ends.

A characteristic example of this was given in 2008, when the pop star Damon Albarn gave an interview to the journalist Bryan Appleyard. The former Blur front man was doing a lot of work in China and was impatient with criticism of the country. "We've got to get over thinking we have the moral high ground," he told Appleyard, "because I just don't think we do." Albarn claimed to have read about the Opium Wars and appeared to believe that every criticism made of modern China could be traced to Western meddling in the country. His interviewer asked him a pertinent question. If all the problems of China could be traced to the Opium Wars, what were we to make of Chairman Mao's killing of perhaps seventy million of his own people? This puts the Opium Wars into the shade, does it not? Albarn—who is admittedly not one of our smartest minds—seemed stumped. Well, he said, "there is also the argument that something like 400 million people were taken out of extreme poverty."[1]

The truth is that unless he could blame the West, Albarn (like so many other cultural and other figures in the West) was stumped to find any explanation for malfeasance in the world. So long as there was a story of Western wrongdoing, that story could suffice to be the founding problem of the country in question.

There are several problems with this reflex anti-Westernism. One is that it ignores what is actually going on in the world today. For instance, almost every anti-Westernist knows that some people from the West were engaged in selling opium to the Chinese in the nineteenth century. But how many of them know that it is synthetic opioids from China that are now decimating swaths of the United States? According to the US National Center for Health Statistics, more than half a million people in America have died in America's opioid pandemic in the last two decades. The Chinese authorities know of this drug production and do little or nothing to halt it.

Among these drugs is Fentanyl, the addictive properties and devastating effects of which are known across the country. George Floyd himself had Fentanyl in his system when he died. Which does not remotely excuse the actions of the arresting officers. But Floyd was just one of hundreds of thousands of Americans hooked on this Chinese drug. In the same year he died, ninety-three thousand Americans died from Fentanyl.[2] Are very many people in America aware of this? Are many people in the wider West or the wider world?

If they are not aware, then it is in part because people have been persuaded that picking over a select group of historical wrongs will help solve problems in their societies today. Whereas the truth is that a better understanding of the issues facing our societies today is a more likely way to help solve those issues. If more people knew about China's present-day opioid war on America, then perhaps lives could be saved. And not just in America. Scotland alone today currently has an opioid death rate almost thirteen times higher than the European average.[3] That is a real-life tragedy. But raking over the past, and judging it as harshly as possible, seems to be so much easier than doing anything practical about problems that face us all today.

All of this is a very unusual game to be playing. No societies outside the West are engaged in the same self-scouring enterprise.

What is the rest of the world doing while the West—with America leading the way—engages in this orgy of self-abuse? The country that is now the only major challenger to America as the world's leading economy is the People's Republic of China. A country which, as is the way with countries with such titles, is not a republic and does not belong to the people. The People's Republic of China has been ruled for over seven decades by the Chinese Communist Party (CCP).

Unlike all the other major powers that tried communism, China is still pursuing a version of that ideology. Unlike them, it has found a way to liberalize its financial system to such an extent that in recent decades it has become the world's second most important economy. While the Chinese GDP has soared, the party elites who run the country have known not to make the same mistake as those of other socialist countries. The CCP has been very careful to keep a rein on any political liberalism, even as it allows a degree of tightly state-controlled economic liberalism. The current president, Xi Jinping, has accelerated this ever since coming to power in 2013. That year he launched a campaign to prevent liberal ideologies entering the public discourse in China. In the name of security, he also introduced a system of "re-education" of ethnic and religious minorities who the party see as an ideological or security threat. To date, more than a million men, women, and children of the Uighur Muslim minority, among others, have been forced into the sprawling network of internment camps—often referred to as "concentration camps"—across the Xinjiang region.

These camps include systematic rape and torture of detainees, as well as forced sterilization of Uighur women. There are also accusations of the forced harvesting of the internal organs of detainees in these and other camps in the Chinese system. The regime tends to dismiss all such reports, but there is nothing surprising about them. The CCP has always denied any and every accusation of human rights assaults within the country.

Some years ago, I had the opportunity to interview Chen Guangcheng, the blind Chinese activist who had caused an international incident by claiming political asylum at the American embassy in Beijing. Guangcheng had come to the attention of the authorities because of his human rights work inside China. He and his family had suffered years of official intimidation, surveillance, and physical abuse. As he said back in 2013, the situation inside China "is far worse than the ordinary Briton or the international community has been told by the Chinese propaganda."

He had come to realize this when he became aware of the grim realities of the CCP's infamous one-child policy. After trying to take a petition to the central government and one to the local government he realized that one of the great cop-outs of communist belief was wrong. It wasn't that the local guys were bad guys and the central government were good guys. The system was rotten throughout. He could not persuade that system to change, in spite of the wealth of evidence he collected against it of women who were found to have had a second pregnancy being dragged away and having their baby "forcefully aborted."

When the authorities found out that a woman was going to give birth to a second child, there were a number of things they could do. If the mother tried to go into hiding, then the authorities would capture all her family members and imprison them for weeks or months until this forced the mother out of hiding. Then the returning pregnant mother could be forced to have an abortion.

What does this mean, to carry out a forced abortion at nine months? Guangcheng explained, "First of all the woman is dragged to the hospital and forced to sign a 'consent' form for an abortion. There are several ways. One way is that they force the baby to be induced—born. Usually the baby is born alive and then they would throw the baby into water and drown it. The second way is they have some sort of liquid poison dosage and they directly inject the needle into the head of the baby and kill the baby directly and let the baby come out." It is a practice, as he said, that happened everywhere. All over China. A system of "family planning by violence." The long-term effects of this, as he saw it, were "the bankruptcy of the culture of respect for human life. People do not respect life anymore."

After causing untold misery, the one-child policy was phased out during Xi's reign. But the camp system in Xinjiang, among much else, shows that human rights have no more purchase in China in this decade than they had in the decades before. If anything, the ability of the CCP to crack down on human rights, whether in Hong Kong or elsewhere, has increased as its unofficial empire has grown.

Because while pursuing its hybrid form of communist-capitalism, the CCP has managed to purchase greater influence and respectability across the world. The elites of America and Europe thought that bringing China into international organizations would push democratic norms into the country. Instead, China has pushed democratic norms out of international organizations. It has used the period since its 2001 entry into the World Trade Organization to especially great effect. In the year 2000, most countries in South America, Africa, the Far East and Australasia, and Europe did more trade with America than they did with China. By 2020, that situation was inverted. In just twenty years, all these parts of the globe were doing more business with China than they were with America. During that period, America had fallen from more than 75 percent of total global trade to just over 25 percent.[4] And eating up all that difference was China, which went rocketing up in exactly the opposite direction.

The country's Belt and Road Initiative seeks to form a network of Chinese infrastructure and investment that covers the globe: an empire in all but name. It has already seen the country buy its way across the Far East, Near East, and Africa. It has also chosen to buy up key infrastructure across the West. Sometimes it is a key port, such as that of Haifa in Israel or that of Piraeus in Greece. In 2019, Italy signed a deal with China to become the first G7 country to be a part of the Belt and Road Initiative. This allows China's Communications and Construction Company to access the Italian port of Trieste and develop the port at Genoa. It will also include Chinese entry into Italy's agricultural, financial, energy, and engineering markets.

These countries are not alone. The UK government gave the Chinese the go-ahead to build and maintain a new nuclear reactor in England. And before a swift reversal, China's government-backed communications firm Huawei was briefly tasked with helping to create the UK's new 5G network. Of course, no country could carry out such a swift global expansion without a key ingredient, and that is elite capture. The CCP's ability to buy up influence among the elites in each of the countries the party is hoping to enter is unparalleled in its scope and munificence. Across the countries of the West, all who have been in need of some postretirement financing, from former prime ministers on down, have found comfortable sinecures thanks to Chinese firms. Even among the relatively lower ranks of political figures in the West, the CCP and its fronts have been busy buying people up.

The Liberal Democrats were the junior partner in the coalition government in Britain between 2010 and 2015. But since leaving office, its senior and junior figures have been hoovered up by Beijing. The party's present leader took funding for his leadership campaign of the Liberal Democrats from Huawei board member Sir Michael Rake. Ryan Coetzec, the former head of strategy for then leader Nick Clegg, ended up joining a PR firm that tried to launder China's international image while it was snuffing out democracy in Hong Kong. And former treasury secretary Danny Alexander, who helped the UK become the first Western country to join China's Asian Infrastructure Investment Bank, joined the bank after leaving government, helping to front the CCP's Belt and Road Initiative.[5] Similar stories have occurred across Australia, New Zealand, Canada, and all other parts of a once solid Western alliance.

As Clive Hamilton and Mareike Ohlberg describe in their book on the subject, *Hidden Hand*, major financial institutions, among others, in the West have competed with each other for the CCP's favors. Often in the most corrupt and flagrant ways. For instance, in the 2000s, Deutsche Bank used bribes and other corrupt practices to gain entry to the Chinese market. And in 2009, the bank beat JP Morgan to a deal because it had been actively hiring CCP "princelings." Among those who the bank had employed was Wang Xisha, the daughter of the current vice premier and member of the Politburo Standing Committee, Wang Yang.[6] Across the West, the same story has unfolded. From New Zealand to Washington, DC, the CCP has been buying up influence both big and small. From making massive infrastructure investments to arranging for the government-run Bank of China to become the largest single shareholder in BHR Partners, set up by Hunter Biden and John Kerry's stepson after Hunter accompanied his father on an official trip to Beijing in 2013.[7] China has also bought its way into elite institutions across the West. Ancient universities including Britain's Cambridge University have welcomed Chinese investment and allowed Chinese authorities the right to decide what should and should not be studied or said in the institutions, and to suppress criticism of the munificent regime that is paying the checks.

Always the country has used its growing financial clout to flex its diplomatic muscles. Early in his time as prime minister, in 2012, David Cameron met the Dalai Lama while the Buddhist leader was on a trip to London. Because the CCP has a disagreement with the Dalai Lama over the issue of Tibet, they responded swiftly to news of the meeting. The British ambassador to China was immediately called into a meeting and given a telling off. In the wake of the incident, the CCP announced that relations with the United Kingdom had been severely damaged. Sure enough, Chinese investment there was put on hold. A trip to the United Kingdom by Chairman Wu Bangguo was called off, and the CCP talked about how "hurt" the Chinese people had been by the meeting.

The British prime minister was understandably spooked and soon afterward announced that he planned never to meet the Dalai Lama again. The British government then issued a formal apology to the Chinese authorities for the offense caused. Normal trade relations were eventually restored. But what struck me most about the affair was an account I was subsequently given of the first meeting between British and Chinese officials after this affair. I was told by a source who had been at the meeting that before the meeting had got underway the CCP officials pushed a copy of the British apology across the table toward their British counterparts, who were then asked to stand up and read it aloud, which they duly did. Sitting down afterward, the lead Chinese official reportedly smiled and said, "We just wanted to know you meant it."

David Cameron certainly learned his lesson and seemed to have discovered where the money and power now lay. A year after leaving office, it was announced that he was taking a leadership role in a new $1 billion investment fund set up to promote and back China's Belt and Road Initiative. A former British prime minister was helping China to develop its empire. Similar stories can be found everywhere in financial and political circles in the West. A couple of years ago, one of the foremost financial authorities in America was trying to persuade an acquaintance to invest in Chinese infrastructure projects. The businessman expressed doubts about the moral efficacy of investing in CCP projects and was told by his American counterpart: "They have already won. I'm just trying to put you on the right side of the ledger."

So China, at any rate, has not wasted the past two decades. It has expanded more than it has managed to expand at any previous point in its history, and if there is going to be any country that overtakes the United States as the global superpower in the century ahead, then China is the only contender. You might have thought, given that competition, that people might have paid some attention to the most basic of comparisons. If the American-led world order is so terrible, what might a CCP-led world order look like? If the United

States and other Western countries are so dreadful, then would the only likely alternative system be any better?

The question might soon be answered for us. China today has a population four or five times the size of that of the United States. It has an economy that prominent figures such as Elon Musk have predicted could reach two or three times the size of the US economy in the very near future. And that is while still expecting GDP per capita in China to be much less than that within the United States. It would only require GDP per capita in China to reach half of that within the United States for the Chinese economy to be twice that of the United States.

So the question "compared to what" might have been a relevant one to have asked in the West in recent decades. Yet very few people asked it. One of the few who did was a late colleague of mine, Clarissa Tan, who wrote in 2014 about the issue of Chinese racism. Although ethnically Chinese, Clarissa had lived for a time in Singapore. As she herself said, there she had been a "banana," which is to say that she was "yellow on the outside but white on the inside"—that is, someone who looks ethnically Chinese but whose thinking was regarded as "Western." As she pointed out, Asia is filled with labels like this, where people are summed up along ethnic lines in ways that are rarely flattering. The terms that are reserved for foreigners, and white people in particular, are especially ugly. They include "*farang* in Thailand, *gaijin* in Japan, *mat salleh* in Malaysia, *gweilo* in Hong Kong." This last one is particularly interesting. *Gwei* means "ghost," and it is meant literally—a white person is not fully human. "Indeed, in many Chinese dialects, the idiomatic term for any foreigner, be they Indian or Ivorian or Irish, contains the ghostly 'gwei'; only ethnic Chinese are constantly referred to as 'ren', which means 'person'. In other words, only the Chinese really exist as full-blooded people."[8] Nor does Chinese society have any of the Western desire to avoid racialized language. Racism against black people remains ingrained and commonplace. And like anywhere, the racism in the present comes from a racist past. One of the most significant reformers in early-twentieth-century China, Kang Youwei, once argued that there should be medals called "Improver of the Race" medals. These would be given to white people or "yellow" people who were willing to marry black people. In time, Youwei believed that this would "purify mankind." Meanwhile, those who were willing to take the "hit" should be honored. If the racism shown to Africans in Africa by their new Chinese masters has roots, they are roots that go back a long way.

Yet for some reason all this is counted up on an entirely different side of the ledger. A fact that suits the CCP enormously well. At the same time that the CCP has been actively engaging in the most appalling human rights abuses, it is clearly delighted that the West has distracted itself with a set of self-abasements of its own. So long as the West is into the masochism business, it will always find a very willing sadist in Beijing. On the national and international stage, China is willing to hit the West—and America in particular—in what it regards as its weak spot. And one of those weak spots is racism.

Consider what happened just weeks into the Biden administration in 2021. America's newly appointed ambassador to the United Nations, Linda Thomas-Greenfield, spoke at the UN General Assembly Commemorative Meeting for the International Day for the Elimination of Racial Discrimination. On that occasion Thomas-Greenfield told the General Assembly that growing up in America she had lived racism, experienced racism, and survived racism. She told the UN General Assembly that America had an "original sin" and that this sin was slavery. Among other deaths, the US ambassador talked of "the senseless killing of George Floyd." She spoke of the justice of the BLM movement and of the importance of dismantling "white supremacy." She also spoke about the "spike in hate crimes over the past three years." The "latest example of this horror," she told the Assembly, was "the mass shooting in Atlanta."[9]

It is worth noting that at the time Thomas-Greenfield said this to the UN, there was no evidence that the Atlanta spa shooting (in which eight people, including six Asian women, had been killed) had any racial component. The suspect being held in custody had previously spent time in a clinic where he was treated for sex addiction, and he later claimed he did not do it for race-related reasons. But the UN General Assembly was left with the clear impression that this was yet another mass racist shooting in the USA. Not content with being racist against the black population, the US citizenry was now also turning on Asian Americans.

Another month later and Thomas-Greenfield was addressing Al Sharpton's National Action Network. There she reminisced fondly about her speech at the UN General Assembly and said that she had wanted to show the UN that she "had personally experienced one of America's greatest imperfections." She continued, "I've seen for myself how the original sin of slavery weaved white supremacy into our founding documents and principles." She also told of her pride at the new administration's decision to seek readmission to the UN Human Rights Council, saying that doing so would advance America's values. But she knew the limits of this approach. "Of course when we raise issues of equity and justice at the global scale we have to approach them with humility. We have to acknowledge that we are an imperfect union and have been since the beginning." She told conference attendees that America had to "do the work" such as "not forgetting our past or ignoring our present."[10]

But it was not clear that America's rivals at the UN shared any of Ambassador Thomas-Greenfield's strategic or moral outlook. Toward the end of her UN speech, she had briefly paused from her litany of American racism to acknowledge that in Myanmar the Rohingya "have been oppressed, abused, and killed in staggering numbers." And she noted that in China "the government has committed genocide and crimes against humanity against Uighurs and members of other ethnic and religious minority groups in Xinjiang." This did not go down well with the Chinese delegation at the UN. Indeed, the country's ambassador to the UN, Dai Bing, swiftly responded from the floor.

"In an exceptional case," Ambassador Bing said, his American counterpart had actually "admitted to her country's ignoble human rights record." And so, he said, "that does not give her country the license to get on a high horse and tell other countries what to do."

A similar note was struck around the same time at the first major America-China bilateral summit involving the new US administration held in Alaska in March 2021. On that occasion, before the world's television cameras, Thomas-Greenfield's boss, the new US secretary of state, Anthony Blinken, briefly expressed to his Chinese counterparts his "deep concerns" over actions by China in Xinjiang, Hong Kong, Taiwan, cyber-attacks on the United States, and the country's economic coercion of allies. His Chinese counterpart, Yang Jiechi, was visibly furious. The United States had no right to lecture China, he explained in an eighteen-minute harangue. "I think that we thought too well of the United States," Jiechi said. "The US does not have the qualification to say that it wants to speak to China from a position of strength."

Waving his hand angrily/dismissively at his counterpart, he continued, "There are many problems within the United States regarding human rights." And these are "admitted by the US itself as well." While China was making progress on human rights, he said, the United States was not. "We hope the United States will do better on human rights." But, echoing the claims of the US's own ambassadors, Jiechi said that "the challenges facing the United States in human rights are deep-seated. They did not just emerge over the past four years, such as Black Lives Matter. It did not come up only recently."

Warning America not to interfere in China's "internal affairs," Jiechi told Blinken that many Americans "actually have little confidence in the democracy of the United States" and that America should look to its own problems "instead of deflecting the blame on somebody else."

The CCP's spokespeople now find this an enormously useful line of attack. In the summer of 2021, the UN Human Rights Council held a session in which developing countries denounced systemic racism and racial discrimination. The UN high commissioner for human rights, Michelle Bachelet, said that denial of historical responsibility by countries that had benefited from the transatlantic slave trade and colonialism was an important cause of ongoing racism and racial violence. The CCP's foreign ministry spokesperson, Zhao Lijian, told the international press that the developed world had to do more to tackle violence against people of African and Asian descent. And Zhao Lijian called on Western countries to address this problem, saying: "We urge relevant Western countries to earnestly respond to the concerns of the international community, deeply reflect on themselves and take concrete measures to address the issue of systemic racism and racial discrimination, so as not only to promote and protect human rights at home, but also to contribute to the healthy development of the international human rights cause."[11]

Yet while the CCP urges this introspection on the West, it engages in no such thing itself. In fact, at the same moment that it demands earnest responses to "systemic racism and racial discrimination" from the West, it engages in bellicose behavior of its own. In the very same month that it made this demand of the West, the CCP was commemorating its one hundredth anniversary. At a highly staged ceremony in Tiananmen Square before a crowd of tens of thousands of people, Xi Jinping declared that China's rise would prove to be a "historical inevitability." He warned that the country would no longer be "bullied, oppressed or subjugated" by foreign powers, and the language he used was characteristically martial. He declared that "anyone who dares to try, will find their heads bashed bloody against a great wall of steel forged by over 1.4 billion Chinese people." The official English-language translation softened this bloodthirsty language in an attempt to mislead the international media. But this is what Xi told the vast crowds in Beijing.[12] Which in itself is a characteristic example of CCP doublespeak. On my last visit to Tiananmen Square, a decade ago, the English slogans being beamed out across the square were all peaceable. Those that were not translated but beamed out across the square in the local language included the slogan "Long live Socialism." There was only so much they wanted their international visitors to learn about them.

But nothing about this is new. The CCP is only weaponizing Western weaknesses in the way that totalitarian regimes and competitors to the West have always operated. In Soviet Russia in 1936, Grigori Aleksandrov and Isidor Simkov created one of the most popular films of the day. *Circus* was a tale of a white woman who has to flee her small-minded town in America, where the locals literally chase her out of town because she has given birth to an interracial baby with a father who is black. The woman runs away with the circus and ends up in Soviet Russia. While the Americans in the movie are portrayed throughout as bigoted and racist, the contrast with the great Soviet people could not be clearer. Indeed, when the heroine's "shameful" secret is exposed in front of an audience at the circus, the entire Russian audience protects the baby. The film ends with them singing a great lullaby to him in which all the Soviet peoples are presented showing that they will protect this little black baby whom the American imperialists have cast out. Then everybody gathers together, holding the baby in their arms, to join in a great parade in honor of Comrade Stalin.

There was nothing any noticeably less racist about Russia in the 1930s than there was in America. Just as there is nothing less racist about China in the 2020s than there is in America. Very much the opposite. And yet it is enormously helpful to China today, as it was to the Soviets in the past, to encourage the perception of America as uniquely racist and China as uniquely virtuous. There are an endless number of reasons why Beijing does this today, as Moscow did in the past. It allows Beijing to get away with grotesque rights abuses of its own. It distracts Western attention. It suggests that the West has no moral legitimacy to act anywhere. And it runs off the claim that the West has not merely done things that every other civilization in history has done, but rather has always been worse than any other civilization, meaning that the West is uniquely unqualified to pass moral judgment today. This in itself relies on two fundamental presumptions, which both turn out to be true. First, it runs on the presumption that knowledge of Western history inside the West is uniquely lacking: Westerners have become increasingly unaware of what is true and what is not about their own past. Second, it runs on the presumption—again also true—that almost nobody in the West has any knowledge of what countries such as China have done throughout history or are doing today.

In other words, the assault on the West's history succeeds because it speaks into a vacuum of vast historical and contemporary ignorance. It speaks to a populace inside the West as much as outside it, which is willing to see the whole of history through a single lens. If anything bad happens in the world, it must be the West's fault, because there is no other legitimate explanation of how things can go wrong, other than explanations involving the West.

Aside from the historical illiteracy of the anti-Westernism of our day, there is something else going on here. It is a gigantic moral presumption. That presumption is the idea that nobody in the world can do anything wrong unless the West has made them do it. A presumption that is quite outstandingly wrong.

When Robert Mugabe came to power in Zimbabwe (formerly Rhodesia) in 1980, the average life expectancy in the country was just under sixty. After his rule, or rather mismanagement, of the country for a little over a quarter of a century, the average life expectancy in Zimbabwe had almost halved. By 2006, the average Zimbabwean man could expect to live to thirty-seven. For women, life expectancy had fallen to thirty-four. The situation got so bad that the average life expectancy for Zimbabwean women fell by two years in two years. Mugabe put his people on a treadmill that got shorter with every step.

Similar stories played out across the world. Six decades ago, Uganda was a net exporter of food, indeed one of the breadbaskets of Africa. In the decades after colonization, it became a basket case, struggling even to feed its own people. Other countries such as Egypt have seen average wages fall lower since colonialism than during it.

And that is not adjusting for inflation, but in simple, practical salary terms.

There are a number of explanations for situations like this, which can be replayed and repeated across Africa, the Middle East, and elsewhere. These explanations include gross mismanagement by postcolonial governments and grotesque corruption and self-enrichment by the governing class, who spent their years in office prioritizing the siphoning off of the nation's wealth to private bank accounts in Switzerland and Liechtenstein. On the other hand, there are countries that have been relative success stories. More than seven decades after independence, India today is not just the world's most populous democracy but one of the world's foremost economies. Although the age of empire lingers over these countries, in few does it remain the salient factor in whether a country has been able to succeed or fail. Some countries succeeded after independence. Some failed.

Naturally, despots who have immiserated their own countries have a clear reason for blaming imperialism for all ills that currently beset their countries. But the only other group to join them in doing so are a portion of people in the West themselves. People who believe that the history of the world is a history of Western malfeasance and non-Western innocence. As well as being an insultingly partial history, it is also one that has absolutely no sense of global or historical perspective. And there is an obvious reason for that. In order to be able to judge the West, you would have to know at least some of the history of the rest. The only thing modern Western populations are more ignorant about than their own history is the history of other peoples outside the West. Yet such knowledge is surely a prerequisite to being able to arrive at any moral judgments.

A poll of young British people carried out by Survation in 2016 found that 50 percent had never heard of Lenin, while 70 percent had no idea who Mao was. Among sixteen- to twenty-four-year-olds, who had all grown up after the fall of the Berlin Wall, 41 percent had positive feelings about socialism, while just 28 percent felt the same sentiments toward capitalism. One possible reason for this is that

68 percent said they had never learned anything in school about the Russian Revolution.[13]

Equal if not greater ignorance can be found in America. A poll carried out in 2020 found that almost two-thirds of Americans between the ages of eighteen and thirty-nine had no idea that 6 million Jews were killed in the Holocaust. According to the study, almost half of Americans in their twenties and thirties could not name a single concentration camp or ghetto established by the Nazis during World War II. About one in eight young Americans (12 percent) said that they had not heard of the Holocaust or didn't think that they had heard of it.[14] And this is about the historical reference point that is most widely and perhaps overused in historical and present-day arguments about politics.

It is worth keeping figures such as this in mind as we see the next manifestation of the war on the West. The assault on Western history.

When people claim that populations are ignorant of the history of the West, they forget that most people are ignorant about almost everything. When critics claim that there is something sinister about their particular area of interest being too little known about, they forget that majorities of young people across the West have no serious knowledge even of one of the greatest crimes in history. So this is a delicate as well as a sinister moment. Because when you are speaking into a great vacuum of ignorance, people with malign intent can run an awfully long way awfully fast. They can tell their listeners things that they will simply believe and tell them what they should not question. And as you speak into a vacuum of knowledge, you can—if you are so ideologically inclined—completely rewrite the history of the West, divorcing it from any proper understanding and certainly from any wider context. All in the hope of persuading the peoples of the West not that they were better than anyone else or that they were the same as anyone else, but that they were uniquely evil and therefore worse than everyone else. That the history of the West is especially shameful.

This is the chief reason that within the course of only a couple of generations, the history of the West has been entirely rewritten. And rewritten in order to tell the people of the West that their history is not especially glorious but instead a source of unimaginable shame. The anti-Western revisionists have been out in force in recent years. It is high time that we revise them in turn.

CHAPTER 2

HISTORY

In her racist speech at Yale in 2021, Dr. Aruna Khilanani made many extraordinary claims. And in an interview around the same time, she made many more. Here is one of the things she told Katie Herzog:

AK: *People of color myself included, suffer from being positioned in the world, psychologically, and the stuff that goes with it: violence, this, that. Now, white people suffer from problems of their own mind. They suffer with trust, they suffer with intimacy, they suffer with closeness, shame, guilt, anxiety. They suffer with their minds. Don't get me wrong, people of color are also neurotic and have their own stuff and ups and downs. But there is a fundamental issue I think that is very unique to white suffering and I think that's their own mind.*

KH: *What would you say is the cause of this?*

AK: *I think it's colonialism. That history. If you do this much lying to yourself it's going to have an effect on your mind. There's no way it can't.*[1]

That may be a characteristically extreme way of putting it. But it is not rare to see someone claim that in all of human history, there is something especially evil about white people.

In recent years, it has become entirely commonplace to claim that white people are somehow deranged by their history. And it is an interesting move for critics of the West to make. Because it demonstrates a need to overturn what such critics see as the mainstream currents of history teaching in the West. These critics have an extraordinary view of what is taught in schools across the West. They believe that young people today are taught one-sided jingoism and nationalistic propaganda. They believe that people in the West are uniquely ignorant of their own history and uniquely ignorant of other peoples' too. They believe that we have spent the last generation covering over the dark parts of our past. Yet nothing could be further from the truth.

For instance, it is the constant assertion of race activists in the United Kingdom that British schoolchildren are ignorant about the legacy of empire in their schools. The claim is demonstrably wrong. The National Curriculum in England and Wales dictates teaching for primary and secondary school pupils in the United Kingdom. The study of the British Empire is a statutory area of study for Key Stage 3. Nonstatutory areas of study include the transatlantic slave trade and Indian independence. And while critics sometimes claim that the fact that these areas are nonstatutory means that they are deemed unimportant, or are somehow "hidden," the claim is nonsense. Other areas of nonstatutory study in English schools include the Magna Carta, the War of the Roses, the Enlightenment, and both World Wars. In fact, schoolchildren in England have as much education in the history of empire as they do in 1066. And when they get to choose which famous people from history to study at Key Stage 1, the handful of suggested figures include Mary Seacole and Rosa Parks.

It is the same in America. It is asserted constantly that Americans are ignorant of the history of slavery. Nothing could be further from the truth. I have gone through all the Advanced Placement exams used in high schools in the United States in recent years. That is the history exam used at the end of high school. In these exams, issues to do with slavery, colonialism, race, and other related rights issues constitute around half of all the subjects that are tested. Out of forty-eight questions in the 2021 AP exam, eight dealt exclusively with racial issues, another four with related racial issues, and another four with economic matters from a point of view that is familiar with anyone who understands the Marxist critique of capitalism. The questions covered every major race-related issue in American history, from the arrival of the colonists to Reconstruction, the civil rights movement, and the effects of racism in the present day.

In spite of the fact that schoolchildren in the West are brought up on a diet of the sins of their forefathers, another narrative has got out there. That is the claim—a claim that ignores all the actual evidence—that insists that our whole history is a pro-Western whitewash. And that it is therefore the job of anyone committed to justice to overturn this narrative. And so, just as the realities of race in the modern West are put through this distorting projection, so the reality of how our history is taught today and what our history was actually like are put through an identical distorting effect. The effort to do this is now going on at the highest imaginable levels.

"REFRAMING" OUR HISTORY

There have been many efforts to rewrite the history of the West in recent years. But few have been as high profile or as pronounced in their intent as a project launched by the *New York Times* in August 2019. "The 1619 Project" could have been launched by any number of institutions (such as a university), but for it to be launched by a newspaper—and one which is still sometimes referred to as a paper of record—is highly unusual. For the project was not a piece of reportage. It was an attempt to reframe, and rewrite, the founding story of

America. That wasn't what critics said about it. It is what the project's founders said about their own project.

The project was launched with a one-hundred-page special edition of the Sunday magazine. In her introductory piece (for which she subsequently won a Pulitzer Prize), Nikole Hannah-Jones made the bold claim that the date of the arrival of the first slaves on the continent should be regarded as the true founding date of America. The introductory paragraph read: "The 1619 project is a major initiative from The New York Times observing the four hundredth anniversary of the beginning of American slavery. It aims to reframe the country's history, understanding 1619 as our true founding, and placing the consequences of slavery and the contributions of black Americans at the very center of our national narrative."

Hannah-Jones, who is a reporter, not a historian, repeatedly made this claim about 1619 being "our true founding." In January 2020, she told an audience at Ann Arbor that "our true founding is 1619 not 1776."[2] And in a conversation with Jake Silverstein (editor in chief of the New York Times Magazine), two months after the project's launch, Silverstein said, "We sort of proposed the idea in a variety of ways that if you consider 1619 as the foundational date of the country, rather than 1776, it just changes your understanding, and we call that a reframing of American history—like you're moving the whole picture over to a new center point."[3] As might be expected, this claim caused a certain amount of pushback. And in response, a number of strange things happened.

Within a year of the project's launch, Hannah-Jones herself claimed that she had never said what she had been saying since the launch. "The 1619 Project does not argue that 1619 is our true founding," she claimed. Though it might be noted that her Twitter banner still had a picture of 1776 with that date crossed out and replaced by 1619. Still, she insisted that the only people who had made this claim about her project's aims were "the right."[4]

Yet there it was. Or there it had been. For as the controversy grew, the New York Times silently edited the web pages in question so that this especially inflammatory claim no longer appeared on them. The words "understanding 1619 as our true founding" were quietly removed. And after they had done this little bit of erasing, the paper's editors then went about pretending that they had never said the words that they had in fact said, or that when they had used the words, they had used them in a way that had a different meaning than the usual meaning such words had. Jake Silverstein, for instance, wrote that what the project was trying to explain was a "rather complex idea" and that when they had said that 1619 was the true founding date of America, they had in fact intended it as a "metaphor." In a generous act of self-back-patting, he noted that some critics had said that this metaphor of his offered "a clearer vision" of American history than had previously been available.[5]

Silverstein then did a little rejigging of his own. In his introductory essay, published in August 2019, he had written:

> 1619. It is not a year that most Americans know as a notable date in our country's history. Those who do are at most a tiny fraction of those who can tell you that 1776 is the year of our nation's birth. What if, however, we were to tell you that this fact, which is taught in our schools and unanimously celebrated every Fourth of July, is wrong, and that the country's true birth date, the moment that its defining contradictions first came into the world, was in late August of 1619?

Soon the online version of this, too, was silently edited. Specifically, the words "this fact, which is taught in our schools and unanimously celebrated every Fourth of July, is wrong, and that the country's true birth date" were deleted. Perhaps Silverstein wondered for a moment whether to pretend that the words "is wrong" was also a rather brilliant metaphor, also praised by many critics. Instead, he fell back on something else, which was claiming that the changes to the text were "so minor as to be immaterial."[6]

In fact, it is hard to think of anything that could be more material than the question of when a country—specifically the most powerful country on earth—was founded. The editors at the *New York Times* ought to have expected that every inch of ground involving the 1619 Project would be fought over, because the project was more than a reframing or a rewriting. The project was a deliberate transposing of American history into a minor key. The move of the founding date was not just about proving that everything that made America exceptional, including its economic power, its industrial power, and its system of democracy, had come out of slavery. It was intended to formalize the idea that the USA was founded on an original sin. It sought to turn a tale of heroism and glory into one of oppression and shame. Perhaps the authors of this project did not expect to get so much attention, or failed to imagine that they would dominate the nation's discourse at such extraordinary speed. But that is what they did.

Within living memory, the story of America had been one of a great leap into glorious liberty, led by some of the most remarkable men of their, or any, age. Now, instead, the American story was rooted in a crime that could apparently never be alleviated. If the authors thought they would get away with this unopposed, then they were wrong. But given the audacity of their efforts, they might have tried to be a little more careful with their claims. Because the work in question was so shoddy that it did not even try to hide its exclusively political aims. A historical study of the many difficult aspects of American history can be easily recognized. That would seek to take complex junctures in the round. It would survey individuals not through the prism of a single phrase or action but through an understanding of what they did throughout their lives. It would look at the circumstances of the time, what other countries and cultures were doing at the same moment, and much, much more.

Hannah-Jones and her colleagues clearly had no desire to do this and would have been unqualified for the role even if they had aspired to it. For instance, in her introductory essay, Hannah-Jones made the claim that one of the primary reasons that the colonists wanted independence from Britain was that "they wanted to protect the institution of slavery." She cites two pieces of evidence (from 1772 and 1775) to justify this claim. The first of these was the British legal case *Somerset vs. Stewart*. But it is quite bizarre to pretend that a British legal case that had no reach in America was one of the major reasons for America's independence. Even stranger was to do so while presuming that the reasons for independence as stated in the Declaration of Independence were unimportant. Until now the reasons for independence given in the Declaration of Independence had been thought to be suggestive at the very least. For the 1619 project, they were not, and so its crack team set out to ignore the historical record and scour the land for anything that could accord with their own preordained theory.

Even worse among the opening essays in the newspaper's project was a piece of work by a sociologist called Matthew Desmond. Perhaps it was inevitable that a sociologist trying to write history would make as many historical mistakes as Desmond did. But what was even more inevitable was that he should have used his contribution to attack capitalism. As the headline read, "In Order to Understand the Brutality of American Capitalism, You Have to Start on the Plantation."[7] The ensuing work attempted, ineptly, to smear capitalism as a whole by claiming that its sources lay in slavery. For example, at one point, Desmond attempted to draw a clear line of association between modern corporations and slave plantations. This is how he did it.

Everything in modern corporations, Desmond wrote, is "tracked, recorded and analyzed, via vertical reporting systems, double-entry record-keeping and precise quantification." According to Desmond, "many of these techniques that we now take for granted were developed by and for large plantations." To put it politely, this is a wildly ignorant argument. Desmond offers no evidence that the plantations were the places where these techniques originated, and that is because there is no such evidence. If the *New York Times'* hired anticapitalist had a wider historical purview, and a less dogmatic anticapitalist standpoint, he might have noticed something else. Which is that many successful enterprises across history share the attributes he describes.

After all, could there be a reason why a system in which things are "tracked, recorded and analyzed" might work better than a system in which things are (for instance) "lost, ignored and forgotten about"?

By now Desmond had the wind in his sails. His anticapitalist critique continued: "When a midlevel manager spends an afternoon filling in rows and columns on an Excel spreadsheet they are repeating business procedures whose roots twist back to slave-labor camps." Indeed, such a line would have to be very long and very twisty. For the midlevel manager could also be said to be doing something that careful bookkeepers have done throughout history, as far back as Pharaonic Egypt and the Mesopotamian Sumerians (neither white). Occasionally the 1619 author tries to summon up someone who will support his assertions. Just about the only person he can locate is one Caitlin Rosenthal, the author of a 2018 book about slavery. Desmond cites her in his defense but fails to note that his own source says, "I did not find a simple path where slaveholders' paper spreadsheets evolved into Microsoft Excel."[8] In other words, Desmond cites a source that says the opposite of what he says to justify his case. Elsewhere, he misunderstands his sources, misquotes statistics, and fails to note a somewhat central fact: the plantation system was not a capitalist system; it was a feudal one.[9] But people who hate the West always hate Western capitalism and are willing to praise or turn a blind eye to the failings of any other economic system so long as they can portray free market capitalism as simply another arm of Western colonialism and oppression.

It appears that Desmond's assignment was simple. It was to smear the capitalist system. Hannah-Jones and the *New York Times* wished to portray everything in American life as having been born in the original sin of slavery, and Matthew Desmond was simply hired to do the hit job on capitalism. But everything else in the project was equally assertive and equally ill-informed. According to Hannah-Jones, America was not even a democracy "until black Americans made it one."[10] Which is the sort of assertion you might make at a rally, but not one normally associated with a historical project—even a historically revisionist project published by a newspaper.

Understandably, this all eventually became too much for some actual historians in the relevant fields. A number of leading scholars of American history (Sean Wilentz, James McPherson, Gordon Wood, Victoria Bynum, and James Oakes) wrote to the *New York Times* to object to the project. While applauding all efforts to look into history, they complained that on "matters of verifiable fact" that "cannot be described as interpretation or 'framing,'" the project had got its history severely wrong. The historians said that the 1619 Project reflected "a displacement of historical understanding by ideology."[11]

From all political sides and none, the corrections to the 1619 Project began to pour in. In an interview with a Socialist website, James Oakes, of the City University of New York, made an interesting complaint about the project from the political Left. He complained that the worst thing about the project's propagandizing was that "it leads to political paralysis. It's always been here. There's nothing we can do to get out of it. If it's in the DNA, there's nothing you can do. What do you do? Alter your DNA?"[12]

As well as moral objections, errors and dishonest summaries in the 1619 Project kept being identified. But still the *New York Times* stuck by its project. Too much had been invested in it. The paper of record had decided that it was going to change the record whether the historians agreed or not and whether the facts supported them or not.

This was neither journalism nor history—but a political campaign.

Unable to answer any of the criticisms of her project's basic historical flaws, Hannah-Jones retreated into two moves. One was to lash out. On Twitter, she derided "white historians" and "LOL"-ed at the idea that they produce "truly objective history." When someone described McPherson as a "pre-eminent" historian of the civil war, she replied, "Who considers him preeminent? I don't."[13] After this, she went for the "wounded" maneuver. She complained that she had not been contacted by any of the scholars privately and insisted that if she had been, she would have taken their "concerns very seriously." Instead, she said, there had been "kind of a campaign" of getting people "to sign on to a letter that was attempting really to discredit the entire project without having had a conversation."[14] By this logic, of course, it might be said that all Americans should feel wounded, because Nikole Hannah-Jones had rewritten their country's birth date and was trying to rewrite the nation's entire history and had done so without really contacting anyone beforehand. Let alone anyone who knew what they were talking about.

But the most interesting thing that happened with the 1619 Project was what happened when it moved from the page onto the street. In June 2020, when protests and riots followed the killing of George Floyd, the *New York Post* ran an opinion piece saying, "America is burning." It described how rioters had already set fire to police stations and restaurants, had looted shops across the country, and were now coming for statues, including George Washington's, which had just been torn down in Oregon. "Call them the 1619 riots," the author wrote.[15] Hannah-Jones noticed this and took to social media to accept the compliment. Call them the 1619 riots? "It would be an honor," she said, as the country was burning. "Thank you."[16]

THE 1619 RIOTS

Just as it is striking how swiftly obscure ideas can spill out from academia, so it is striking how swiftly ideas pumped out in the media can make their way onto the streets. Around the time that the 1619 Project came along, America was clearly ripe for a reframing by those opposed to nearly every aspect of its founding. In 2020, a survey showed that by that year 70 percent of self-identified "liberals" wanted to rewrite the US Constitution into one "that better reflects our diversity as a people."[17] Basic tenets of American history that Right and Left had agreed on until now, and which had for generations united Americans of every background, were suddenly subjects of fundamental disagreement. Nowhere was this clearer or more visceral than in the spate of statue toppling that burst out from the summer of 2020 onward. For in no time, that movement shifted its attention from contested figures in American history to every single major figure at the heart of the American experiment, from the founders onward.

It started at the contested margins with the Confederates. In the days that followed the death of George Floyd, the city of Birmingham, Alabama, removed a Confederate monument erected 115 years earlier. In Alexandria, Virginia, the authorities removed the Appomattox statue erected by the United Daughters of the Confederacy in 1889. Across the country, similar actions were taken. The University of Alabama announced that it would remove several plaques dedicated to Confederate soldiers who had attended the school. And in Jacksonville, Florida, after a Confederate statue commemorating the Jacksonville Light Infantry was vandalized, a crew of cranes moved in during the early hours of the morning and took the statue apart. There were not many objections to all of this. Few people wished to defend the maintenance of Confederate statues. And even fewer wished to do so in the immediate aftermath of a horrible, apparently racist, killing. But the authorities and crowds that started on the Confederate statues soon found it very hard to know where their iconoclasm should stop.

The statues of Christopher Columbus were a major focus of their ire. Though this was hardly the first time that the explorer had been in the sight line of anti-Western activists. During the 1990s and 2000s, there had been eruptions of anti-Columbus sentiment in America. But all of this picked up in 2020, with statues of Columbus being assaulted and pulled down across the country. During the great iconoclastic rage of that year, statues of Columbus were either torn

down by crowds or preemptively removed by the authorities in Chicago, Pittsburgh, Boston, Minnesota, Virginia, and dozens of other
places across America.

As the days went on and the crowds searched for more and more
stone victims, they got ever nearer to the holy spots of American history. Within under a month after George Floyd's death, a crowd in
northeast Portland pulled down a statue of George Washington and
graffitied it with the words "You're on native land" and "Genocidal
colonist." They also marked it with the letters "BLM." Plus, the
date "1619." On that occasion, the crowd also set fire to the statue's
head, draped it in an American flag, and then set that on fire too.
During the same period, a crowd pulled down a statue of Thomas
Jefferson outside a high school named after him, spray-painted him
with the words "slave owner," and also wrote the name of George
Floyd over him.

Soon it was George Washington's turn again, with a statue of him
being covered in red paint and then torn down in the downtown area
of Los Angeles. In San Francisco, it was Ulysses S. Grant who was
targeted, with a crowd assaulting the monument to the president
who led the Union armies in defeating the Confederacy. And it was
by this stage that it looked as though all American history was in the
crosshairs. The statue of Spanish missionary Father Junipero Serra
was soon torn down in Los Angeles, as was that of Francis Scott
Key, the lyricist of "The Star-Spangled Banner."

So comprehensive was the destruction in some cities that the authorities were frantically removing statues to try to get ahead of the
crowds. After assaults on statues of Abraham Lincoln in other parts
of the country, the authorities in Boston announced that they would
take apart and remove their statue of Abraham Lincoln and a freed
slave which stood in Park Square. While at Hofstra University in New
York, the university authorities moved a statue of Thomas Jefferson
on the campus in response to a "Jefferson has gotta go" movement.
In 2018, the university authorities had rejected student calls for Jef-

ferson to be removed. But a little over a month after George Floyd's death, the authorities removed it of their own volition.

One of the students behind the campaign to remove Jefferson said that the removal, and relocation, of the statue was not enough, but that at least it would stop her parents having to spend "sleepless nights worrying that their eldest daughter would be lynched by white supremacist groups validated by Hofstra's decision not to remove the sculpture."[18]

It seemed in that moment as though American history in the round was being erased. Statues of Confederates were coming down, but so were those of Union leaders. People who had owned slaves were coming down, as were those who had never owned a slave. Statues of those who were in favor of slavery were coming down but so were those of people such as George Washington, who came to oppose slavery and freed his slaves. And it wasn't just the founders, but almost everybody who came after them who was being treated in this way. At Princeton, the Woodrow Wilson School of Public and International Affairs announced that it was dropping Woodrow Wilson from its name. Until then, Wilson had been best known for his peace plan for Europe at the end of World War I and for being the instigator behind setting up the League of Nations. But now, like everybody else, he stood accused of "racist thinking," and so the university where he had studied and been president before reaching a higher office decided it had no further use for his name. The death of George Floyd was offered as the explanation for speeding up a consultative exercise that had been going on for some years.

A new way of thinking about and looking at America had washed through the country. So much so that the then president decided to give a speech from Mount Rushmore trying to reestablish the American narrative. And doubtless hold it close to himself ahead of an election. But in some ways what was most striking about President Trump's speech at Mount Rushmore on Independence Day weekend 2020 was not anything he said himself, as he rattled through the accomplishments of Washington, Jefferson, Lincoln, and Theodore Roosevelt on the rock face behind him.

What was most striking was what CNN's correspondent said as the network went live to Mount Rushmore ahead of the speech. Here is how Leyla Santiago described the upcoming events: "Kicking off the Independence Day weekend, President Trump will be at Mount Rushmore, where he'll be standing in front of a monument of two slave owners and on land wrestled away from Native Americans." She went on to report that the president was expected to focus on efforts to "tear down our country's history." Santiago appeared not to realize that her own words were at least as suggestive as anything President Trump had to say.

For even a couple of years earlier, it would have been inconceivable for an anchor at one of the main networks to use language entirely lifted from the most radical, revisionist figures in America. If Mount Rushmore is "stolen," then what is the rest of the country? Before the modern era, the whole history of our species was one of occupation and conquering. One group of original peoples were replaced by another group of other peoples. And someone outside the American continent was always going to "discover" America.

What exactly were Columbus and subsequent Europeans meant to do after making their discovery? Should they have returned home and said that there was nothing to see? Should they have kept their discovery to themselves, waited for someone else to find it, or declared America a place with no potential? The ineluctable conclusion of this narrative is that it would have been better if Columbus had never discovered America. Or that it would have been better if it had been found and settled by some more suitable civilization. Such as the Chinese or Japanese. But these notions are not just ahistorical. At this stage, they are also completely self-destructive. For if the land you are on is simply stolen, the Founding Fathers were simply "slave owners," the Constitution needs to be rewritten, and no figure in your history deserves respect, then what exactly holds this grand quarter-millennial-long project together?

NONE OF THIS IS NEW

In a period of such rich iconoclasm, it is easy to think that the present anti-Western moment came from nowhere. In fact, it has been bubbling up for decades. Specifically, since the postcolonial period, when the European powers were in retreat and America was struggling with the problem of how to be a superpower without acquiring an empire.

Throughout this period, perhaps it was inevitable that a certain anti-Western attitude would advance. The postcolonial period got off to a variety of starts. In some places, the withdrawal was smooth; in others, it opened up vacuums that consumed everything in the vicinity. But wherever the case, as the West retreated, anti-Westernism advanced. A correction was due. But in no time, that correction became an overcorrection. People in the former colonies who praised or emulated aspects of the colonial era were suddenly pariahs. And in the West itself, the pendulum also swung. Where once many people had thought that the West could do nothing wrong, the West entered an era where it became dangerous to concede that the West had ever done anything right.

To the surprise of no one, this was whipped along and otherwise encouraged by intellectuals. Specifically, by those who, though unwilling to lose a drop of blood themselves, seemed keen on considerable bloodletting among other people.

One such figure was Jean-Paul Sartre, who in early 1963 wrote the preface to a posthumous work by the Martinique-born anticolonialist Frantz Fanon. From his first page, Sartre mocked the Western powers for their efforts to create a native elite in the countries they had once ruled. Sartre claimed that the West had imbued these people with "the principles of Western culture," including "grand glutinous words that stuck to the teeth" leading natives to be "sent home, whitewashed." Such people had become "walking lies," wrote Sartre.[19]

For Sartre, Fanon by contrast offered another way—"Revolutionary socialism all together everywhere."

And so Sartre correctly stated that Fanon puts his readers "on guard" against "Western culture." And all this was admirable in Sartre's eyes. For Sartre was a man who claimed to believe that "the only true culture is that of the revolution."[20]

Sartre talks about people "who are rather too Westernized" and absorbed the "witchery" of Western culture.[21] And he seems almost panting at the prospect of conflict to come. "In the past we made history," he writes, "and now it is being made of us. The ratio of forces has been inverted; decolonization has begun; all that our hired soldiers can do is to delay its completion."[22]

The man who Sartre raised the curtain for was equally vengeful. Fanon, who was a huge figure in his day, and remains much quoted by anticolonialist authors, said that when "the native" hears about Western culture "he pulls out his knife" and "laughs in mockery when Western values are mentioned." He wrote that "in the period of decolonization, the colonized masses mock at these very values, insult them, and vomit them up."[23] Reading Fanon now, one is struck by how much the claims that he made in the 1960s have been built upon in the decades since. For instance, Fanon wrote that "the wealth of the imperial countries is our wealth too . . . Europe is literally the creation of the Third World." According to Fanon, the docks of Bordeaux and Liverpool owe their renown only to their traffic in slaves and so "when we hear the head of a European state declare with his hand on his heart that he must come to the aid of the poor underdeveloped peoples, we do not tremble with gratitude. Quite the contrary, we say to ourselves: 'It's a just reparation which will be paid to us.'" For the people of underdeveloped counties, all such payments are "their due." The "capitalist powers . . . must pay."[24]

Likewise, in arguments that would soon become familiar, Fanon condemned the entire Western bourgeoisie as "fundamentally racist."[25] Yet he also feared the potency of the ideas that the West exports. Because of the import of Western films, literature, and more, he was worried that "the young Africans are at the mercy of the various assaults made upon them by the very nature of Western culture."[26]

Fanon didn't know how to deal with this, other than to tell people not to imitate Europe, but to create "the whole man" who Europe "has been incapable of bringing to triumphant birth." In his rousing conclusion, he claims, "Two centuries ago, a former European colony decided to catch up with Europe. It succeeded so well that the United States of America became a monster, in which the taints, the sickness, and the inhumanity of Europe have grown to appalling dimensions."[27]

There are several interesting things about this. Not least that Fanon, like many other postcolonial writers who became famous in the West, is not really interested in restoring the cultures of the non-Western countries he claims to care about. He is not interested in returning African nations to an era of tribal customs or any other precolonial Indigenous tradition. What he is interested in is analyzing these cultures through a Marxist lens and then "saving" them by applying a Marxist ideology to them. Naturally there is something perverse about this. For Marx was a Western thinker, with next to no knowledge—let alone experience—of non-Western cultures or societies. Just one of the ironies of the postcolonialist thinkers is that so many take the same path as Fanon. Intent in shrugging off the legacy of Western colonialism, they find an answer for every non-Western society in Western Marxism.

Other arguments in Fanon have also become familiar through the West in the decades following. There is, for instance, the argument that the West is especially rapacious—and that in this regard, it is wholly unlike all other cultures. There is the argument that the West is wholly without virtue, even while it is strangely, indeed dangerously, alluring. And then there is the insistence that revenge is called for and that the West needs to pay for what it has done. Finally, there is the curious fact that the rage against the imperial powers of the nineteenth century does not stop at the nineteenth-century imperial powers, but extends to a country that never had an empire: America. An interesting truth can be discerned here. There may be many reasons to criticize the European powers for their empires. But if this is seen as a founding sin, and Western countries that did not have empires are lumped in with those that did, then it would seem that it is not in fact empire that is the problem in the eyes of such critics, but the West itself.

The strength and style of Fanon's writing has kept it being read. Though its appeal seems mostly to lie in its lust for violence, specifically vengeance against the West. But there is another thinker, after Fanon, whose central idea reached even wider, and whose interest in the Middle East ended up with him writing a crucially hostile reframing of the West. That writer is Edward Said, a Christian Palestinian, born in 1935, who had an unprecedented impact on the way in which significant portions of the West thought about themselves.

Like other postcolonial writers, Said's central claim is singularly anti-Western. He is uninterested in crimes committed by non-Western powers. And that disinterest helps lead him to believe that every aspect of the West—even or especially its intellectual and cultural curiosity—is to be not just condemned but derided. His central work explaining this trend—*Orientalism*, published in 1978—has become one of the most widely cited books across disciplines in academia. Said's central critique is an attempt to prove that when Westerners encountered other societies, they did so through the lens of the societies they came from. Despite the intelligence and style that Said could bring to his writing and his public debates, this central point is wholly unremarkable. After all, through what other lens might Western travelers and scholars have been expected to look at the Orient? Could they have been expected to look at the Middle East through Chinese eyes? Or Middle Eastern eyes? And why should Western explorers, linguists, and others be held to such a strange standard? It would be curious indeed to expect Arabs to have looked at Europe through European eyes. Or for the Chinese to look at the Middle East through Aboriginal eyes. Everybody approaches a different culture through references they have picked up in the culture they are from. There is nothing sinister about this. It is inevitable.

Yet for Said, so long as the people doing the looking are Western and the cultures being looked at are not, it is very sinister indeed.

Everything about the West, even the learning of its scholars, is held against it. For instance, Said wishes to blame Westerners for their allegedly narrow worldview. He ignores the fact that the Orientalists who he spurns were remarkable men and women: people who learned the languages and dialects of faraway societies and who studied these cultures almost always because they were fascinated by and admired them.

Indeed, a significant strain in Orientalism always came from Westerners who admired non-Western culture more than the culture they were from. Often as an escape from their own culture. In nineteenth-century Germany, there existed a significant strain of thought that looked to the Orient as a place to give balm to the soul. Yet Said dismisses all of this, and instead levels sinister accusations against the West for all its interactions with the East. He constantly laments the Western tendency to "essentialize" the East—that is, to not draw precise enough delineations between one group and another. A tendency to lump a disparate group of people under one umbrella.

Again, there is nothing so terrible about this. All descriptions must by necessity include some generalization. Not every sentence can be the length of a dissertation. Concepts that sum up large swaths of peoples—including "the West"—are useful even if they cannot sum up everything contained therein. But an interesting aspect of Said's judgment in this is that while he loathes essentializing in others, he indulges in it frequently himself. For instance, at one point in his most famous work he says, "It is therefore correct that every European, in what he could say about the Orient, was consequently a racist, an imperialist, and almost totally ethnocentric."[28] Every European? Every single one? Where is the evidence to support that fact? If you replaced the word "European" in that sentence with "African," "Arab," or even "Palestinian Christian," what might you be called? Elsewhere Said refers in passing, perfectly blithely, to an "average nineteenth-century European."[29] What is that, you wonder? It essentializes an awfully large array of people.

But there was always in Said a tendency to single out Western man and woman for a unique form of attack. This included extraordinarily hostile and ungenerous attacks on two of the great female writers of the nineteenth century: George Eliot and Jane Austen. Said's attack on Jane Austen in one of his later books is a classic of anti-Westernism. For there Said tries to smear Austen as a supporter of the slave trade. He does so through a solitary reference to slavery that appears in *Mansfield Park* during a conversation between Edmund and Fanny. In an exchange that takes up no more than a few lines of text, Austen's heroine and her husband-to-be discuss the fact that there had been "such a dead silence" the night before, when Fanny's uncle (who had just returned from a plantation in Antigua) had been asked about the recently abolished slave trade.[30]

Said believes that this single reference means that Austen is praising the slave trade. He makes his argument through two means. The first is that he attacks Austen by referring to later novels by other authors, including Joseph Conrad's *Heart of Darkness*, saying that if we read Austen in their light, that single reference "acquires a slightly greater density than that of the discrete, reticent appearances it makes in the pages of *Mansfield Park*." Doubtless that is so. By the same light, we might try to apply Holocaust literature to the pages of *Pride and Prejudice* and marvel that this, too, would take on a similar "density."[31] But it would still be a strange thing to do. Stranger still is that Said should choose to use one statement by a character in a novel—a statement that incidentally suggests that the character in question is an abolitionist—to smear not just that character but her creator, Jane Austen, as embroiled in the great sin of slavery.

But through intellectual sleights of hand like this, Said provided a playbook for others who wished to criticize the West. Among his most important techniques was to interpret everything in the West—including the most delicate and perfect works of art—through a lens that was not just interrogative and hostile but amazingly ungenerous. In doing so, he held the West to standards expected of no other society and then castigated the West for failing to live up to these standards. He also helped to create an interpretation of the world in which the non-Western peoples were people to whom things were done, while the Western people were people who did things. And terrible things at that.

Coming out of the postcolonial period, Said gave added impetus to a feeling that was already underway. A feeling that the West itself was overdue for some justice or, rather, revenge.

EMPIRE

In April 2015, there were a set of protests at the University of Cape Town in South Africa. The university had a statue on its campus of the famed nineteenth-century imperialist Cecil Rhodes. The statue was there because Rhodes had donated the land for the university to be built on. But for some years, students and others at the university had argued that the statue was a symbol of colonial aggression and white supremacy and so should come down. Eventually a "Rhodes Must Fall" movement was formed by students and others. The University Council finally voted for the statue's removal, and down it came.

As ever in the present era, what happens in one continent swiftly spreads to another. In this case, it transferred swiftly to England and the University of Oxford. One of the things that Cecil Rhodes provided for in his will was the endowment of a scholarship scheme so that students from the United States, Germany, and the then British Empire would be able to study at Oxford. He insisted on a number of stipulations for the scholarships. One of these was that "no student shall be qualified or disqualified for election . . . on account of race or religious opinions."[32] The first black student won a Rhodes scholarship five years after Rhodes's death. Since then, students from around the world, not least from South Africa, have benefited from the scheme.

Nevertheless, in recent decades there had been growing unease about the legacy of such an unabashed imperialist. In 2003, Nelson

Mandela agreed to have his name appended to the scholarship scheme. That year, the Rhodes scholarships officially became known as the Mandela Rhodes scholarships. Asked about why he would agree to have his name linked with the great imperialist, Mandela said that South Africa's new constitution includes an injunction "for us to come together across the historical divides, to build our country together with a future equally shared by all."[33] But more than a decade after this gesture of reconciliation was agreed to, it seemed to have done nothing to placate a new generation of students. Not least the South African students in Oxford publicly involved in the Rhodes Must Fall campaign, who appeared keen to use the international attention the issue brought to make names for themselves back home.

Oriel College, Oxford, was founded in 1326, and Cecil Rhodes studied there in the 1870s. Before his death in 1902, he arranged a considerable financial bequest to the college. In addition to the scholarship scheme, his will allowed for a new building to be built for the college. It was completed in 1911 and was adorned with several statues, including one of Rhodes himself. There, high above street level, his statue stood unmolested for over a century.

However, after the campaign success of Rhodes Must Fall in Cape Town, the same campaign was effectively transplanted to Oxford. The main impetus for it came at first from a number of South African students, one of whom—Ntokozo Qwabe—was actually on a Rhodes scholarship at the time. Many well-meaning students from Britain and around the world joined the South African student leader who claimed that the statue was an example of "structural violence" and that this violence was not limited to a statue on a building. According to Qwabe, "The structural violence is like the curriculum, the lack of black professors. Those things are not just exceptions. They go to the very heart of how Oxford is configured and how Oxford as a space is, to be quite frank, racist. And this is what we are saying—that that blatant violence and assault and racism is unacceptable at a university that purports to be inclusive."[34]

Soon the claims of the anti-Rhodes campaigners grew. The Rhodes

Must Fall petition in Oxford claimed that by failing to remove the statue of Rhodes, Oriel College and Oxford University as a whole "continue to tacitly identify with Rhodes's values, and to maintain a toxic culture of domination and oppression." The petition attracted a considerable number of signatures from across the university. Subsequent demonstrations attracted large numbers of students. To a great extent, these students, short on time, were mobilized by things that the anti-Rhodes campaign claimed that Rhodes himself had said. These quotes were immensely helpful for growing the campaign against Rhodes. For they were short, pithy, and abhorrent.

The petition to the authorities at Oxford University cited several quotes from Cecil Rhodes. Describing him as an "apartheid colonialist" they claimed that his statements included this one: "I prefer land to niggers . . . the natives are like children. They are just emerging from barbarism. . . . one should kill as many niggers as possible." These quotations were then picked up and used by other media when reporting on the petition and protests.[35] And they are terrible quotes indeed. For they showed Rhodes to be not only a racist but someone advocating genocide against black Africans. At such moments, with such damning material put in front of everyone, it is not easy to even query such material. But a small number of people at Oxford did, including students. They began to look at the sources of the quotes that the anti-Rhodes campaign was using and look into their claims about Rhodes's life. What they found revealed a deep dishonesty.

The anti-Rhodes petition itself offered no sources for its quotations. But the quote did turn up, ellipses and all, in a book review in the *Times Literary Supplement* in 2006. The author of that piece, Adekeye Adebajo, happened to be a former Rhodes scholar himself, and was quoting from a book under review by Paul Maylam.[36] That book makes it clear that the three phrases were all said at different times. But all three parts of the quote turned out to be unstable in their sourcing. These include a work from 1957 that is not a work of scholarship and in which the author admits in the introduction that he has not given references in footnotes "so as not to interrupt the continuity of the story."[37] The first statement is said by Maylam to have been made by Rhodes to Olive Schreiner at a dinner. But the only source is Schreiner herself, who used the phrase in a novel of hers in 1897,[38] and claimed that it came from Rhodes's mouth during a speech to the Cape Parliament. It has been shown that Schreiner herself had a faulty memory on the matter and was almost certainly referring to a speech Rhodes gave to the Cape House in 1892 on taxation and governance in which he said: "You want to annex land rather than natives. Hitherto we have been annexing natives instead of land."

The second part of the alleged quotation comes from a speech by Rhodes to the Cape Town Parliament in 1894. The full paragraph reads:

> Now, I say the natives are children. They are just emerging from barbarism. They have human minds, and I would like them to devote themselves wholly to the local matters that surround them and appeal to them. I would let them tax themselves, and give them the funds to spend on these matters—the building of roads and bridges, the making of plantations, and other such works. I propose that the House shall allow these people to tax themselves, and that the proceeds of their taxation shall be spent by them on the development of themselves and of their districts.

But the third part of the quotation ("One should kill as many niggers as possible") is surely the most reprehensible quote of all. Again, the Rhodes Must Fall campaign made no attempt to reference where it came from. Again, the source would appear to be Adebajo's review of Maylam. And yet this is not what Rhodes is quoted as saying in that work. There Rhodes is alleged to have said, "You should kill as many as you can." There is no use of the N-word. That word has been inserted by the activists of Rhodes Must Fall. As for the rest of the quote, Maylam cites a 1913 biography of Rhodes as his source. And if we look at this source, then the context of the quote becomes clear. The 1913 biography quotes an unidentified officer who heard Rhodes say, after an especially bloody battle with some rebels, "Well you should not spare them. You should kill all you can, as it serves a lesson to them when they talk things over at their fires at night."[39]

In other words, the statement attributed to him by Rhodes Must Fall activists (and assumed to be true by the vast majority of people who will have read it) was a wholesale misrepresentation. Indeed, it was more than a misrepresentation. It was a lie. The quotation was not a single quote from Rhodes, but a conglomeration of three alleged quotes: the first of which was from a novel, the second of which was from a speech advocating for increased African self-determination, and the third of which is an outright fabrication.[40]

Why do these details matter? Rhodes was certainly a colonialist. He was certainly a believer in the British Empire. Would a critique of this not be enough? Why would anybody need to lie and exaggerate the offense? Certainly, there are people who claim that there is an overdue reckoning or rebalancing needed for historical figures such as Rhodes. But why would they decide to base such a reckoning not on the rights or wrongs of empire, or a weighing up of its human costs and benefits, but rather on an outright lie? Or, rather, on a set of lies? Why would a reckoning with the legacy of empire not be enough? Why is it necessary to slip in racist epithets in order to make the past worse than it was and to make important figures in it all come out looking like racist monsters?

Among those who started to carry out his own research was Nigel Biggar, the Regius Professor of Ethics, who is also a canon at Christ Church Cathedral in Oxford. As well as being deeply unassuming and polite, he is also a famously rigorous scholar. When the Rhodes Must Fall campaign began, he started by doing what any diligent scholar might do and read the essay on Rhodes in the *Oxford Dictionary of National Biography*. From there, he developed a growing interest, not just in Rhodes but in the whole way in which empire was being approached. Without issuing any political pronouncements in any way, he suggested that the university could best respond to current turmoils by doing what universities are meant to be best at: scholarship.

He proposed that the university should set up a project, composed of historians and others, dedicated to looking into "the ethics of empire." Biggar suggested that this was a serious and understudied area. This much was provable. One reason why the Rhodes Must Fall campaign went so far so fast was precisely because the study of empire had become unfashionable and so—whatever people's views on it—institutional and individual knowledge of what had happened and who had said what had been slipping away for more than a generation. If the university, and the wider country, was interested in working out its attitudes toward the past, then it should study the past. The rise of postcolonial studies had been a necessary correction within academia, but that period itself now needed interrogating. For to assess the legacy of empire, it is necessary to assess the period in the round. Just as a previous period had been unable to admit to any flaws in empire, so the postcolonial period had been unable to recognize anything positive that had happened. Leading to claims that were ahistorical and just plain wrong. But a second problem Biggar identified was that this solely negative view of empire that led to a feeling of guilt among former colonial powers had in turn led to a reluctance to deal with any of the world's present-day problems. Former colonial powers that had found themselves constantly compared with the worst regimes of the twentieth century might easily find themselves denuded of the will or confidence to act even against serious rights abuses going on around the world today. The result, in other words, could be Western inertia. Something over which other powers might happily seek advantage.

A similar point had recently been made by another academic— Bruce Gilley, who rather remarkably was employed at Portland State University. In 2017, Gilley had published a paper in *Third World Quarterly* titled "The Case for Colonialism" that argued that recent attempts to turn the term "colonialism" into a wholly negative concept were a mistake. As he wrote, "The notion that colonialism is always and everywhere a bad thing needs to be rethought in light of the grave human toll of a century of anti-colonial regimes and policies." He argued that there was a need to accurately reevaluate the past in order to improve the future. In both cases—Biggar and Gilley—this call for levelheadedness and historical fairness did not go down well with their respective critics.

In the case of Gilley, there was such a backlash to his article that fifteen members of the thirty-four-member editorial board of the journal that published it resigned in protest. Despite having gone through all the necessary peer-review processes before publication, petitions and even threats of violence against the journal's editor led to the article being withdrawn and the publication apologizing for ever having published it. Gilley himself was also attacked, accused of "white supremacy" by fellow academics, and subjected to death threats.[41]

Biggar did not get off much more lightly. After he announced his intention to launch a program looking into the ethics of empire, a collection of more than fifty of his fellow academics at Oxford wrote a joint letter to *The Times* condemning his initiative. They said that it was not possible to create a balance book of positive entries to counterbalance (for example) the Amritsar massacre. They accused Biggar of ignorance, of misstating the current state of the debate, and indeed of talking "nonsense." Other academics associated with the project were pressured to resign and did so. According to the anti-Biggar scholars, "No historian (or, as far as we know, any cultural critic or postcolonial theorist) argues simply that imperialism was 'wicked.'"[42] Which simply suggested that the signatories had not read very far.

This letter was then joined by a further letter from more than 170 scholars around the world who wrote condemning Oxford for even considering giving a berth to Biggar's proposed program. These critics accused Biggar of being "a long-time apologist for colonialism" and of aiming to provide "a rehabilitation of the British empire." A student group aiming to challenge "racism and colonialism" claimed that Biggar's project was yet more evidence of Oxford racism.[43] An academic at Cambridge referred to him as a "gnarled old racist" and on the announcement of the course declared on social media with great academic rigor: "OMG, this is serious shit. We need to SHUT THIS DOWN." Elsewhere Biggar's scholarship was dismissed as "supremacist shite"; he was called a "racist" and a "bigot" and told that whatever came out of his mouth was "vomit."[44]

The treatment of Biggar, like the treatment of Gilley, suggested something more than normal academic disagreement. The backlash suggested that these scholars had crossed over some unspoken threshold. And, of course, they had. Just as in the early twentieth century the default consensus at a university such as Oxford would have been that the empire was a force for good, so by the early twenty-first century it had become the default position at such places that the empire was solely a force for bad. The dogma had simply shifted. So now it was not even possible to try to weigh up the moral complexities of empire without being accused of being an apologist for, or supporter of, colonialism. Inadvertently, these critics showed the fragility of their arguments.

Because other people—not least in the countries that had been colonized—were capable of thinking with far greater nuance. For instance, the Nigerian novelist and hero of anticolonialism Chinua Achebe said in 2012, "The legacy of colonialism is not a simple one but one of great complexity, with contradictions—good things as well as bad." And in his final book, *There Was a Country* (2012), Achebe wrote, "Here is a piece of heresy. The British governed their colony of Nigeria with considerable care. There was a very highly competent cadre of government officials imbued with a high level of knowledge of how to run a country . . . British colonies were, more or less, expertly run. . . . One was not consumed by fear of abduction or armed robbery. One had a great deal of confidence and faith in British institutions. Now all that is changed."[45] Achebe is not alone in his assessment. Scholars and writers such as Nirad C. Chaudhuri and Dr. Zareer Masani have argued eloquently in the case of India that what the empire left behind was not just the railroads and the Indian civil service but the scholarship of men such as Sir William Jones and James Prinsep, who unlocked the classical language of India and handed that civilization back to itself.

Many others have made a similar case. Bishop Michael Nazir-Ali, born in Pakistan in 1949, has pointed out that in India and Pakistan there is a common recognition of this complex legacy. As he has said, while there is no doubt that "white nabobs" made themselves wealthy at the expense of the local population, there were also those such as Sir Charles Napier who abolished slavery in the province of Sindh while he was governor in the 1840s and who famously outlawed the practice of "suttee" (the burning of a widow alive on her husband's funeral pyre). The Punjabis called Sir John Lawrence "the saviour of the Punjab," and General John Jacob created the irrigation system around the city of Jacobabad which made the whole area fertile.[46]

The oddity of those who argue against weighing up the various merits and demerits of empire is twofold. First, they say that it cannot be done: there is no way to form the moral calculus necessary to work such things out. Then, they insist that in any case because of a specific terrible thing that happened, any positives must be discounted. In the case of the academics at Oxford who objected to the study of empire, the whole idea of weighing up the merits of empire was obscene because of the Amritsar massacre of 1919. But the example they give highlights the absurdity of their position. After all, there is a reason why the Amritsar massacre is so well known that it is still remembered over a century later.

The brutal shooting at a crowd that led to the deaths of 379 people would not have been remembered if it had been carried out in the twentieth century by Japanese or Chinese troops. It would not have been remembered if it had been carried out by Russian troops, and it would hardly have registered if it had been carried out in the twentieth century by German troops. It is remembered because the massacre was carried out by British troops. It was not just an exception but one which caused deep anger and shame in Britain even as it happened. The General responsible for ordering the soldiers to fire on the unarmed protestors—General Dyer—was removed from his command, forced into retirement, and stripped of his pension. Among the many people in Britain who expressed horror at his actions was Winston Churchill, who told the House of Commons in a debate in 1920 that the massacre at Amritsar "appears to me to be without precedent or parallel in the modern history of the British Empire. It is an event of an entirely different order from any of those tragical occurrences which take place when troops are brought into collision with the civil population. It is an extraordinary event, a monstrous event, an event which stands in singular and sinister isolation."[47]

It may not be possible to answer, but is it not an interesting question to ask why this one monstrous event—or any number of others—could not be weighed up against any good the British Empire did? Does it get outweighed by the British Empire's decision not only to abolish slavery in its colonies but to police the seas in order to outlaw it across the world? If not, then why not? And if the sins of the West are ineradicable, then are the sins of all other peoples ineradicable too? Or is it only Western crimes that are judged in such a light? Nobody appears to know the answer to these questions. More sinister is the fact that nobody is even meant to ask them.

As it happens, there were several codas to the Rhodes Must Fall campaign. Oriel College promised to scrap the Rhodes statue and then promised to save it. The college then agreed to have it withdrawn and also agreed not to do anything about it. This is where the situation currently stands. Since coming to fame for his Rhodes Must Fall activism, Ntokozo Qwabe returned to South Africa, where he briefly made headlines in May 2016, when he boasted in a Facebook post about something "so black" and "wonderful" that had happened that he couldn't "stop smiling." The wonderful thing was that in a restaurant with a friend, he had bullied a white waitress, telling her he would give her a tip "when you return the land." When the waitress burst into tears, he laughed and dismissed her tears as "typical white tears."[48] Later, back at the University of Cape Town, Rhodes having gone, Qwabe was involved with the new "Fees Must Fall" campaign and was reported to have whipped a white student with a stick while racially abusing him. Qwabe took to Facebook to object. He admitted that he had hit the student's phone out of his hand with a "protest stick" he always carries around with him for "cultural purposes," but he said that he had not whipped the student. However, Qwabe added, "I wish I'd actually not been a good law-abiding citizen and whipped the white apartheid settler colonial entitlement out of the bastard." The white student told the media that he did not want to be identified. "It's a month to exams, I just need to pass," he pleaded.[49] Meanwhile, in Cape Town, the Rhodes Must Fall campaign went from strength to strength, even after Rhodes had fallen. The following year, Rhodes Must Fall activists burned artwork, set a bus and other vehicles on fire, and petrol-bombed the offices of the university's vice chancellor.[50]

SLAVERY

In recent years, the critics of the West have marked themselves out through a set of extraordinary claims. Their technique now has a pattern. It is to zoom in on Western behavior, remove it from the context of the time, set aside any non-Western parallels, and then exaggerate what the West actually did.

The case of slavery is a pertinent one. For slavery has been a constant in almost every society since the dawn of recorded history. In antiquity, slaves came from Ethiopia and then farther afield. When the Muslim empires arose, they expanded the trade. As the Muslim empire spread across West Africa during the Middle Ages, it made possible the trading of black slaves across the Sahara. Some ended up in Muslim Spain and Portugal. But when Ferdinand of Aragon and Charles V agreed to a couple of hundred, and then four thousand, slaves to be shipped to the New World they can have had no idea of the change that they were bringing about. From the 1400s to the 1800s, somewhere between ten and twelve million Africans were transported across the Atlantic to the new world. The slaves that were brought out of Africa not only suffered the indignity of being ripped away from their homeland and taken abroad without their permission. They suffered the additional indignity of having been sold by their neighbors and families. There were times when the Portuguese, among others, seized slaves after a military campaign in Africa. But the overwhelming majority of slaves taken out of Africa during these centuries were a result of "man-stealing" and selling, where neighbors, enemies, and sometimes families of Africans would sell other Africans on. Some of the few slave memoirs, such as that of Olaudah Equiano, attest to this fact.

Yet this fact among others is a testament to the fact that the history of slavery is far more universally morally compromising than the current discussion is remotely willing to concede. For while historical attention is now almost exclusively interested in one direction of slavery, throughout the last millennium (as throughout history) the horror went in every direction. And while huge attention has been paid in recent years to the trade in slaves that went west, very little has been expended on the trade that went east. So little indeed that estimates on the numbers of African slaves who were put into the Arab slave trade are even wider (as well as higher) in their range than the transatlantic trade. The best available figures, proposed by scholars such as Professor Ralph Austen of the University of Chicago, is that somewhere between eleven and seventeen million Africans were traded east in the Arab-run slave trade. One reason why the numbers are so difficult to discern is that unlike the transatlantic trade, the slaves the Arabs traded were systematically castrated after being brought from Africa. Which of course ensured that there was neither a second generation of slaves nor any other descendants. Why is this trade so little focused upon? The scholar Tidiane N'Diaye is one of those who has questioned this, in *Le Genocide Voilé* (*The Veiled Genocide*, 2008). He proposes that Arabs have an obvious desire to downplay their thirteen centuries of uninterrupted trading in human beings from sub-Saharan Africa. He also suggests that they ignore it because the Arab nations would much rather maintain pressure on the West by continuing to encourage a focus on the transatlantic trade. It is interesting that almost all the scholarship on this area is now being carried out by French or French-speaking historians and anthropologists. The English-speaking countries appear uninterested in the matter.

Other areas get almost as little attention. For instance, in the modern interest in slavery, very little attention is paid to the fact that between the sixteenth and nineteenth centuries Barbary pirates (that is, Muslim pirates mainly from North Africa) carried out constant raids not just on European ships but against coastal towns and cities across Europe. During these years, the Barbary pirates raided and stole inhabitants of the countries on the northern side of the Mediterranean—including Italy, Spain, Portugal, and France. But they also stole people from as far away as Britain and the Netherlands. The people captured—all white Europeans—would then be either used for ransom or sold into slavery. Over the years during which the Barbary pirates operated, it is believed that they stole as many as one and a quarter million Europeans from their homes.

Of course, there is no movement of reparations for those people or their descendants, and no European has seriously suggested trying to find out where any bill for compensation should be sent. To the extent that it is known about today, it is recognized to be just one of the many bloody and brutal things that went on in the centuries before our own. Worse for the people who suffered it than other forms of slavery, but no morally better or worse in itself. If it is agreed that everybody did bad things in the past, then it is possible to move on and even to move past it. Who wants to litigate or relitigate a past in which nobody's ancestors were saints?

Some people do, and they have decided that they can do so by reframing the history of slavery through their own specifically anti-Western lens. Consider Ibram X. Kendi writing about slavery. In his most famous work, he curtly acknowledges that other societies apart from America and European nations also engaged in slavery. But he then sets up a new stratification of bad slavery and worse slavery. In *How to Be an Antiracist*, he writes: "Premodern Islamic slave traders, like their Christian counterparts in premodern Italy, were not pursuing racist policies—they were enslaving what we now consider to be Africans, Arabs, and Europeans alike. At the dawn of the modern world, the Portuguese began to exclusively trade African bodies."[51]

Even here, for Kendi, the question of diversity is of foremost importance. A form of slavery that involves the enslaving of one racial group is the worst of slavery's forms. While a form of slavery that has diversity at its heart is somehow better slavery.

It is not just that this is a strange standard to apply; it is also a moral retrofit. Kendi applies a current attitude to the past in order to fit the past into a narrative of constant, otherwise universally uncommon Western racism.

Other examples of similar bad-faith arguments can be found everywhere in the current debate on slavery and empire. For example, it is now common to hear the Atlantic slave trade being described as though it had been an act of genocide. Though this is, on its own terms, a nonsensical argument. Appalling as it was, the transatlantic slave trade was dedicated to getting as many living people as possible from Africa into the New World. Though many people died on the way, the aim of the exercise was not to kill the slaves but to get them to the Americas alive so that they could be put to work. That is a great wickedness in itself. But it is far from being a deliberate attempt to wipe out a people. Had the Americans or Europeans ever wanted to attempt such a thing, they might have taken a leaf out of the Arab traders' playbook and castrated all their slaves. Had they done so, then there would be no descendants of slaves in America, just as there are none today in the Middle East.

Similar hyperbole has been attached to every aspect of empire and colonialism. In recent decades, it has become increasingly common to talk of the European settlement in Australia, New Zealand, Canada, and America as though they involved—by intent—the genocide of the local Indigenous populations. Most of the time, this includes reference to the Indigenous populations having been wiped out or significantly diminished by the deliberate spreading of disease. This, too, relies on a distortion of events.

For at some point, someone else in the world was going to discover the New World. And whoever did so was—like the Europeans—likely to enter with a level of immunity to disease that the native populations (being more homogenous and having had less exposure to outside peoples) would not possess. The natural spread of diseases brought in by Europeans could not have been deliberate because the Europeans had no knowledge of immunology, what diseases they themselves were carrying, or how those diseases might spread. Still, none of this has stopped propagandists and academics from asserting that what happened in post-Columbus America, as well as Australia and New Zealand and Canada, was not just genocide but the worst genocide ever. Here is an academic with tenure at a British university speaking on the subject: "What is the first act of Europe in the Americas? It is the largest genocide that has ever existed on the planet . . . I actually don't understand the science of this, but apparently there were so many people killed, the temperature of the earth actually rose."

Claiming that the Holocaust was not unusual in the West, he went on: "It's not an outlier at all, it's the complete logic of the West. Just the only difference is that it was brought to bear in Europe with people we would consider white, right? If you actually think about the mechanics of what the Holocaust was—genocide, killing millions of people because they'd been deemed racially inferior—we'd seen that before. This was not new. This was not a novel thing. This is kind of the foundation of what the West is."[52]

Every aspect of the colonial era is now routinely discussed in the same light. So it has been claimed, for instance, that the British deliberately starved the Indian population on the subcontinent—a claim that is not just without documentary proof, but that runs counter to a most obvious fact: that the Indian population boomed under the period of British rule. Still, this argument, like others, is not enough for the West's detractors.

In fact, the forgotten history of slavery, like colonialism, is not the history of what the West got wrong but the history of what the West got right. While the history of slavery in the West is obsessively pored over, and demands for reparations naturally flow from it, the history of the rest of the world is ignored. Independent Brazil continued to encourage the slave trade right up to the 1880s. The Ottoman Empire continued it even longer. Still today in Saudi Arabia and across the Middle East, black people are referred to as *Abid'* (plural *Abeed'*), which literally means "slave." Being "black" and being a slave still means the same thing to millions of people in the region. In other parts of the world, slavery continues still. I have met slaves myself. I have spoken with them and seen their tears. But those academics such as Siddharth Kara who try to highlight this fact today get a fraction of the attention accorded to those who want to talk only of Western slavery from centuries ago.

Slavery persists today, in countries including Mauritania, Ghana, and South Sudan. In recent years, the world watched the Islamic State put thousands of Yezidi women and children into slavery, killing husbands and bartering wives and children in slave markets. In 2020, a Samoan chief in New Zealand was sentenced to eleven years in prison for slavery. He was caught luring people from Samoa to New Zealand, where he would then bind and enslave them in order to enrich himself. In the West, this is unusual and punished when discovered, but in much of the world, the modern slave trade goes utterly unpunished. There are estimated to be over forty million people living in slavery around the world today. In real terms, this means that there are more slaves in the world today than there were in the nineteenth century.[53] So this is not a question of historic what-aboutery. It raises the question of what might practically change for people today if we spent even a portion of the time that we focus on past slavery focused, instead, on present-day slavery. And what we might be able to do about this modern horror.

Anyone interested in looking into historical mistreatment of people in any century before our own will find a great amount of material. It happens that our age has decided to burrow down on a couple of issues in particular. But doing so means we have lost the whole context in which these horrors themselves occurred. When we say a person was "of his time," we mean the beliefs of those times, but we also mean the hardships of those times. The current interest in slavery alongside the obsession with "privilege" (especially "white privilege") elides the fact that white Europeans during this time were not living in some type of privileged paradise. For instance, the working classes in the United Kingdom throughout the early nineteenth century, when slavery was still going on, were in absolutely no position of privilege themselves. When you look at the charge sheet now leveled against the West and everything in its history, you cannot help noticing the complete lack of context as well as the grotesque lack of balance that exists.

What was the situation of a coal miner in England in the 1800s? How much freedom did he have to make life choices, or escape the background into which he had been born? What of those forced into child labor in countries such as England, pushed before the age of ten into dangerous textile factories or agricultural work? As one recent author on slavery conceded, the life expectancy for slaves in Demerara was exactly twice the life expectancy of an industrial worker in Lancashire or Yorkshire at the same time. Is there anything to learn from this? In the case of that particular historian, the only thing to do was once again to talk about the blame of "white men" and to issue the groveling compulsory confession that as a white man he must "do better."[54]

It is strange to still read of such genuflections, after all these years, simply based on race. For if one race of people should be expected to make them, how could any race avoid them? Not just the peoples who traded but the peoples who sold. What answer can there be, even after all these centuries, to the challenge Voltaire utters in his *Essai sur les moeurs*, where he made the observation that while the white Europeans were guilty of buying slaves, far more reprehensible was the behavior of those Africans who were willing to sell their brothers, neighbors, and children ("On nous reproche ce commerce: un peuple qui trafique de ses enfants est encore plus condamnable que l'acheteur" [They reproach our trade: a nation that traffics its children is even more to be condemned than the buyer]).[55] Does this absolve the West of its responsibility? Of course not. But it is a reminder of how strange it is to see only one group of people consistently in the dock for a crime that everybody took part in.

There is, too, the question of balance. For it must surely be the case that if there are examples of historical sins, then there are also examples of historical virtues, and that even if the one does not fully wipe out the other, then it stands in some mitigation at least? For instance, it is true that Britain engaged in the slave trade and that it took part in a trade in human beings that was appalling. But as we've seen, Britain also led the world in the abolition of that trade. And Britain not only abolished that trade for itself but used its navy to seek to wipe out that trade in all parts of the world the navy could reach. If Britain's decision to abolish slavery in 1807 was unusual, more unusual by far was her decision to send the Royal Navy around the world, establish the West Africa Squadron based at Freetown, and grow the fleet until a sixth of the ships and seamen of the Royal Navy were employed in the fight against the slave trade.

The cost of this extraordinary decision was not only financial. It was paid for in British lives as well. Between 1808 and 1860, the West Africa Squadron captured 1,600 slave ships and freed 150,000 African slaves. They also lost a huge number of personnel themselves. More than 1,500 men of the Royal Navy were killed in action during this period, and the acts of bravery and selfless heroism of those men is worthy of some note, surely? Anthony Sullivan's recent history of the operations of the Royal Navy's West Africa Squadron is one rare work to highlight the extraordinary bravery of these British sailors, chasing boats across the oceans, boarding them, and fighting for their own lives and for the lives of the slaves that they invariably found stowed away in the holds of ships bound for a wide variety of countries.[56] It was a game of cat and mouse across the high seas, with standoffs and guessing games about slave ships trying to pass themselves off as other vessels. Until the British sailors boarded the ships and searched for themselves, they never had any certainty that they were right in this high-risk strategy. It is a tale of great heroism that carried on for six decades. Do these efforts count for anything? In the retributive anti-Western game that is currently going on, it seems they do not.

Instead, we hear only of guilty men. Such as claims made by activists that Britain's greatest maritime hero—Admiral Lord Nelson—was an ardent believer in the slave trade. Such claims are invariably made in order to demand (as it was on that occasion) the removal of Nelson's Column in Trafalgar Square, London. In fact, when this campaign erupted in 2020, it soon transpired that the letter "condemning" Nelson as a slaver was in fact a forgery. Specifically, it had been forged by the anti-abolitionist movement when the slavery debate in England was still ongoing. But by the time this came out, the drive-by shooting on another hero of the West had been achieved. BLM activists had used a forgery created by anti-abolitionists to bolster their own, more contemporary cause. It was an ethical and a scholarly failure.[57] But not many people stayed around for this debate.

Still, to see the full unfairness of the anti-Western game of our time, it is enough to note simply how one individual is now judged. And that individual the greatest of them all.

CHURCHILL

One of the historic figures who has received the most targeting in recent years has been a person who on the face of it might seem a surprising target for "cancellation." Until the last few years, Sir Winston Churchill had generally been revered as one of the most successful and admirable figures in Western history. His arrival into the position of prime minister of the United Kingdom in May 1940, at the very moment that Adolf Hitler began to unleash his blitzkrieg on the West, was later described by Lord Hailsham as the one time he could discern the hand of God intervening in human affairs.

Churchill had been right on many things in his long career, as he had been wrong on some, but identifying the menace of Hitler early on in the 1930s and urging rearmament and facing down the appeasers made him—even before his conduct of the war—one of the great figures of any period in history. Many people talk of fascism and antifascism, but here, without doubt, was the twentieth century's greatest antifascist. If anything, his reputation only grew in the decades after his death. In 2002, he beat off all competition to be voted by the British public as "The Greatest Briton" of all time.

But in recent years, there has been a slow but steady assault on Churchill. While Hollywood movies such as *Darkest Hour* (2017) have continued to play the heroic Churchill out to packed cinemas, a slower burning, but equally virulent strain of anti-Churchill sentiment has spread. There are many things that distinguish this movement, but among the most interesting is how extraordinarily historically ignorant its proponents are.

Take a panel discussion that took place at Churchill College, Cambridge, in February 2021. This event, at a college named after Winston Churchill (the only time a living person has been so honored) was titled "The Racial Consequences of Churchill." The three panelists—Dr. Onyeka Nubia (University of Nottingham), Professor Kehinde Andrews (Birmingham City University), and Dr. Madhusree Mukerjee—were united in their virulent hatred of Churchill. The person who chaired the discussion was one Priyamvada Gopal, who happens to be a teaching fellow at Churchill College. In recent years, she has distinguished herself on Twitter through her antiwhite race-baiting. This has included such gems as "abolish whiteness," "white lives don't matter," and her claim that she has to "resist urges to kneecap white men every day."[58]

None of the participants are specialists in twentieth-century history. One of them is principally a physicist. But none of this prevented the participants from acting as supreme judges on Britain's wartime leader. Their lack of expertise showed itself in the fact that the participants made the most basic historical errors. For instance, at one point Dr Nubia made the schoolgirl error of confusing Ernest Bevin with Aneurin Bevan, perhaps believing that the two men were one and the same. In any case, Aneurin Bevan was not even in office at the time that Dr. Mukerjee claimed he was responsible for British government policy. Still, it was not in the details but in the vast, sweeping claims that these nonspecialists leveled that something important could be discerned.

For instance, throughout the event, Professor Kehinde Andrews, one of the panelists, made claims such as these: the British Empire was "far worse than the Nazis"; the war would have been won without Churchill; Britain would have won with almost anyone else in the position of prime minister; the Holocaust was not unusual in recent history; and, in any case, the victory of the Allies over Nazism was not especially significant because "all we really did was we shifted from an old version of white supremacy to a new version of white supremacy."[59]

There were no depths to which the participants would not sink. At one point, one of the participants started to snark at Churchill for being a coward: "I mean, was it Churchill out there fighting the war? 'Cause I'm pretty sure it wasn't; I'm pretty sure he was at home."[60] You must wonder how hostile somebody must be to ask why a prime minister who, as a young man, saw action on four continents and volunteered to fight in World War I, should, in his sixties, have fought on the front line of the conflict like some medieval warlord. Among other attempts to denigrate Britain's wartime leader, the participants strangely also taunted Churchill for losing the 1945 general election.

This is of a piece with recent Churchill criticism. In 2021, a new book attacking Churchill used every possible line of attack, including attacking him for drinking too much. Elsewhere the book's author claimed that Churchill "was never really a well-travelled man."[61] Which makes you wonder what a well-traveled man would look like if not like Winston Churchill.

Although all these claims show a deep animus, most are essentially frivolous. But the most serious allegations made against Churchill are accusations that have in recent years also come to the fore.

When the BLM movement spilt out from America into Britain in May and June 2020 the statue of Churchill in Parliament Square immediately became one of the focal points for protestors. The statue was repeatedly graffitied and otherwise defaced. At one stage, a BLM banner was taped around the statue's waist and the statesman's name was crossed out with black spray paint. Then, beneath "Churchill," the words "was a racist" were added in more black paint. It was in reporting this protest that the BBC ran the headline "27 Police Officers Injured during Largely Peaceful Anti-racism Protests." A headline only bettered in our time by CNN, a month later, having its reporter standing in front of a burning city with the tagline "Fiery, but Mostly Peaceful Protests."

Such was the sensitivity around the BLM attacks on the wartime leader's statue that it was soon boarded up and then completely encased in a metal box so that protestors could not get at it. A spokesperson for the mayor of London, Sadiq Khan, promised that the status of the statue would remain "under review" by the Greater London Authority and the Met police. During a visit to London by Emmanuel Macron in June, the shamefaced British authorities took down the coverings around Churchill's statue. The French president's visit was to commemorate the eightieth anniversary of General de Gaulle's appeal to the French people to resist the Nazi occupation of their country. So the British authorities may have been aware of the impression it would give if, eighty years after that occasion, London could not even display a statue of its own wartime leader.

But no sooner was Churchill allowed out than he was defaced

again. In September, the words "is a racist" were added to the base
of his statue, this time in yellow paint. And nor were such attacks
limited to the United Kingdom. In the heart of Churchill Square,
in Edmonton, Canada, is a life-size statue of Churchill unveiled by
his daughter in the 1980s. In June 2021, it was the turn of this statue
to be attacked. Activists poured red paint over the figure so that it
dripped down the bronze and covered everything from the statue's
face to its base. One local activist who had previously called for the
statue's removal responded by saying, "Here's an idea—maybe let's
not celebrate, commemorate, and otherwise memorialize warmon-
gers and genocidal maniacs. Stick him in a museum where he belongs
with a proper chronicling of his views and atrocities."[62] The best that
the local mayor in Edmonton could do in response to the attack was
to say: "I don't know the intent behind the vandalism, but I know
historical monuments and sculptures, here and elsewhere, are at the
heart of an emotional debate regarding what legacies and stories we
venerate as a society. I believe there are more productive ways to
move society along towards a more inclusive and uplifting future."

One reason why such mealymouthed criticisms became the norm
was for the same reason that websites like the BBC's started to insist
on putting "the case for the prosecution" under any piece explaining
such attacks on Churchill's reputation. The attacks tended to follow
the line that *Foreign Policy* magazine did when it allowed one of its
authors to describe Churchill in passing as an "avowed racist." As
though this question were not even arguable, simply settled.[63] Or as
CNN did when it ran a piece justifying the Churchill statue defacement in London with the headline "Yes, Churchill Was a Racist. It's
Time to Break Free of His 'Great White Men' View of History." The
article went on to accuse Churchill of "white supremacism."[64]

The accusations against Churchill always boil down to the same few
things. The first is that he occasionally expressed views which were
nineteenth-century in their attitudes. As a product of nineteenth-
century England this is hardly surprising. But the tactic against him
is to seize something in his life that he got wrong or said wrong and

use it to wipe away everything else. As with Rhodes, much of this relies on outright lies.

For instance, Noam Chomsky, among others, has claimed that Churchill advocated the gassing of Iraqi civilians in 1919. What such critics fail to realize is that Churchill was advocating the use of tear gas, not mustard gas. Then there is the example of the Bengal famine of 1943–44. This terrible famine, in which official estimates say that upward of 1.5 million people died, was started when a cyclone hit Bengal and Orissa, destroying the rice harvest. Local officials failed to deal with the problem, as did the viceroy and others. The cabinet records in London show that Churchill insisted that "famine and food difficulties" in the area be "dealt with." Churchill's recent critics accuse him of failing to send sufficient grain to India to alleviate the famine, distort the historical record, and fail to note that the truth is that even at the height of World War II, Churchill personally saw to it that emergency grain supplies reached India from Iraq and Australia.

While the claims against him have been made by utterly inept figures, infinitely better qualified figures including Tirthankar Roy and Amartya Sen have proved how false such claims are. Ordinarily the evidence of such experts would have proved conclusive. But in recent years, even without any grounding in fact, the claims against Churchill have grown. Activists have built on the work of sloppy writers to claim that Churchill didn't bother with the famine in Bengal, that he wanted there to be a famine, and even that he was gleeful that people starved so long as they were Indians. Such claims are wholly disproved by the historical record but have gained some currency thanks to the ferocity of their repetition. As Churchill's most recent biographer, Andrew Roberts, has written with Zewditu Gebreyohanes, "It is unrealistic to imagine that anyone else in [Churchill's] place could have given more attention to the famine than he did when a world war was being waged on multiple fronts."[65]

It sometimes seems as though there is nothing that Churchill could have done to please his latest critics. In 2019, the then Labour shadow chancellor, John McDonnell, was questioned about Churchill during a public event in London. "Winston Churchill: hero or villain?" he was asked. McDonnell, a self-described Marxist and socialist, replied simply "Tonypandy. Villain." This referred to an incident in South Wales in 1910 when Churchill as home secretary sent police in to deal with riots that had erupted over a miners' picket line. One miner was killed in the ensuing violence. And there is surely something extraordinary in this: a wholesale lack of ability to weigh up good and bad. The events at Tonypandy are disputed, and nobody would seriously lay the death of that one miner at the hands of Winston Churchill. But so what if they could? If that one Welsh miner did die because of the direct decision making of Winston Churchill, did nothing that Churchill achieved in the decades after 1910 make up for that? Does his central role in defeating fascism count for nothing against this?

Historical judgment calls like this tend to come with complications. The first is that they are so astoundingly one-directional. While he was shadow chancellor, McDonnell was happy to praise Mao Zedong and wave his Little Red Book in the House of Commons, recommending its contents to the House. During his life and career, Chairman Mao is estimated to have been responsible for the deaths of around sixty-five million people. Yet this fact can be brushed aside by Labour politicians such as McDonnell and former shadow home secretary Diane Abbott, who once said that "on balance Mao did more good than harm," because "he led his country from feudalism." It seems right to ask exactly what accounting system is going on here? How can it be that a left-wing dictator can kill tens of millions of people yet still be praised for great leaps forward in agricultural matters, whereas Winston Churchill can help save the world from fascism yet be forever damned because of a Welsh miner's death three decades before? There is something so outrageous in this that it must be put down to a desire to win some other political fight.

Something else is going on in the attacks on Churchill, which are a possibly deliberate attempt to cause enervation. It is almost impossible to look at people trying to weight the scales of history in such a fashion and not sigh with exhaustion.

If what Churchill did in his life doesn't count for anything, then it is hard to see how any human action counts for anything.

If Churchill's good points cannot outweigh any bad points, then no one can ever do enough good in their lives. In other words, if we cannot get Churchill right, and get him in a proper perspective, then there seems little point in trying to do so with anyone else. Finally, there seems little point in trying to do anything good ourselves. The attacks on Churchill make all human endeavor seem futile, because if even defeating the greatest evil in history will count as nothing, and you will not be lauded for it in your own country even half a century after your death, then what good deed could ever count for anything?

Still, this doesn't quite answer why Churchill should attract so much opprobrium. Why it should be the case that on issue after issue his reputation has been smeared and sullied and his achievements so dishonestly assessed. To understand what is going on here, it is necessary to consider this not at a historical level but at a religious level. Since World War II, Churchill has been revered across the Western world. Perhaps more than any other single figure, he has been seen as an example of a great man—and a great man produced by the West. He is a figure in whom the public still feels huge pride. The knowledge of him, and the memory of him, stirs them. They may not believe in God, but they believe in Winston Churchill. That is why cinema audiences got to their feet and cheered at the end of *Darkest Hour*. It is why books on Churchill and memorabilia to do with him still sell so strongly. Because his story is a heroic story, demonstrating the greatness that mankind can aspire to and the heroism that men can achieve.

This, then, is the reason why Churchill must be particularly assaulted. Because as long as his reputation stands, the West still has a hero. As long as his reputation remains intact, we still have figures to emulate. But if Churchill can be made to fall? Why then one of the great gods, perhaps the greatest of the West, falls. And then? Well, anything might be forced upon a people so subjected and demoralized. The academics and others who assail Churchill know what a holy being he is. They know how much he is revered. And it is for precisely this reason that they assault him. Because they want to kick the "white men," they want to kick at the great man view of history. They want to kick at the holiest beings and places of the West. They choose their targets well.

STATUES

In Britain, as in America, this kicking at the foundations has taken on a special fury in recent years. Just as the Floyd protests in America began with debatable figures and then roared right toward the center of the nation's history, so in Britain it burned from the outside in at a record pace. In the days immediately after the death of George Floyd, a crowd in Bristol attacked a statue of Edward Colston (1636–1721), a local merchant and philanthropist who had been involved in the slave trade. As the police looked on, the crowd pulled the statue from its plinth, rolled it down the street, and hurled it over the docks into the harbor. As in America, there was a clear elation in the air, a feeling that here—in this permissible vandalism—was something to do. A way to right something.

Like their American counterparts, the British authorities also began to remove statues preemptively, hoping to stay one step ahead of the mob. A statue of the merchant Robert Milligan was removed from its plinth at London's Docklands because of his connection to the slave trade. The mayor of London—Sadiq Khan—announced the setting up of a commission to look into what statues and monuments might need to be removed across London. The Robespierreian title of the commission was "The Commission for Diversity in the Public Realm." The likely conclusions of the commission could be guessed at fairly easily. Its members included Lynette Nabossa, a "community builder" who had claimed that white supremacy was a uniquely British thing and that the United Kingdom is "the common denominator in atrocities across the world."[66] There was also Aindrea Emelife, who had already expressed her approval of "guerrilla style" statue removal,[67] and another member, Toyin Agbetu, who had distinguished himself in the past by turning up to a service at Westminster Abbey where he had heckled the archbishop of Canterbury and the Queen before threatening to punch a black security guard as he was being removed.[68] A finely unbalanced panel, in other words.

Just as a guilty verdict had already been declared on the statues that were still standing, so the verdict was also already in on what memorials should replace them. The mayor who had put together the commission pledged that just as the old statues would come down, so new ones would go up. He said that new memorials for London would include ones for the Windrush generation and one for Stephen Lawrence, a black teenager who had been murdered thirty years earlier, as well as a National Slavery Museum.[69] In other words, once again, the whole national story was to be turned upside down.

As with the 1619 Project, a story of accomplishment was to be turned perfectly deliberately into one of oppression. A story of heroics would be turned into a narrative of bigotry. And anyone who did not agree to go along with this shift in the narrative could expect to come under fire themselves, however unknown they might be.

After the protests in Washington, DC, a video went around online of three women, who happened to be white, trying to scrub BLM graffiti off the Lafayette Building. The video showed the women being berated by a passing motorist. "Why do you want that to come off?" demanded the woman in the car. "Because this is a federal building," said one of the women. "So you don't care about black lives then?" said the woman doing the interrogating. "That's not at all what we're saying," one of the women said. "We certainly do care about black lives." "Not enough to leave up a message," shot back the woman in the car. Making the removal of graffiti yet one more entry in the ever-lengthening list of racist acts.

Similarly, after one of the BLM protests in London, a group of young British people turned up to clean graffiti off the public monuments in Whitehall with their own hands. The young men and women turned out to be members of the Household Cavalry, who came around after the protests had dwindled and began to scrub the graffiti off the statue of Earl Haig on Whitehall. This was shortly after at least one other protestor had been pictured clambering over the Cenotaph and defacing Britain's memorial to the fallen of the two world wars.

These and other Whitehall monuments had been spray-painted with "ACAB" (All cops are bastards) and other BLM slogans. A young woman with a camera-phone sought to "shame" the young men and women for cleaning the monuments. Other protestors taunted the young soldiers for their acts. First, for clearing away some of the protest banners that had been left littered around Whitehall. And, second, for daring to try to clear the graffiti. "Couldn't even wait a day," one woman taunted them. "Not one day. Because of their precious memorial."

Of course, for any British person, these memorials are indeed precious. They represent the sacrifices that every family in the nation made to keep their country free from tyranny. For most British people, the sacrifice that previous generations made on their behalf isn't a funny or shallow thing, or something to be derided. It is deep and not up for negotiation.

But this desire to mock the West's holy places seems almost unassuageable. And it has spread everywhere. In Canada, during the BLM summer, crowds had already pulled down a statue of Sir John Macdonald, Canada's first prime minister and the nearest thing the country has to a founding father. In the summer of 2021, there was a revived burst of this anti-Western iconoclasm. Until 1982, Canada had celebrated Dominion Day on the first of July. But "Canada Day" was deemed to be more inclusive, and that agreement almost held until 2021, when the anti-Canada feeling inside Canada was growing. Another statue of Macdonald was pulled down and then, on the day itself, crowds of people gathered on Parliament Hill to chant "Shame on Canada." Prime Minister Justin Trudeau ordered the flying of the national flag at half-mast. And across the country, protestors seemed keen to rip out any and all monuments to the country's Western past. A statue of the explorer Sir James Cook was pulled down and then in Winnipeg huge crowds armed with ropes and hooks pulled the vast throned statue of Queen Victoria off her plinth. They then performed the same ritual act of vengeance on a statue of the present monarch, Queen Elizabeth. In only a few years, a day of celebration of Canada's confederation as a country had turned into an opportunity for an orgy of anti-Canadian-ness.

During this strange stampede in Canada, as in so many other cases, the whole history of the country and the wider West became strangely perverted. Both truths and lies were exaggerated and then spun along through a cycle of outrage. Assumptions of obvious guilt were made, followed by a scouring search for culprits to blame. Always the indictable force is the West, and the institutions and ideas that have made up the West. History becomes the history of Western sins. And ignorance reigns not only over anything good the West ever did but over anything bad that anyone else has ever done.

THE GREAT DIVESTMENT

Fixed in this narrative is a stampede inside the West to rid itself of its own history. And for some years now, strange outbursts have begun to break out. For instance, in recent years, universities and other public institutions have started to order historical audits of themselves to see whether—or to what extent—they might have benefited from the slave trade or empire. The guilty verdict is always preordained. But precisely what should be done to make amends is never clear.

In the meantime, these strange spasms can break out anywhere. In 2019, Cambridge University announced that it was going to carry out an audit over whether or how it may have benefited from the slave trade. One consequence came in May of that year when it was announced that St. Catherine's College had removed a bell that it had on display. The bell in question was held under suspicion for having once been on a slave plantation, and so it was "shuttered off" from public view pending further investigations into the inanimate object. At such moments, you can begin to wonder whether we are getting into the realms of Narnia-like magic. Do such items carry some sort of dark matter with them? Will the plantations come back if the bell is rung? It remains unclear. A senior tutor at St. Catherine's simply stated that the college wanted to "reflect on our commitment to diversity, inclusion and asking challenging questions."[70]

What is clear is that no institution can afford to get left behind in the current moment. In London, the British Museum has been put under pressure once again. In August 2020, it caved to pressure to remove the bust of the museum's founding collector. The bust of Hans Sloane was removed from its pedestal and resituated to a cabinet because, it was explained, his collecting "was partly financed from the labour of enslaved Africans on his wife's sugar plantations."[71] This inevitably led to renewed calls for the museum to return various items in the collection. For once, the demands to return the Parthenon Marbles to Athens were overshadowed by demands to return the Benin bronzes to the country that is now Nigeria, from which the bronzes originally came in the 1890s. An influential book followed, erroneously claiming that the bronzes were "looted" by an expedition of British men in an example of "racism," "corporate extractive capitalism," and "proto-fascism." In fact, the bronzes were seized as war booty after an expedition of British men were butchered ("perhaps lost their lives," the author of *Brutish Museums* puts it). In fact, the four British men were sacrificed by the Oba of Benin, who was still operating a slave market. The severed heads of the British men appeared a day later with stick-gags in their mouths.[72]

But as with so many other occasions in the present moment, nearly all actual knowledge of what had happened at the point in question had been long forgotten. The history had been rewritten in the same one-note tone as everything else: a story of Western racists taking advantage of innocent natives. Such was the pressure on one institution that another institution soon buckled. In April of the following year, the Church of England (C of E) announced that it was sending back to Nigeria two Benin bronzes that were in its collection. It transpired that these two bronzes had in fact been given to the former archbishop of Canterbury, Robert Runcie, in 1982. The gifts had been given by the University of Nigeria. So now, in a fit of guilt, the C of E announced that it was returning some recent gifts, as though to get stolen property off its hands.

INTERLUDE:
REPARATIONS

What can the West do with such a catalogue of sins being leveled at it? What could anyone do? How can these wrongs be righted without punishing the innocent and rewarding the unworthy? It is a puzzle that hovers over any and all historic injustices. And it requires a considerable amount of care to wield this moral scalpel at all. Let alone to wield it without killing the patient during surgery.

The first thing to do is to work out whether the wrong has actually occurred. And what the extent of that wrong might be. Next, it is necessary to work out who the person is who has been wronged and who the person is who has done the wrong thing. If forgiveness or apology is required, then who can offer it and who can accept it? If some kind of compensation or restitution is required, then where will it come from and who will it go to?

These are just some of the questions that linger in the debate over the history of the West. And this process of questioning is not in itself unusual. All of history, and geography, is claim and counter-claim about who wronged who and which group of people still owes another group of people for a historic wrong. Sometimes those fights end up being territorial, as in Cyprus or the Western Sahara. Sometimes they are about which group is seen to have come out on top in the same society. Throughout history, such conflicts have died out and been capable of being reignited again with extraordinary ease. It is not difficult to whip up animosity against a particular group by portraying them as having unfairly benefited to the detriment of others. History is chock-full of versions of how this plays out. So an extraordinary amount of care is required if you are going to make claims of wrongdoing against whole groups of people, let alone whole ethnic groups.

It might be no surprise that none of the necessary moral finessing is performed in the current day when it comes to the West, or when it comes to the ethnic group that has made up the majority in the West. Quite the opposite, in fact. The opponents and competitors of the West seem thrilled not only to be able to say whatever they like about the West but to make extraordinary demands of it. The more outrageous the better.

Again, none of this is especially new, but it has picked up pace in recent decades. Demonization of the West and of Western people is now the only acceptable form of bigotry at international forums such as the United Nations. If demonization of the African nations was the norm, then this would be easily identified. The same would go for any other culture. Except for the West.

Anyone who doubts that should cast their minds back just two decades to an event that happened in the coastal city of Durban, South Africa. The "World Conference against Racism, Racial Discrimination, Xenophobia and Related Intolerance" took place between August 31 and September 8, 2001. Unsurprisingly for such an event—under such auspices—the conference was less about tackling racism and intolerance than it was about showcasing these things. The state of Israel came in for particularly virulent attack, to such an extent that some of the Western countries even began to get so uncomfortable about the amount of abuse being leveled at a conference meant to tackle discrimination that the United States and Israel walked out. Other Western countries threatened to walk out but stayed. The outrages of this conference—which took place under the auspices of the UN—were soon overshadowed by the greater outrages that happened in New York, Washington, DC, and a field in Pennsylvania just three days after the conference ended. But everything that happened in Durban should have been better understood. Because every detail of it demonstrated the orgy of anti-Westernism that not only set the scene for 9/11 but had already become the acceptable default position of anti-Westerners around the globe.

The self-important "declaration" that was published at the end of the conference ticked all the right boxes for the various anti-Western powers who made most of the running at the event. Although the anti-Semitism that had run through the conference was downplayed in the final document, it took it as proven that there was no wrong in the world that could not be laid at the West's doors. Every endlessly rehearsed crime of the West was used as the sole explainer for global racism and discrimination. Any and all negative aspects of life in Africa, the Middle East, the Far East, and elsewhere were either ignored or put on the West's tab regardless.

For instance, the final declaration at Durban pronounced, "We recognise that colonialism has led to racism, racial discrimination, xenophobia and related intolerance." It claimed that the African people still suffer the consequences and that not only should colonialism be "condemned" but its reoccurrence should be "prevented." Something that African leaders notably failed to do over the following two decades as they sold their countries to China's Belt and Road project. Elsewhere the declaration condemned "the transatlantic slave trade" (the only such slave trade that was singled out and named). It also called for reparations to be made by the countries that were responsible for these atrocities.[1] In some ways, these conclusions were mild, given the nature of the conference that had led up to the final document.

Because there had been many highlights in the anti-Western frenzy that was the Durban conference. For instance, there was the sight of Robert Mugabe's government (then terrorizing and murdering white farmers in Zimbabwe) calling on Britain and America to "apologise unreservedly for their crimes against humanity." Someone called

Matthew Coon Come, a chief of Canada's "First Nations," told the
UN delegates that he and his fellow natives were victims of "a racist
and colonial syndrome of dispossession and discrimination." This
went down very well with the delegates. When Mr. Coon Come
claimed that the government in Ottawa had only a year before ordered "white mobs" to attack the people of the First Nations (a figment of Mr. Coon Come's imagination) the delegates applauded
loudly. Of course, the government being accused of these crimes had
paid for Mr. Coon Come's airfare to go to Durban and make these
allegations against the Canadian authorities. But this irony had to
join a long queue at Durban.

The Syrian foreign minister was among the other progressives who
used the conference to make their pitch against the West for its xenophobia and prejudice. The term "techno-racism" was invented at the
conference to try to claim that capitalism was in its essence a racist
enterprise. The biggest ovation of all was reserved for Fidel Castro,
who was introduced to the conference as the leader of "the most
democratic country in the world." By 2001, Castro had neglected to
hold a free and democratic election in Cuba for four decades. But
that did not matter to the attendees at Durban. In fact, nothing mattered to them, other than attacking the Western democracies, blaming them for all the world's ills, and lauding anyone seen as an enemy
or antagonist of the West. Perhaps the only meaningful disagreement
at Durban came over who the reparations should be paid to. Various African American attendees thought that reparations should
be paid to individuals. Whereas, as Mark Steyn observed at the time,
the African presidents in attendance seemed to believe that "it would
be more convenient if the West just dropped off one big check at the
presidential palace."[2]

There was even a moment when the Organisation of African
Unity stated that reparations for the slaughter of the Tutsi tribe by
the Hutu tribe in Rwanda in 1994 should be paid out by the government of America. Rwanda gained its independence from Belgium
in 1962.

Anyone familiar with the operation of the UN Human Rights Council in Geneva will be familiar with this system of values. There, Israel, America, and the European powers are consistently berated for historic crimes by such luminaries of human rights as Iran, Syria, and Venezuela. Most of this can be put down to posturing and distraction techniques. As it was in 2020, when North Korea called the United States a "human rights wasteland" and a country of "extreme racists," citing the BLM protests and the death of George Floyd as justification.[3] It is hard to imagine a country anywhere in the world in which racism is as instilled into the general population as it is in North Korea. As I saw for myself on a visit to the country some years ago, the idea of the racial supremacy of the North Korean peoples is instilled from birth. As is a racialized contempt for Americans, Westerners in general, the Japanese, and many others. It is a country that actively fears miscegenation and has gone to extraordinary lengths to ensure that North Korean blood is not "diluted."[4]

International bodies such as the Human Rights Council are perfect places for oppressive states to deflect attention from their ongoing crimes and focus instead on the historic sins of the West. Most totalitarian and even many nonaligned countries find it useful to cover for each other's abuses in this manner. But just because some claims for reparations are cynical and opportunistic does not mean that all of them are. In recent years, in America in particular, there has been a serious and growing call for some form of reparations to be paid, and it should be seriously considered. These include calls for reparations for the descendants of the victims of empire and reparations for the descendants of those who suffered from the transatlantic slave trade.

For many years, these ideas sat on the Fanon-ish edges of the Far Left. They were regarded as unfeasible and so hardly worth discussing seriously. Then in 2014, Ta-Nehisi Coates wrote a cover article for *The Atlantic* called "The Case for Reparations" that made a serious argument for a historic wealth transfer from one set of racial groups in society to another.[5] In his 15,000-word essay, Coates

claimed: "Something more than moral pressure calls America to reparations. We cannot escape our history." The history that particularly called for reparations was the existence of slavery and the Jim
Crow laws. His claim was that because black Americans still under-
perform white Americans in household income, this inequity could
be put down to the legacy of racism in the United States.

On the point that he did raise, Coates was wildly imprecise about
exactly how any such reparation transaction could be carried out. He
even claimed that he didn't think that reparations could be achieved.
But the essay changed the weather around the discussion. In fact, five
years later, the *New Yorker* said that the article had "chang[ed] the
world." Not least by making reparations a major subject of debate
among Democratic presidential candidates.[6]

Portions of the Left across the West also picked up the theme. In
a short time, the subject of reparations moved from being politically
unfeasible to politically credible. In Britain, the 2019 Labour Party
manifesto committed Her Majesty's opposition to "conduct an audit
of the impact of Britain's colonial legacy." The resulting 234-page
investigation into the British state, published by the Labour Party in
2021, declared that Britain "should make an unreserved apology to
all of the countries of the world that the Empire invaded and negatively impacted" and that "the British state should set up a reparations fund . . . to communities across the world that can show loss
and detriment as a result of the actions of the British state."[7]

In America, the issue came even closer to the political center. And
it makes the demands of the British Labour Party look straight-
forward. For it is in the United States that the talk of a wealth transfer is not about an international money transfer but a transfer of
wealth from one set of racial groups within the country to another.
The Democratic contenders for the presidential nomination in 2020
talked about it. And one of President Biden's first acts in office, in
February 2021, was to give his support to Democratic lawmakers attempting to pass legislation that would create a commission to examine slavery in the United States and its ongoing effects and to look

into possible remedies. The possible remedies listed included financial payments from the government to the descendants of slaves, to compensate them for unpaid labor carried out by their ancestors.[8]

Wittingly or otherwise, such people, and US authorities, are dealing with a question deeper than they realize. In his *Atlantic* piece on reparations, Ta-Nehisi Coates talked about German reparations to Israel as a type of model for what reparations might look like in the United States. Since he, too, chose to employ a World War II parallel, perhaps a tale from the same period might be used to exemplify the depth of the problem that any discussion about reparations must deal with.

In 1969, the Holocaust survivor and celebrated postwar Nazi hunter Simon Wiesenthal published a work called *The Sunflower: On the Possibilities and Limits of Forgiveness*. It is an account of something that Wiesenthal says happened to him at the Lemberg concentration camp. In 1943, Wiesenthal was one of a group of forced laborers and one day is plucked from the line and taken to the bedside of a Nazi soldier who is dying. The man, called Karl S in the book, turns out to have joined the Hitler Youth and from there moved up the Nazi ranks all the way to the SS. During this time, he participated in one particular atrocity. He confesses to the Jewish man at his bedside that his unit had at one stage in the war destroyed a house in which there were around three hundred Jews. The SS unit had set the house on fire, and as the Jews inside tried to escape from the burning building, by leaping from the windows, Karl S and his comrades shot and killed them all.

This is described in considerable detail, and if this was all *The Sunflower* was then it would simply be yet one more tale of the countless number of tales of Nazi atrocities carried out against Jews during World War II. But Wiesenthal's book is not about that. It is about what happens next. Because it is clear that Karl has asked for a Jew to be brought to his bedside because he wants to confess to this crime in particular and to a Jew in particular, because he wants to get this particular atrocity off his chest before his imminent death.

It is something in the way of a deathbed confession. And it is what happens next that makes Wiesenthal's book so memorable. For after the SS soldier has finished his tale, and the reader perhaps expects some type of reconciliation, Wiesenthal gets up and leaves the room without saying a word.

Later, Wiesenthal meditates on whether he did the right thing, and the second half of the book is given over to a symposium involving a range of thinkers and religious leaders who contributed their thoughts on the events that Wiesenthal has described. It is noticeable, incidentally, that many of the Christians who contributed to this symposium believed that Wiesenthal should have offered some kind of forgiveness to the soldier. But the broader consensus that emerges from the contributors is that Wiesenthal did the right thing. And if there is a reason that this comes down to, it is this: that Wiesenthal, although he was a Jew, like the soldier's victims, had neither the right nor the ability to forgive the soldier for what he had done.

In order for true forgiveness to occur, the parties involved must be not only the one who has done the wrong but the one to whom the wrong has been done.

Wiesenthal may have been a Jew, like the victims, but he does not have the right to forgive on behalf of his fellow Jews who were gunned down by the soldier as they jumped from a burning building. Wiesenthal is not these men, women, and children. He is not even a close relative of these men, women, and children. These victims may never have wanted to forgive their killers. Perhaps they would have hated their killers forever and not wanted them to die in peace. The SS soldier had participated in such a terrible end for them, so what right did Wiesenthal have to say on behalf of all of these people that the SS soldier is forgiven? Why should the SS soldier die with even a part of his conscience cleared? After taking no care about the consciences of so many other human beings.

Within this is a very powerful and important point almost totally lost in the debate about forgiveness in the modern world. In recent years, the prime ministers of countries including Australia, Canada, the United States, and Britain have all issued apologies for historic wrongs. Sometimes, as when the direct victims of these wrongs are still alive, this can ameliorate suffering and provide a form of closure for the victims. But when we are talking about apologies for things done centuries ago, we enter a different ethical territory. In such cases, neither the people claiming to be victims nor the people assuming the mantle of perpetrators are any such thing. When it comes to apologies for the slave trade or for colonialism, we are talking about political leaders and others making apologies for things that happened before they themselves were born. And apologizing to people who have not suffered these wrongs themselves, though some may be able to point to some disadvantage they can claim to have suffered as a result of these historic actions.

Any apology begins to consist of people who may or may not be descended from people who may have done some historic wrong apologizing to people who may or may not be descended from people who had some wrong done to them. In the realm of reparations, this becomes messier still. For at this stage, the divide in the West is by no means clearly between victims and perpetrators. Whereas the governments in almost every non-Western country are strikingly ethnically homogenous (consider the political leadership in India, China, or South Africa), governments in every Western country are now made up of people of a wide variety of ethnic backgrounds. No Western cabinet would be able to work out the victim-oppressor divide even at the table around which they sit. Nor would any political party. Just consider the difficulty merely of working out what Elizabeth Warren may or may not be owed.

The issue of reparations now comes down not to descendants of one group paying money to descendants of another group. Rather, it comes down to people who look like the people to whom a wrong was done in history receiving money from people who look like the people who may have done the wrong. It is hard to imagine anything more likely to rip apart a society than attempting a wealth transfer based on this principle.

Perhaps that is why the difficult questions on this are ignored by everybody who has argued for reparations to occur. For instance, were any such scheme to operate in America, the country would have to carefully determine which racial groups in the country have been most harmed by American history. It may determine to limit the scope of its attentions solely to the issue of people who are the descendants of slaves. Though there is no reason why it should limit itself to that. But if it did, then the prelude to reparations would have to be the development of a societal, genetic database. It could be that this would only be necessary to create for the black population of the United States. It would then have to determine how to apportion the funds available. Anyone who thinks voter ID laws or vaccines are intrusive should prepare for the questions that will follow this process.

For instance, after the genetic database is created, it will have to be decided whether or not the only recipients should be those who are 100 percent descended from slaves—if any such people can be identified. Should these people alone be given a full stipend? Should someone who is only descended from slaves on their mother's side receive 50 percent of the same sum? Will the restitution process try to operate the "one-drop rule," and if so, how will it ensure that nobody is taking advantage of the financial spigots that would result? And, of course, all of this would be predicated on the idea that a vast wealth transfer from one racial group to another racial group in America in the 2020s will bring racial harmony and will not cause any igniting or resurgence of racial ill feeling. Can anyone be sure that this is the most likely result?

Only around 14 percent of the US population is black. As of 2019 more than half of that population (59 percent) were millennials or younger (that is, under the age of thirty-eight).[9] During their lifetime, it has been illegal to treat people differently because of their skin color. Jim Crow laws were decades in the past before this group was born. The official prohibition on the further importing of slaves into the United States had been signed two centuries before this group was born. To begin to apply reparations to this community would require a clear differentiation between black Americans who are descendants of Africans brought forcibly to the United States and black Americans whose ancestors voluntarily came to the United States in the centuries after slavery was abolished.

And what about the people doing the paying? There will be many people who have come to America's shores since slavery ended—most of America's Jewish, Asian, and Indian populations, for instance— who may make an objection at this point. Why should those whose ancestors played no part in a wrong be made to forfeit a part of their tax dollars in paying for something that happened generations before their family came to America? Should people whose ancestors died in the Civil War fighting for the North get any special dispensation? Should those whose ancestors fought for the South pay disproportionately more?

There are very obvious reasons why people might call for reparations: for political convenience or in genuinely seeking to right a historic wrong. But there is an equally obvious reason why they can almost never be drawn into giving any details of what the process might look like. That is because it is an organizational and ethical nightmare.

We also know that no matter how much is done to address the issue it will never be enough. We know this not least because Britain's attempt to make up for the slave trade is over two centuries in the past and the issue of further reparations being made is still raised. Indeed, the subject is discussed as though critics either do not know or know and do not care how many resources Britain poured into abolishing slavery in the 1800s. The British taxpayer paid a hefty price for the abolition of the slave trade for almost half a century. And it has been proven that British taxpayers spent almost as much suppressing the slave trade for forty-seven years as the country profited from it in the half century before slavery was abolished. Meaning that the costs to the taxpayer of abolition in the nineteenth century were almost certainly greater than the benefits that came in the eighteenth century.

The British government of the day spent 40 percent of the entire national budget to buy freedom for the people who had been enslaved.

At the time, the only way that the British government could get the consensus needed to abolish the trade was to compensate those companies that had lost income because of the trade. This sum was so large that it was not finally paid off until 2015. And while some campaigners have used this to show how recent the trade in human beings was, it rather better exemplifies the unprecedented lengths the government was willing to go to in order to end this vile trade.

Two of the scholars who have done some of the complex math required here have estimated that the cost of abolition to British society was just under 2 percent of national income. And that was the case for sixty years (from 1808 to 1867). Factoring in the principal costs and the secondary costs (for instance, the higher prices for goods that the British had to pay throughout this period), Britain's suppression of the Atlantic slave trade, it has been claimed, constituted "the most expensive example" of international moral action "recorded in modern history."[10]

Several things could be learned from this. But one thing worth noting is that such actions appear in the current era to be almost entirely unknown. What is more, they appear to buy Britain—and the wider West—absolutely no time off in the purgatory of the present. The British may have actually overpaid in compensation for their involvement in the slave trade, but it appears to count as nothing; demands for reparations internationally and domestically still continue.

Is there any end to this? Are there even any means to an end to this? The British precedent suggests not. If America were to find a way to pay reparations today, why would the same demands not rearise two centuries later, as they have done in relation to Britain? If the great reparations machine were to pour out money, why should it be a once-in-a-lifetime opportunity? It is not a problem that is unique to the British or American examples.

Whenever a country such as Greece gets into financial trouble, politicians there can always be found who are willing to say that

Germany must pay Greece for its occupation of the country during World War II. Indeed, Prime Minister Alexis Tsipras made precisely this demand again in 2015. There are not many ways to see how this would stop. Other than Greece never getting into financial difficulties ever again.

The same applies to the payment of reparations for empire or slavery. It will always be the case that there will be African politicians who will claim that the problems of their country are not to do with any mismanagement of their own, but because of colonialism. The late Robert Mugabe was a fine example of this genre. The only way for such demands to stop would be for every former colony to be thriving and well run for the rest of time with governments that are always and everywhere strangers to corruption.

Likewise, in the American context, what would it look like for reparations to have been paid off? Even writers, such as Coates, who have argued for reparations have joked about the likely consequences of doling out large sums of money to black Americans. Dave Chapelle did a skit on this, showing black people spending their reparations payments on fancy cars, rims, clothes, and more. It would be a good time to buy shares in Nike. But the serious fact is that it could only be deemed that reparations had worked if black Americans either performed equally to or actually outperformed all other racial groups. And not just in the aftermath of payments but for every year in the foreseeable future. If black Americans underperformed, then it could always be argued that reparations had not so far adequately occurred because inequalities still existed. In order for demands for reparations to go away, any and all wealth disparities would have to disappear not just once but forever. Until then, it is hard to see how the demands for financial compensation will be able to stop.

In the meantime, it is impossible not to note how fantastically one-sided, ill-informed, and hostile this debate has become. No world forum ever concentrates seriously on any form of reparations that does not involve the West. And there is an obvious reason why there are no calls for reparations to Africans abducted into the slave trade that went East. Which is that the Arabs deliberately killed off the millions of Africans they bought. But there is little explanation as to why it is that today it is only Western former colonial powers or former slave-owning countries that are expected to pay any sort of compensation for sins of two centuries ago. Modern Turkey is not expected to pay money for the activities of the Ottoman Empire. An empire that, incidentally, ran on for twice as long as the empires of Europe did. After all these years, it is still only the sins of the West that the world—including much of the West—wish to linger over. It is as though when looking at the many, multivariant problems that exist in the world, a single patina of answers has been provided that is meant to explain every problem and provide every answer.

In 2021, during a discussion with, among others, a black American filmmaker and a prominent black media academic from South Africa, I was told by the latter that "we" live in a "white supremacist, patriarchal society." I asked Asanda Ngoasheng (whose work was described as focusing on the decolonization of the curriculum and attempts to "amplify conversation about race, power and gender") what "we" meant in this context. My counterpart was living in, and speaking from, South Africa. That country has certainly had its own uniquely benighted history. If you had said that South Africa under apartheid was a white-supremacist society, then you would have been correct. But, I asked my colleague, did she honestly mean to claim that the whole world, including South Africa today, is a white-supremacist society?

"Yes," she said, "that is what I am saying." And, she added, "not just in South Africa, but globally." And I wondered in what sense it can possibly be said that today's South Africa—a country whose cabinet is entirely composed of black South Africans—is a "white-supremacist society." The country certainly has its own wide array of problems. But white supremacy seems to me not to be among them. I was told that as a white non–South African I had no right to say that South Africa today is not a white-supremacist society. Minutes earlier, the same person had felt free to tell me that Britain is "the home of racism."[11] Not for the first time, I marveled at the fact that generalizations about the West remain the only generalizations acceptable to make. Whereas specific questions about specific claims made about non-Western countries are batted away as though they could not possibly contain any merit and are in fact presumptuous even to raise.

What is anyone from the West—let alone a white person from the West—to do in such a setup? To date only a few options have been made available.

One is to raise the next generation of people in the West with a sense that they are the heirs of an illegitimate, ill-gotten fortune. That to the extent that they have any benefits in their lives, these benefits have been dishonestly accrued in a uniquely wicked way. This seems to be the option employed by an increasing number of institutions, particularly in Australia, Canada, and America.

In the summer of 2020, when the COVID crisis was still ongoing and university education continued to be disrupted, first-year students everywhere began the process of getting heavily in debt. Most were doing so virtually. At the University of Connecticut, first-year students were greeted by a set of online events. At one of these events, the students were instructed to download an app to their phones. This app asked students to type in their home address. The app then informed them which Native American tribe their home had been "stolen" from.[12] So that is one way to do it. To imbue people with an endless sense of unalleviable guilt and shame.

Another option is to try to alleviate or otherwise pay down that guilt. But how to do it? In her book on white privilege, the black British broadcaster and writer June Sarpong (who is a deeply privileged person herself) has suggested a number of actions that white people can take. One is to "educate yourself about the past."

Black History Month is not enough, according to Sarpong. Instead, she says, black history should be taught 365 days of the year.

What more can white people do? Sarpong writes, "First, you can look to fill the gaps left by an incomplete teaching of black history from your own education," such as the British Empire, she suggests. More importantly, she tells people that they can lend support and make cash donations to a number of black groups she names. Finally, white people should lobby their politicians to remove statues and monuments to people "who should not in the twenty-first century be venerated." But even this is only so long as "you remember that there are bigger battles than statues that need to be fought and won if we are to defeat systemic racism once and for all."[13]

Otherwise, it may be possible to arrive at equality by giving "non-Western" people a freer pass and carrying out acts of vengeance on "Western" people. Arlington County's attorney recently said that she plans to "find ways to reduce the incarceration of black people" by explicitly taking race into account in prosecutorial decision making. The former chief prosecutor has condemned this, saying that it "makes a mockery of blind justice and corrodes confidence in the criminal justice system."[14] Which indeed it does. Parisa Dehghani-Taft appears to be keen to ensure that any past wrongs are righted by creating fresh wrongs.

Others also see this as a route to justice. In 2020, San Francisco passed the CAREN Act, which made it a hate crime to make a "racially motivated" 911 call against a black person "without reasonable suspicion of a crime."[15] The name comes from the derogatory term "Karen," which in recent years has come to mean a white woman with entitled energy. The act makes it a potential crime to call the cops on a person who is black and makes white people doing so have to wonder whether it will be they who the police take in for questioning. It is also noteworthy, in passing, that in the current era, racial slurs are actually cool and can be written into law so long as the people they demean are white women.

Both of these actions, in Arlington and San Francisco, are explicit departures from the Fourteenth Amendment's guarantee of "equal protection of the laws." Both take the form of explicitly unequal treatment on the basis of race. Taking this further would certainly be one form of revenge, if not reparation. But a grander, more common form of revenge is what is now taking place and sweeping across the culture.

This process carries forward one of the central claims of those who attacked Western Civ courses in America in the 1980s. Which is that the best and easiest form of revenge is to trash the entire Western canon and tradition. There are various ways to do this, but the one that has become popular in recent decades is to lambaste the Western tradition for failing to take into account or otherwise integrate the experiences of outside voices, making it effectively worthless. This movement claims that marginalized groups were never allowed into the Western pantheon and that it has always been hermetically sealed for bigoted reasons. It claims that a tradition that started with Plato and Socrates could have no understanding of same-sex attraction. That a history that included Helen of Troy, Sappho, the Madonna, Jane Austen, and Marie Curie had no place for women. Most importantly, it asserts that Western history, instead of being almost incomparably outward-looking and diverse, is in fact a tradition that is historically insular and exclusionary.

From this wholesale attack on Western history, it can be seen that every discovery made by the West, whether it is the discovery of new lands or the discovery of the atom bomb, can be used against it. As though it were obvious that had any other group of people got there first, the results would have been more peaceful, equal, and socially just. There is no evidence whatsoever for this. Indeed, there is a great amount of evidence that things would have gone far worse and more bloodily had the West not been first in a whole range of discoveries.

Still, it seems that it is not enough to attack the West merely by attacking every aspect of its history. It is also necessary to attack every other aspect of its inheritance. That includes its religious and philosophical pillars. In an effort to pretend that one of the richest traditions on earth is in fact deserving of nothing but destruction. The tools being used to carry out this act of revenge will by now be very familiar.

CHAPTER 3

RELIGION

In 2012, a few years before he was attacked in London for being white, General Jim Allen was in Afghanistan. To be precise, he was on television across the country in which he was stationed, appealing to "the noble people of Afghanistan." A serious incident had arisen in the country. For it had been rumored—not confirmed, just rumored—that some Muslim holy books, including Qurans, had been improperly disposed of at a US air base north of Kabul. For the time being, nobody knew exactly what had happened, but riots were already starting, extremist clerics were getting their boots on, and the world's press was gearing up, or battening down, for a major Quran-desecration story.

"We are thoroughly investigating the incident and are taking steps to ensure this does not ever happen again," General Allen promised, with an unmistakable note of pleading. Swearing that there was nothing intentional in the actions, he promised that as soon as allied forces had "learned of these actions, we immediately intervened and stopped them." He announced that "the materials recovered will be properly handled by appropriate religious authorities."

You may be critical of the general or praise him for that speech. It may have been supplicating, or it may have been diplomatic. What nobody could say was that the era was capable of ignoring a reported Quran burning. Wherever in the world Qurans were reported to have been disrespected, riots and much more reliably followed. In 2010, when a whack-job Florida pastor threatened to burn a Quran, there was an intervention from General David Petraeus himself. In other words, there was nothing overblown about General Allen's fears.[1]

By contrast, in August 2020, at least one Bible—possibly more—was burned on camera in Portland, Oregon. At first, the American news media decided that this was a nonevent. Then, some claimed that the reports were actually Russian disinformation. The details of what happened in Oregon after midnight on August 1 are much disputed. At least one Bible was seen being burned in footage streamed on a live feed on the platform Ruptly. The story immediately went around the world. The idea that a Bible burning should have been one of the features of what had become nightly "Antifa" protests in America was at least suggestive to a lot of national and international commentators. Certainly, and inevitably, some Russian megaphoning sites took up the cause. It was only at this stage that the *New York Times* and others began to write up the story to highlight how Russian-backed news websites aim to "fuel grievances and deepen political divisions." Several prominent Republicans had tweeted about the story, at least one claiming that a stack of Bibles had been burned. But as the *New York Times* wrote: "The truth was far more mundane. A few protesters among the many thousands appear to have burned a single Bible—and possibly a second—for kindling to start a bigger fire."[2] So nothing really to see here.

It is quite the contrast that. On the one hand, if there is even a rumor anywhere on the globe of the mishandling of an Islamic holy book, the top brass of the American military immediately pronounces a DEFCON 1 situation. But if a Bible is burned in an American city, the country's paper of record says there's nothing to see here, because it was only a couple of Bibles, and, besides, they were only being used as kindling. Of course, it is true that Muslim communities around the world can be more combustible around these issues than the average Christian or post-Christian societies any longer are.

It serves as a reminder that the West is now willing to protect and revere almost any holy places, so long as they are not its own.

In part, this is because of the historic falloff in affiliation with the Christian churches in the last generation. In the United Kingdom, church attendance fell by more than half in the last forty years, while the number of Americans who identified themselves as Christians fell by over 12 percent in the last decade alone. The same trend can be seen across every country in the Western world, and where there are any anomalous rises or even plateaus of Christian belief, this maintenance is nearly always the result of immigrant communities. The withdrawing of Christianity is one of the most significant stories of the last century in the West, affecting nearly all its major institutions and populations. You may deplore or celebrate that, but the fact is undeniable.

Still, it is not the case that the resulting gap is left vacant. Into that gap many religions and pseudoreligions have flooded. As Christianity has withdrawn, so one new religion in particular has found its way into the cultural mainstream, starting off in America and flooding out from there across the Western world. It is what the linguistics teacher from Columbia University John McWhorter has called the new religion of antiracism. This new belief system has much in common with that of other religions in history and is, as McWhorter has written, "a profoundly religious movement in everything but terminology." It has an original sin ("white privilege"), it has a judgment day ("coming to terms with race"), and it has "the excommunication of the heretic" (social-media shamings and more).[3]

Like those of all new faiths, the followers of the religion of antiracism look with scorn on the main belief system that existed in their society before them. They regard it as barbaric and unenlightened. They look down on those who have not joined their group of the elect, especially those who they believe have seen what they have seen and yet come to different conclusions. Crucially, this new religion constitutes *something to do*. With any and all other grand narratives collapsed, the religion of antiracism fills people with purpose and a sense of meaning. It gives them drive and allows them to see where they are going. It allows them to imagine a perfectible upland toward which they and everyone else on earth might strive. It imbues them with confidence, and consolation, dividing the society they are in between saints and sinners in a way that gives them the illusion of great perception. Perhaps most crucially, it also allows them to war on what were their own origins. The appeal of this conflict should not be underestimated. It is a very deep-seated instinct, the instinct to destroy, to burn, and to spit on everything that has produced you. And, of course, there is one final appeal. The opportunity to treat other people badly beneath the guise of doing good.

Still, it is remarkable that the new religion believes not just that it owes nothing to its origins but that its origins are in fact part of the problem. There is a reading of social justice theory and antiracism that could grow out of the Western traditions—not least from Western Christianity. A true social justice movement might recognize these traditions as having given birth to its own self and continue looking to the traditions of antiracism, anticolonialism, and antislavery within the Christian heritage. They might even look to such traditions to give answers for ways out of whatever predicaments people currently find themselves in—seeing them as holding out a store of wisdom and knowledge that could be worth drawing upon now, as people have drawn upon them in the past.

Yet this is exactly what followers of the new religion do not do. The West's sources—the traditions of Athens and Jerusalem—are in fact the last place that the new devout would look to for guidance or consolation. And that is not entirely a surprise. A strange pattern reappears here: something that is itself a long-standing element of the Western mind.

That is a willingness to celebrate and sanctify anything so long as it is not part of the Western tradition, and to venerate anything else in the world, so long as it is not part of your own heritage. It is the trend that leads young Americans and Europeans to travel the world to find the temples of the Far East, while failing to spend any time in the cathedrals on their own doorsteps. Sometimes this manifests as a simple admiration of the exotic. Sometimes it comes across as a form of loathing for Western society itself.

Certainly, it has a long and distinguished tradition. In his "Sermon of the Fifty" (1762), Voltaire performed a masterly attack on what he saw as the contradictions, absurdity, and evident untruth of the Christian religion. Of other faiths, however, he took a different view. His essay "On the Manner and Spirit of Nations" (1756) considers the religion of Islam and finds its teachings to be beautiful and admirable in their simplicity. A similar trail has passed through Western thought for centuries. It exists not only in an exaltation of other religious traditions. Most often, it exerts itself by using other peoples and cultures as a way to show how lacking in admirable traits we are in the West.

As Edward Said showed, it is not just easy but rewarding to survey five centuries of Western thought and claim that it has always been dominated solely by a sense of superiority or superciliousness toward other cultures. But at least as clear has been a Western tradition of venerating—indeed idealizing—any culture so long as it is not Western. Though naturally this creates an ideal that nobody could possibly live up to.

The first explorers who studied the cultures of the countries they stumbled upon very often saw the natives in exactly this light. Indeed, they viewed them as so enviable that they often saw them as living in something like Eden. Christopher Columbus himself described the tribes he first met in the Caribbean in exactly this way—as living like Adam and Eve. Such tribes seemed to be living in paradise, and Europeans were as likely to view them with awe and envy as anything else. That was certainly the case with Louis Antoine de Bougainville when he came across the men and women of Polynesia in the eighteenth century. All this played into what is clearly a deep-seated need in human beings: to think of a place that is unspoiled. To believe that a place exists where all is peace and where the woes and struggles of civilization can be escaped.

But the Western mind did not just idealize such societies. It consistently used them in order to lambaste Western societies for their failures. At times this took an almost comic form. For instance, in his 1516 work *De orbe novo*, Peter Martyr d'Anghiera, a humanist and prelate, compared the Spanish conquistadores with extraordinary negativity to the people they encountered in the New World. D'Anghiera criticized the Spanish for their greed, for their cruelty, and for their intolerance. By comparison, the natives were to be admired and, in many ways, envied. D'Anghiera asserted that among other things: "They go naked, they know neither weights nor measures, nor that source of all misfortunes, money; living in a golden age, without laws, without lying judges, without books, satisfied with their life, and in no wise solicitous for the future." They lived, he thought, "in the golden age."[4]

As time went on, it became clear that Western writers did not even have to travel to other places in order to compare them favorably against their own. In his famous essay "On the Cannibals" (ca.1580), Michel de Montaigne, one of the most educated and cultured men in history, relayed what he had been told about people beyond Europe's shores. Specifically, about tribes who had been accused of cannibalism: "I find (from what has been told me) that there is nothing savage or barbarous about those peoples, but that every man calls barbarous anything he is not accustomed to; it is indeed the case that we have no other criterion of truth or right-reason than the example and form of the opinions and customs of our own country. There we always find the perfect religion, the perfect polity, the most developed and perfect way of doing anything!"[5]

That may have been true in Montaigne's day. But it was not true for much longer in the West. As the centuries went on, a different trend emerged. Whatever were the opinions and customs of the West—these were the worst. Whatever the religion of your own society—this was the worst. What Montaigne asserted became exactly inverted in the centuries after his death. And it was in part because of an oddity he expressed in that same essay. At one point Montaigne said of cannibal tribes: "[We] surpass them in every kind of barbarism. Their warfare is entirely noble and magnanimous; it has as much justification and beauty as that human malady allows . . . They are still in that blessed state of desiring nothing beyond what is ordained by their natural necessities: for them anything further is merely superfluous."[6]

That is quite the claim to make: that even the warfare of other people is "entirely noble and magnanimous." Yet repeatedly the philosophers of the West—some of the most cultured and culturally enlightened people of their day—made similar claims whenever they had the chance. Other societies provided a blank slate onto which could be written all the habits, manners, and virtues that were seen as lacking in the West.

Nobody excelled in this habit quite so much as Jean-Jacques Rousseau, a man of extraordinary learning and skill. There was nothing he could not develop a theory on, especially whenever he had no firsthand knowledge of the issue in question.

For instance, while Rousseau himself never traveled in far-off countries, he had many theories about the people who lived in them. Specifically, he believed that they lived in a state of nature in which all men were essentially equal. This is one of the most important themes in his influential "Discourse on Inequality" (1755). In the state of nature, people do not have the troubles that they have in places such as Rousseau's home societies of Switzerland and France. At the same time, Rousseau was wise enough to know that he was indulging in a dream. At one point, he says that the state of which he writes "no longer exists . . . perhaps never existed . . . [and] will probably never exist."[7] Still, he left a way to dream that others picked up in centuries to come.

The great twentieth-century French anthropologist Claude Lévi-Strauss was just one of those who venerated and guarded the flame of Rousseau. Lévi-Strauss once described him as "our master and our brother" and repeatedly demonstrated his feeling that the people who came after Rousseau were not worthy of him and had not honored him enough.[8] But as a number of astute critics of both Rousseau and Lévi-Strauss have pointed out, Rousseau did not glorify the state of nature simply for its own sake. He did so because he wanted to compare it with the Paris of his day—and to do so to the detriment of Paris. The noble savages were admirable to Rousseau, but more important is that they were useful. They were a foil for his jousts against the society he inhabited.

Yet there were many people who took him at his word, among whom there were also some who came to regret it. In 1772, the French explorer Marc-Joseph Marion du Fresne was on an expedition to New Zealand. One of his officers was Julien Marie Crozet. These men were to varying extents still high on the theories of Rousseau and believed in the innocence of the state of nature. They had to learn the hard way what Rousseau had imagined the easy way. Marion du Fresne and many of the ship's men were butchered in an apparently unprovoked Maori attack. The reverence of the survivors for Rousseau's theories did not survive this early encounter with the Maori people, who had not performed as Rousseau had expected them to.

Yet the tendency to extol all non-Westerners survived Rousseau and Marion du Fresne. In the twentieth century, the vogue for using non-Western natives as a means to criticize the West has continued. If anything, it has sped up, with the added oddity that by now so much of what had been asserted in centuries past not merely was provably wrong but also could be seen to be insultingly naive.

Perhaps inevitably the tendency thrived especially in academia. For instance, in the late 1980s a professor at the University of Kansas could still be found waxing lyrical about non-Western native peoples. Writing about the Maori people, Allan Hanson could not resist comparing them with white people. Specifically, white "Western" people in New Zealand. In a paper in *American Anthropologist* (which inevitably cited Said's *Orientalism*), Hanson wrote that white people "have lost the appreciation for magic and the capacity for wonder." What was more, he asserted, "white culture" is "out of step with nature" and "pollutes the environment" and lacks "a close tie with the land."[9]

In a 2001 work, the dissenting Australian academic Roger Sandall sent up this strain of thinking, correctly identifying it as having an especially strong hold in his own country, as it weathered the debates over its own history. At the opening of his 2001 book *The Culture Cult: Designer Tribalism and Other Essays*, Sandall relayed the story of the actress and ex-model Lauren Hutton, who a few years earlier had taken her two young sons with her to visit the Maasai in Africa. Among their adventures, she took the children to see a witch doctor. Their mother tasted the witch doctor's potions, and the family then saw a cow being slaughtered and watched the red-robed Maasai warriors drinking the blood from its carcass. Hutton herself was enthralled by the whole thing, apparently accompanying these rituals with cries of "Wow." The children, by contrast, appeared to have been traumatized for life. Neither of them smiled, and one of them burst into tears.

Hutton had defended her decision by saying that she wanted her Westernized children to learn a form of enlightenment from their visit to the Maasai "vision seeker." Naturally these things are more attractive to dip into than they are to live in. But that lesson has gone unlearned for many Western anti-Westerners, and the trend still persists. It is a trend that, as Sandall writes, "yearns for romantic simplicity" and a "radical simplification of modern life." This perspective takes "a sour view of modernity" and in the process forgets the benefits that modern Western civilization has conceived, created, and exported. It may be amazing to visit the Maasai, but how many people want to go raise cattle with them in Tanzania? How many immigrants head voluntarily into their tribe? Would they even be allowed? As Sandall said, the achievements of modern Western civilization are far from insignificant. They include, though are not limited to, a system that "allows changes of government without bloodshed, civil rights, economic benefits, religious toleration, and political and artistic freedom." The alternatives to Western civil society do not enjoy or perpetuate any of these things to any significant extent. As Sandall wrote, "Most traditional cultures feature domestic repression, economic backwardness, endemic disease, religious fanaticism and severe artistic constraints."[10] Just for starters.

Yet the appeal of everywhere but home will not die. By the last decade, it has become so common as to have become cliché that whenever a Western writer is in search of a ready-made answer to their critique of everything in the West, there is always a tribe somewhere, just waiting to impart some homespun wisdom that can be repackaged, commodified, and sold in its turn by some wily anticapitalist. Such writers present the native well as being extraordinarily deep, no matter how shallow it actually is. Popular films and television series continuously fall into the same trap: showing Western, white society in all its flaws and then some new ones, while the life of native peoples outside the West is presented as an Elysian world, full of truths that Westerners can only dream about. The popular series *White Lotus* (2021) offered a characteristic example of this. All the rich white Westerners in the HBO series are unhappy and empty, while the world of the native Hawaiians is held out as a vision of Edenic truthfulness the Westerners can only dream of accessing.

Another fine recent example of this trend was presented by Naomi Klein in her 2017 book, *No Is Not Enough: Defeating the New Shock Politics.*

There Klein presented a vision of a West in utter crisis, brought on principally by the dominance of capitalism and the absence of socialism. But Klein is not only general. She can also be specific. For instance, after 250 pages of searing critique of Western capitalism, she has several answers for how to fix what she terms "the corporate coup described in these pages, in all its dimensions," a "crisis with global reverberations that could echo through geologic time." As opposed to any other sort of time. But Klein has answers too. "We need to do more to create liberated cities for migrants and refugees," she says at one point.[11] But as she struggles for ideas or practical conclusions, you can just sense where she is going to head to find the answers she needs.

Inevitably at this point we learn of Brave Bull Allard, the official historian of the Standing Rock Sioux tribe. Klein calls her the "legendary Lakota elder LaDonna Brave Bull Allard" who opened a camp on her land called "Sacred Stone Camp." Klein is transfixed. Rousseau himself might have balked at her descriptions. "Eyes still sparkling, betraying not a bit of fatigue despite playing den mother to thousands of people who had come from across the world to be part of this historic movement." Her camp is for Indigenous youth but also for "non-Indigenous people who realized that the movement called for skills and knowledge most of us don't have." And what can people learn here, as they escape from the capitalist West at this spot of sacred wisdom?

"My grandkids can't believe how little some of the white people know," Brave Bull Allard tells Klein, who describes her saying this "laughing, but without judgment." Then, presumably still laughing nonjudgmentally, Brave Bull Allard tells a besotted Klein, "They come running: 'Grandma! The white people don't know how to chop wood! Can we teach them?' I say, 'Yes, teach them.'" Brave Bull Allard herself patiently taught hundreds of visitors what she considers basic survival skills, including how to keep warm in the winter.[12] The thermostat does not feature.

But it is not just Brave Bull Allard who has such wisdom to teach the white man. Other members of the Standing Rock Sioux tribal council have done their bit too, including helping to stop a local pipeline. Council member Cody Two Bears tells Klein about "the early days of European presence on these lands," when his ancestors educated the visitors on how to survive in a harsh and unfamiliar climate. "We taught them how to grow food, keep warm, build longhouses." But the taking never ended, from the earth and from the Indigenous people. And now, Two Bears says, "things are getting worse. So, the first people of this land have to teach this country to live again. By going green, by going renewable, by using the blessings the Creator has given us: the sun and the wind. We are going to start in Native country. And we're going to show the rest of the country how to live."[13]

Perhaps it is wisdom like this that leads Klein to the great summary of her book, in which she stumbles along the revelation that saying no is not enough and that instead we must learn to say yes.

ALL PHILOSOPHERS ARE RACIST

Perhaps it is just as well that there is still some Native American wisdom to draw upon. Because given the course of recent years, it seems fairly likely that Native Americans' philosophy may be the only one that people in the West or anywhere else will still be allowed to access. Coming as it does not just from a purer and simpler place but also from a place unmolested by the system of cancellation that has afflicted absolutely everything else to date.

I first became aware of the erasure of almost all Western philosophers after a talk some years ago at a university in America. During my remarks, I had, in passing, mentioned Immanuel Kant, most likely as an example of a philosopher who—beyond the categorical imperative—is exceptionally difficult to understand. At the end of my talk, one of the students queuing up to ask questions raised the fact that I had mentioned Kant. "Did you know that he used the N-word," the student asked. I have to admit that it flummoxed me at first. Would the N-word have been in operation in German in Kant's day? Surely not. "Negro," or an eighteenth-century German variant of it, perhaps. But the actual N-word would have surprised me. I think I expressed my doubt to the student as I struggled around trying to work out the import of the question. Suddenly it dawned on me. Of course. If Kant used the N-word, then you don't have to read him. Gone are the necessity of weeks spent plowing your way through the *Critique of Pure Reason* or the *Metaphysics of Morals*. Instead, you can skip all that, label Kant a racist, and move swiftly on. You have to work to know Kant, but you could know he was a racist for free.

As it happens, Kant did indeed use some terms in eighteenth-century Prussia that would not be used at a progressive university in the West in the 2020s. In December 2020, one academic at the University of Warwick called Dr. Andrew Cooper denounced Kant, saying that "in several of his essays on natural history he makes some shocking racist remarks, and seems to endorse pro-slavery texts." Elsewhere the same university decided, after advice from "an equality working group," that Kant's racist views should be taught to students "as an example of how people can succumb to racism."[14]

This was not an original critique. In fact, it was the same claim that has been made in recent years against almost every one of the pillars of the Western philosophical tradition, going right back to the ancient Greeks. For instance, in 2018, the *Washington Post* ran a hit piece on Aristotle, accusing him of being the "father of scientific racism." Later in the piece, he was transformed into "the granddaddy of all racial theorists." The various charges laid against Aristotle included the sinister fact ("worth noting") that Aristotle has been named by Charles Murray (coauthor of *The Bell Curve*) as his favorite philosopher. Kant could be condemned for texts he endorsed in his own day. But Aristotle could be condemned for someone admiring him almost two and a half millennia after his death. It was enough. In this and other ways, the author of the *Washington Post* piece claimed that Aristotle had laid the groundwork for "race science." Furthermore, in the first book of his *Politics*, Aristotle stands charged with having used "taxonomies to justify the exclusion of certain people from civic life." A truly shocking fact in a work written around the year 300 BC. As a result, Aristotle was linked with "the alt-right" and its "chilling" embrace of "Western civilization."[15]

If the Jerusalem pillar of Western civilization has been the Judeo-Christian traditions, then the Athens pillar of Western civilization has been the tradition of philosophy garnered from the ancient Greek and Roman worlds. Any serious attempt to bring the Western tradition low requires both of these pillars to be assaulted simultaneously. To lambaste the ancient Greeks as well as the Christian tradition. To go for Aristotle as well as the Bible. So each successive strand of the Western tradition has been picked off in turn.

Consider the assault in recent years on the tradition of the Enlightenment. This was the movement, or set of movements, that occurred across Europe around the eighteenth century and saw some of the greatest leaps forward in human history, providing, among other things, the philosophical bases for the principles of toleration, the utility of reason, and the separation of church and state. The value of this project used to be recognized across the various political sides. Writing in the *New Left Review* in 1994, the late Eric Hobsbawm was already warning of an interpretation of the Enlightenment as "a conspiracy of dead white men in periwigs to provide the intellectual foundation for Western imperialism." Hobsbawm—who was a lifelong apologist for the crimes of communism—understood the importance of protecting the Enlightenment. For, he warned his readers, in spite of its downsides, the Enlightenment provides "the only foundation for all the aspirations to build societies fit for *all* human beings to live in anywhere on this earth."[16] Since writing this, Hobsbawm has become a dead white man himself, so he knows what it feels like. But it is striking that as recently as the 1990s, it was possible for a major figure on the international Left to defend the Enlightenment fulsomely. Those who have come after him do not have the same reverence for the foundations of reason that Hobsbawm still possessed. Instead, they have been going through a process of iconoclasm of the most gleeful, ravening kind.

One by one, they have sought to bring low the philosophers of the Enlightenment. In June 2020, a statue of Voltaire was removed from in front of the Académie Française in Paris after it was repeatedly vandalized, including being covered in red paint. On that occasion, the charge against the great figure of the French Enlightenment was that he had personally invested in the French East India Company. Others pointed out that he had made a racist comment about Africans in his 1769 work *Les lettres d'Amabed*. One critic claimed a direct linkage between comments of Voltaire's discussions with Frederick the Great and Adolf Hitler's plans for the Third Reich. Writing in *Foreign Policy*, Nabila Ramdani claimed that Voltaire "spread darkness, not enlightenment."[17] Ramdani and other critics of Voltaire ignored entirely his devastating attacks on the immorality of slavery, not least in *Candide*. So out goes Voltaire, his 1763 *Treatise on Tolerance*, and all the rest of it. Onto the dustheap with everything else.

As Voltaire is attacked in France, so every figure of the British Enlightenment has been attacked in Britain. John Locke owned stock in companies that were connected with the slave trade. And so, *A Letter Concerning Toleration* (1689) has been transformed from one of the great advances of humanist thought into a guilty man's meaningless hypocrisy. One by one, the same techniques have been used. If a person cannot be found to have invested inappropriately in the companies of their day, then their work can be scoured for anything not fitting the mores of the modern world these men helped to create.

In *How to Be an Antiracist*, Ibram X. Kendi attacks "Enlightenment philosopher David Hume." He quotes Hume as saying: "I am apt to suspect the negroes and in general all the other species of men (for there are four or five different kinds) to be naturally inferior to the whites. There never was a civilized nation of any other complexion than white . . . Such a uniform and constant difference could not happen, in so many countries and ages, if nature had not made an original distinction between these breeds of men."

It is clear even from Kendi's own footnoting that he did not stumble upon this quote during a routine read through of Hume's collected works. He sources it to a chapter titled "'A Lousy Empirical Scientist': Reconsidering Hume's Racism" in a book titled *Race and Racism in Modern Philosophy*.[18] This work, described by its own publishers as "an innovative and substantial intervention in critical race theory," is intent on answering the question "Is modern philosophy racist"? People might guess at the answer.

Such details matter for several reasons. One is that Kendi cites the above as though it were a central tenet of Hume's work. In fact, the comment is contained in a single footnote in his essay "Of National Characters." It is in all editions of his work and is notorious among Hume scholars. None ever offer any defense of it.

If a defense were attempted, it might mention that Hume was of course not a sociologist and had no knowledge of African cultures. More importantly, the sentiment runs entirely contrary to that in so many other parts of his work, not least his denunciation of slavery in "Of the Populousness of Ancient Nations." Furthermore, as the scholar Jane O'Grady has persuasively argued, thinkers such as Hume and Kant set the foundations in their work for the arguments that would make racism untenable. They helped to expose its fundamental flaws. For instance, Hume argued "that morality is based on humans' natural attunement to one another's feelings and a discomfort at sensing others' discomfort that can be elevated into more impartial justice."[19] Until very recently, Hume was revered—most commonly in the country of his birth—for his radical empiricism, skepticism, and application of reason in works such as *An Enquiry Concerning Human Understanding* (1758).

What seems obvious to the entire world now, especially to these philosophers' critics, was not obvious before Kant and Hume. Not in the West, and not anywhere else.

None of this stands as a defense, and a solitary footnote is enough to wipe away the attainments and advancements of one of the eighteenth century's most important thinkers. After the inevitable guilty verdict comes the equally inevitable sentence. In the summer of 2020, a petition got underway to persuade the authorities at Edinburgh University to rename the David Hume Tower on campus because of the philosopher's "comments on matters of race." The petition's organizer insisted that "we should not be promoting a man who championed white supremacy." A former holder of the David Hume

Fellowship at the university denounced Hume as "an unashamed racist." And so the tower, which happened to be the tallest as well as one of the ugliest 1960s buildings on the campus, was promptly renamed. The university's "equality and diversity committee" and "race equality and anti-racist sub-committee" made the announcement, saying that Hume's comments on race "rightly cause distress today" and that their work had been "energized" since the death of George Floyd and the BLM movement. The building would henceforth be known by the poetic moniker "40 George Square."[20] The university subsequently announced a review of all of its buildings and their possible connection to the slave trade so that it could take "practical steps" to reflect "diversity."[21] Pressure immediately grew to remove the statue of Hume on the Royal Mile, and in the meantime various campaigners hung an excerpt from Hume's notorious footnote around his neck so that passersby could know that he was tarred.

Of course, such renamings and reevaluations might be regarded as being simply part of the normal run of things. Times change, and as the centuries pass, things always emerge in a different light. But one of the oddities of the attack on many of the preeminent figures in Western thought is that the same accusations are leveled at them whatever their views. So, for instance, it has become as common to read denunciations of John Stuart Mill as it has been to read denunciations of Hume. This despite the fact that in his work Mill argued vociferously and explicitly exactly the opposite case to that mentioned by Hume in his one fatal footnote. The case leveled against Mill in recent years has been based on accusations that he was in favor of empire.

Such critics fail to take into account Mill's career-long efforts to discredit the racial theories of his day or his belief that education would alter all those things that were claimed to be inherited characteristics.[22]

The anti-Mill-ians also fail to address his attitude to the question of the American Civil War *as it was going on*. Critics have leveled many accusations against Mill.[23] Yet nearly all of these have been comprehensively answered in the critical literature, and none of the accusations against him should detract from his consistent and principled defense of racial equality for American "negroes" during the war and its aftermath.[24] It is not easy to get things right as they are going on, not least when they are going on in the nineteenth century on another continent. But Mill got the American Civil War about as right as it was possible to get it, worrying of what would happen if the South gained independence, concerned that the African slave trade Britain had spent so much of its treasure abolishing could be brought back, and fearing that the "barbarizing" consequences of a Southern victory would warrant intervention from Europe. As a result, Mill did more than defend the actions of the North. He would not be a pacifist. As he wrote, "I cannot join with those who cry Peace, peace. I cannot wish that this war should not have been engaged in by the North."

Mill was "not blind to the possibility that it may require a long war to lower the arrogance and tame the aggressive ambition of the slave-owners." But, he said: "War, in a good cause, is not the greatest evil which a nation can suffer. War is an ugly thing, but not the ugliest of things: the decayed and degraded state of moral and patriotic feeling which thinks nothing worth a war, is worse."[25]

It is interesting, incidentally, that the figures who have been most assailed over recent years should so conspicuously be those who are connected with the European Enlightenment. Indeed, it is so conspicuous that there must be a reason. In fact, there are a number of reasons.

It is possible that the West's critics presume that the manners and morals of Plato or Aristotle are too far back to be worth assailing with the same tools. The argument "But that was more than two thousand years ago" may still hold some water, whereas the argument "That was only two hundred and fifty years ago" may not. But it is also possible—it certainly seems possible—that several things are going on here.

The first is the possibility that there is genuinely a reckoning against the thinkers of the Enlightenment that has never before been carried out. That claim could be made, but it would also be inept. For example, nobody who has read Locke is unaware that his concept of tolerance did not extend to Catholics and atheists. Just as nobody could read various German thinkers of the eighteenth and nineteenth centuries and imagine that all of them were philo-Semites. No scholar of Hume is unaware of that one footnote. It seems right to assume that there is something else going on.

One possibility is that all these thinkers were living and writing at a time when what have become the two great sins of the West—slavery and empire—were going on and that a reckoning on this is overdue. But being alive at the same time as other events does not make someone central to the darkest aspects of those occurrences. Yet that is the claim of the new assailants of the Enlightenment. For instance, the British writer and academic Kehinde Andrews claimed in a public debate in 2021 that:

> a defence of liberalism is the worst possible thing you want to do. Because liberalism is the problem. It is the Enlightenment values which really cement racial prejudice. If you actually think about all the Enlightenment scholars . . . all of them had a racial theory with white people at the top and black people at the bottom. It was universal across all the different countries. It was such an important part of the Enlightenment. But it gets embedded into the way that we think in a way that we don't even think about it as racist. So we take someone like Immanuel Kant's universal values of human rights—which is deeply racist—and then we wonder why the world is still racist.[26]

Aside from Andrews's attack on both the Enlightenment and liberalism, the most interesting aspect of this analysis is how remarkably ahistorical it is. As the historian Jeremy Black, among others, has noted, there was a very significant debate going on throughout the same period as the Enlightenment. It was a debate that people did not need to engage in but that was going on beneath them all the same. That is the debate between monogenesis and polygenesis.

Those who defended monogenesis believed that human beings, despite their racial differences, all came from the same genetic stock. The followers of polygenesis, by contrast, believed that the different races were not racially connected. It was a debate that continued throughout the 1700s and after. America's Founding Fathers were caught up in it, but even the greatest among them did not have settled views on the matter. After attacking David Hume, Kendi points out that Thomas Jefferson "seemed" to believe that "all men are created equal." But he goes on to fault Jefferson. Because "Thomas Jefferson never made the antiracist declaration: All racial groups are equals. While segregationist ideas suggest a racial group is permanently inferior, assimilationist ideas suggest a racial group is temporarily inferior. 'It would be hazardous to affirm that, equally cultivated for a few generations,' the Negro 'would not become' equal, Jefferson once wrote, in assimilationist fashion."[27]

This assault on Jefferson is emblematic of the uncharitable and ignorant approaches the critics take. The source of the quote is a private letter of Jefferson to the Marquis de Chastellux, written in June 1785. It is not a clause in a constitution, or part of a declaration. It is not something that Jefferson toured the country preaching to people. He is simply turning over in his mind in a letter to a fellow philosopher and military general one of the unanswered questions of their day. Perhaps because it does not fit his effort to portray Jefferson in the most unsympathetic possible light, Kendi does not bother to quote what Jefferson writes in the same letter. But it is interesting. Jefferson writes: "I believe the Indian then to be in body and mind equal to the whiteman. I have supposed the blackman, in his present state, might not be so. But it would be hazardous to affirm that, equally cultivated for a few generations, he would not become so."[28]

Rather than a racist assertion, Thomas Jefferson wrote what a defender of American blacks would say to a skeptic. He's recommending against thinking the thing Kendi accuses him of. It is dishonest in a multiplicity of ways to claim that because of this fact figures such as Jefferson must essentially be dethroned and discarded.

It would have been an unusual figure who lived through past centuries and saw every part of them with all the varieties of insight that the rearview mirror provides. It would have been an uncommon figure in the 1770s who without making it their special area of study—or even if they had—could have come to the conclusion that peoples they had rarely if ever met, or even read about, were without doubt from the same genetic stock as themselves. It also assumes that the issues that exercise us today must de facto have been the same issues that should have preoccupied not just some people, but all people, in the times before our own.

Perhaps the thinkers of the Enlightenment should have preoccupied themselves exclusively with the issues that preoccupy us today. But they were busy with other things. Much of Voltaire's energies were expended against the clergy of his day. Much of Hume's energy was spent (like other thinkers of the era) devising ways for society to emerge from a period of superstition and corruption. Kant's energies were spent attempting to divine and delineate a universal ethic. Might they have spent more time applying themselves to what was happening on continents they never visited? Perhaps. Might they have applied themselves to questions of rights among peoples they had never met? Quite possibly. But it is a high demand to make, and a presumptuous one.

Even today's champions of speaking out have not spoken out on every injustice. The number of human rights violations that American television host Joy Reid, for example, has not spoken out about must be literally immeasurable.

In addition, in our own age, the developed West sees it as wrong to talk of superior or inferior people. But in the eighteenth century, it was not unusual to compare one civilization to another and categorize them as superior or inferior to each other. If we have a special abhorrence for such trends today, then it is because we live after the twentieth century. An eighteenth-century philosopher in Königsberg did not know everything that we know now. Nor did he know nothing. It does not mean that we have the right to condemn him, teach students only about his errors, or fool ourselves—for the sake of ease—into thinking that we have nothing to learn from him.

There is one other possibility to explain the oddity of the Enlightenment thinkers ending up so prominently in the firing line of our era. And that is this: The European Enlightenments were the greatest leap forward for the concept of objective truth. The project that Hume and others worked away on was to ground an understanding of the world in verifiable fact. Miracles and other phenomena that had been a normal part of the world of ideas before their era suddenly lost all their footholds. The age of reason did not produce the age of Aquarius, but it put claims that were ungrounded in fact on the back foot for the best part of two centuries.

By contrast, what has been worked away at in recent years has been a project in which verifiable truth is cast out. In its place comes that great Oprah-ism: "my truth." The idea that I have "my truth" and you have yours makes the very idea of objective truth redundant. It says that a thing becomes so because I feel it to be so or say that it is so. At its most extreme, it is a reversion to a form of magical thinking. Precisely the thinking that the Enlightenment thinkers chased out. And perhaps that is why the Enlightenment thinkers have become such a focus for assault. Because the system they set up is antithetical to the system that is being constructed today: a system entirely opposed to the idea of rationalism and objective truth; a system dedicated to sweeping away everyone from the past as well as the present who does not bow down to the great god of the present: "me."

WHY DO THEIR GODS NOT FALL?

Yet there are many oddities in all of this. Kant, Hume, Jefferson, Mill, Voltaire, and everyone else connected to racism, empire, or slavery must fall. And yet a strange selection of historical figures does not. And in this fact, we get to the roots of something that is happening in the anti-Western moment.

In Highgate in London, one of the largest monuments in the cemetery is a great bust on top of a huge stone pillar. On the front are quotes from *The Communist Manifesto* ("Workers of all lands unite") and from the *Theses on Feuerbach* ("The philosophers have only interpreted the world in various ways. The point however is to change it"). The man whose tomb this is—paid for by the Communist Party of Britain in the 1960s—is of course Karl Marx. To this day, it remains a place of pilgrimage for people who think that Marx changed the world in a good way. All have their own spin for dealing with the fact of the roughly one hundred million people who were killed in trying to change the world along Marx's lines.

Yet it stands there still, and there have been no serious efforts to topple it or destroy the bust. Occasionally it has been daubed in red paint—with such vandalism always condemned by cultural and political figures alike. But through the events of recent years, there have been no online petitions or crowd efforts to pull it down and kick it into a nearby river. There may be a reason for that, of course, which is that it is a tombstone, and even the most doctrinaire people might find it distasteful to desecrate a grave. Yet the monument in Highgate is not the only memorial to Marx or Marxism that stands. As recently as 2016, Salford University unveiled a new memorial on its campus. The huge bust of Friedrich Engels—coauthor of *The Communist Manifesto*—was made into a feature of campus life. In part to commemorate the fact that Marx and Engels used to drink in a nearby pub when they lived in the area in the 1840s. The university authorities paid for the vast five-meter-tall sculpture as a tribute to the two men.

As recently as 2018, on the two hundredth anniversary of his birth, a vast new larger-than-life statue of Marx was unveiled in the town of Trier in the southwest of Germany, just near the borders with Luxembourg, Belgium, and France. The fourteen-foot-tall bronze statue was donated by the authorities in China, and the hundreds of guests at the unveiling included a delegation from the Chinese Communist Party. It seems as though a connection with Marx or Marxism is no ethical problem, perhaps even a plus. In April 2021, when students at the University of Liverpool forced the university authorities to rename a building named after the nineteenth-century prime minister William Gladstone (because of his father's links with slavery), they renamed the hall after a civil rights campaigner and lifelong Communist Party member called Dorothy Kuya.

There is no special effort to eradicate, problematize, decolonize, or otherwise act in an "antiracist" manner against the legacy of Karl Marx and his circle. And this is strange because as anybody who has read the work of Marx will know—especially anyone who has read his letters with Engels—Marx's reputation by the lights of our own age ought to be toast by now.

Consider the racism in Marx's letters to Engels, where the two great communists converse privately about the issues of their day. Here is a letter from Marx to Engels written in July 1862:

> The Jewish nigger Lassalle who, I'm glad to say, is leaving at the end of this week, has happily lost another 5,000 talers in an ill-judged speculation . . . It is now quite plain to me—as the shape of his head and the way his hair grows also testify—that he is descended from the negroes who accompanied Moses' flight from Egypt (unless his mother or paternal grandmother interbred with a nigger). Now, this blend of Jewishness and Germanness, on the one hand, and basic negroid stock, on the other, must inevitably give rise to a peculiar product. The fellow's importunity is also nigger-like.[29]

Of course, this is not a nice way to speak about anybody. But a charitable interpretation, such as has been denied to David Hume, might say that this is just one ugly thing said by Marx in a private letter and that we shouldn't judge him harshly on it. Yet this is not the only occasion that such a sentiment came from Marx's pen. Here is another letter to Engels, written four years later (in 1866), in which Marx describes a recent work he believes Engels might benefit from. By this stage, both men are aware of the discoveries of Charles Darwin, whose work on the origins of species, natural selection, and much more were of course unavailable to the philosophers of the Enlightenment. Marx is interested in Pierre Trémaux and his *Origine et transformations de l'homme et des autres êtres* (Paris 1865). By now the monogenesis argument (that is, that human beings are all related and are not different species) was winning the intellectual war. Frederick Douglass and others had made highly persuasive, and ultimately successful, interventions into the debate. And yet even now still Marx is playing around with the polygenesis argument. As he tells Engels of Trémaux's work: "In spite of all the shortcomings that I have noted, it represents a *very significant* advance over Darwin. . . . E.g., . . . (he spent a long time in Africa) he shows that the common negro type is only a degeneration of a far higher one."[30]

Perhaps this was just a blind spot for Marx? Perhaps he had a problem with black people but not with other groups?

Here is Marx in another letter to Engels, where he manages to get onto the subject of Jews: "The expulsion of a Leper people from Egypt, at the head of whom was an Egyptian priest named Moses. Lazarus, the leper, is also the basic type of the Jew."[31]

Of course, there is another way in which this also could be defended. It might be said that Marx was not writing for public consumption in these letters. His reflections on the "degenerative" nature of the "common negro" and the "leprous" nature of the Jewish people are ugly, certainly, but they are private reflections in a private letter written privately to a friend. Like the letter that Thomas Jefferson sent to the Marquis de Chastellux. But the problem with Marx is that he didn't just keep his racism to his private correspondence with his coauthor on *The Communist Manifesto*.

In 1853, in one of his pieces for the *New York Tribune*, Marx wrote of the Balkans that it had "the misfortune to be inhabited by a conglomerate of different races and nationalities, of which it is hard to say which is the least fit for progress and civilization."[32] In 1856, he could be found writing in the same paper that "we find every tyrant backed by a Jew" and claiming that there exists always "a handful of Jews to ransack pockets." Starting from the time of Jesus and the throwing of the moneylenders out of the Temple, Marx tells his audience that "the loan-mongering Jews of Europe do only on a larger and more obnoxious scale what many others do on one smaller and less significant. But it is only because the Jews are so strong that it is timely and expedient to expose and stigmatize their organization."[33] And these proto-Hitlerian views are not from a single period of Marx's life. Rather, they are consistent throughout it. Over a decade earlier, in 1843, Marx writes in "On the Jewish Question": "What is the worldly religion of the Jew? *Huckstering*. What is his worldly God? *Money*. . . . Money is the jealous god of Israel, in face of which no other god may exist."[34]

Well, you might say, perhaps Marx simply didn't like Jews very much? Except that he didn't seem to like other races very much either and had just as little respect for their great histories as he did for the history of the Jews. In 1853, he is telling his audience in America, "Indian society has no history at all, at least no known history." And while Marx is simultaneously damning and utterly ignorant of Indian civilization, he does seem to favor British rule in India. "The question," he says, "is not whether the English had a right to conquer India, but whether we are to prefer India conquered by the Turk, by the Persian, by the Russian, to India conquered by the Briton." One role of Britain in India, Marx asserts, is to lay "the material foundations of Western society in Asia." He is inclined to think that they can do it. For although Marx notes that other civilizations had overrun India, these earlier "barbarian conquerors" had been unequal to the task. Whereas "the British were the first conquerors superior, and therefore, inaccessible to Hindoo civilization."[35]

Still, Marx may have been antiblack, anti-Semitic, anti-Indian, procolonialist, and racist both in public and in private. But at least he cannot be connected with the other great sin of the West. Alas, as though proving to posterity that Marx could get every issue wrong, here he is writing about slavery in 1847, ahead of the American Civil War and already very much on the wrong side of that conflict: "Slavery is an economic category like any other."

Marx weighed up the bad side and what he called "the good side of slavery." And he found a lot of good to say about it: "Without slavery North America, the most progressive of countries, would be transformed into a patriarchal country. Wipe North America off the map of the world, and you will have anarchy—the complete decay of modern commerce and civilization. Cause slavery to disappear and you will have wiped America off the map of nations."[36]

Why is it worth reeling off this incomplete list of what are—in our own era—an almost clean sweep of offenses? Not simply because they demonstrate that the most significant figure in the history of left-wing thought, indeed its genesis figure and prophet, perhaps even its god, was guilty of every one of the vices leveled at all non-Marxists in the West. But in any analysis, Marx was far worse than any of the people who largely leftist campaigners have spent recent years lambasting. Marx's anti-Semitism is more noxious than Immanuel Kant's. His career-long record of racism makes a single footnote in the work of David Hume look very slight. His language of superior and inferior races was of a kind that progressive thinkers such as John Stuart Mill already abhorred and worse than anything Thomas Jefferson engaged in.

The only defense that might be made of him by his defenders and disciples is that he was a man of his time. That Marx lived in the nineteenth century and therefore held on to a number of the era's more unpleasant attributes. And yet this defense is packed with explosives waiting to go off in the face of anyone hoping to use them. First, because who is not a man of their own time? Every person whose reputation has been brought down in the cultural revolution of recent years was also a man or woman of his or her own time. So why should this excuse be successful when used in defense of Marx, yet dismissed when used in defense of Voltaire or Locke? With Marx,

there is another problem in his defense, which is that for his defenders, he is not simply another thinker. He is not even to be compared
with Hume or the sage of Königsberg. For his followers, Marx is the
last or (depending on how you count it) the originating prophet. He
was not just a thinker or a sage—he was the formulator of a world-
revolutionary movement. A movement that claimed to know how to
reorder absolutely everything in human affairs in order to arrive at a
utopian society. A utopian society that has never been achieved and
has cost many millions of lives in not being achieved but that activists across the West still dream of instituting next time: always next
time.

It may be said that a prophet should be held to a higher standard
than a mere philosopher, antiquarian, or botanist. A 2019 biography
of Marx was reviewed in the *New York Times* under the headline
"Karl Marx: Prophet of the Present." The paper's reviewer (while
noting in passing some of Marx's less seemly comments about Jews)
concluded that the work "makes the case for taking Marx seriously
today as a pragmatic realist, as well as a messianic visionary" who
"never lost his belief in a redemptive future."[37] Which is a beautiful
idea, of course. And entirely divorced not just from every detail of
the consequences but from the reality of the man in question.

What becomes clear in analyzing the differences between the
treatment of Marx and the treatment of almost every other thinker
of the West is that the game is worse than inconsistent. It exists to
cut a swath through every thinker or historical figure in the Western
tradition. To lambaste them for holding on to one or more of the attitudes of their time that our own age holds to be abhorrent. And at
the same time to ensure that figures whose work is helpful in pulling
apart the Western tradition, even to the point of demanding revolution to overturn it, are never treated to this same ahistorical and
retributive game. Marx is protected because his writings and reputation are useful for anyone wishing to pull down the West. Everybody
else is subjected to the process of destruction because their reputa-
tions are useful for holding up the West. After all, remove every other

philosopher from the field, take down all their monuments and the tributes to them, and ensure that their thought is taught primarily (and ahistorically) as a story of racism and slavery and what is left standing in the Western tradition?

For anyone who doubts that this is the game that is being engaged in, perhaps one other example may suffice. Among the modern thinkers who have the most impact on contemporary thought almost none sits higher than Michel Foucault (1926–84). He remains the world's most cited scholar, across an array of disciplines. His work on sexuality, and especially on the nature of power, has endeared him to generations of students. His ideas make him the most important name to drop for any scholar engaged in the activist studies of recent decades. For black studies, queer studies, and others, he is the indispensable figure. Among the reasons is that, taken in its totality, his work is one of the most sustained attempts to undermine the system of institutions that had made up part of the Western system of order. Foucault's obsessive analysis of everything through a quasi-Marxist lens of power relations diminished almost everything in society into a transactional, punitive, and meaningless dystopia. Among those to push Foucault's work from an early stage was Edward Said. The two would inevitably have been attracted to each other because underneath the work of both men was an effort to destabilize if not deconstruct the idea of the Western nations as having almost anything good to be said for them.

It is always unpleasant—as well as unwise—for thinkers to lambaste each other because of the habits of their personal lives. The personal is not always political and is certainly not always philosophical. Yet in March 2021, a most interesting fact emerged about the personal life of Foucault. During an interview, his fellow philosopher Guy Sorman revealed a fact that had long been rumored. Sorman revealed that in the late 1960s, when Foucault was living near Tunis, Foucault would have sex with the local children. Sorman said that on a visit to Sidi Bou Said, near Tunis, he witnessed young children running after Foucault asking him for the money he offered other children before raping them. According to Sorman, these boys of eight, nine, or ten years of age would have money thrown at them by Foucault, who would arrange to meet them late at night "at the usual place." The usual place turned out to be the local cemetery, where Foucault would rape the children on the gravestones. As Sorman said, "The question of consent wasn't even raised." Foucault would not have dared to do this in France, according to Sorman, but there was "a colonial dimension to this. A white imperialism."[38]

One of the many oddities of these revelations is that, to date, they seem to have done nothing to dent Foucault's reputation. Nor has the fact that along with other French intellectuals, he once signed a letter recommending the age of consent in his country be lowered to twelve. His work continues to be cited. His books continue to be published, and there is no significant campaign to have them pulled. Indeed, a final, previously unpublished volume in his *History of Sexuality* was published after these revelations came out. The repercussions of Foucault's theories continue to be felt, and nowhere has there been any recantation by his disciples in disciplines across America or anywhere else because of the revelations of racially motivated child rape.

Like the double standard over Marx's racism, this fact is suggestive. For it would surely be different if it had worked the other way around. If one of the twentieth century's great conservative thinkers had been revealed to have traveled to the developing world in order to rape young boys on a tombstone in a graveyard at night, it might be considered suggestive. The political Left would likely be unwilling to let the issue slide by completely. Nor would they be willing to pass up the opportunity to extrapolate some extra lessons. They might say that this habit was revealing of a wider conservative mindset. That it revealed the pedophilic, rapist, racist tendencies at the heart of traditional Western thought. They might even try to point out that a whole cultural movement or societal tendency was tarred by association with this nocturnal and noxious habit. But with Foucault, no such thing has happened. He remains on his throne. His work continues to spill out. And nobody to date seems to think there is anything especially telling about one of the founding icons of the anti-Westernism of our time having found personal pleasure in purchasing native children of foreign countries to satisfy his sexual desires.

It is in such omissions and double standards that something crucial can be discerned. Which is that what is happening in the current cultural moment is not simply an assertion of a new moral vision but the attempted imposition of a political vision on the West. One in which only specific figures—whom the West had felt proud of—are brought down. Meanwhile, those figures who have been most critical of the Western traditions of culture and the free market are spared the same treatment. As though in the hope that when everyone else is brought low, the only figures who will still remain on their pedestals (both real and metaphorical) are those figures who were most critical of the West. Meaning that the only people left to guide us would be the people who will guide us in the worst possible directions.

WOKE CHURCHES

Ordinarily at a time of great cultural flux, people might hope to find solace in institutions that have weathered similar storms before. In the Western tradition, few institutions have held onto a truth, and proclaimed that truth, for as sustained a period as the Christian churches. For two thousand years, they have held themselves out as the possessors of a sacred flame—one with a gospel, teachings, and truths of their own. While Athens might fall, Jerusalem would not. The times may change, but the church remains the same.

In reality, the churches have often shifted with the cultural tides. As the mores of the times have changed, so the churches have had to shift. But rarely have they shifted so swiftly as they have in joining the war on the underpinnings of the West. The story is playing out across denominations. A decision by the churches to throw their lot in with the anti-Western fashions of the day and to apologize not just for their own pasts, but for their own unique cultural gifts to the world.

The Church of England has long led the way in this trend. For a generation, it has found itself in a position of having to apologize for spreading its gospel around the world and being embarrassed by its former missionary zeal. In recent years, it has also decided to take upon itself the most hostile possible critique of itself.

In February 2020, the archbishop of Canterbury, Justin Welby, gave a speech to the General Synod of the Church of England. In it he apologized for the "institutional racism" of the Church of England. The archbishop said, "I am sorry and ashamed. I'm ashamed of our history and I'm ashamed of our failure. There is no doubt when we look at our own Church that we are still deeply institutionally racist."[39] At the time that Welby gave this speech, the next most important bishop in the church besides himself was John Sentamu, the then archbishop of York. Despite his number two hailing from Uganda, nobody seemed to think there was anything off about this description of the church. In fact, the archbishop and the hierarchy of the church persisted, and throughout a year in which every church in the land was shut due to COVID restrictions, the church authorities worked away on a "task force" to look at the question of racism.

The results, published in a report titled "From Lament to Action," was spurred by the death of George Floyd, who it described as "a 46-year-old practicing Christian, who worked to mentor young people and oppose gun violence." This was perhaps the only generous estimation in the report. In its draft form, the report was rife with warnings about the racism of the dwindling (and at that point literally shuttered) Anglican church. It warned that racism is "whispered in our pews." It had often been joked that the C of E was the Tory party at prayer. But by 2021, the church's own self-estimation seemed to be that it was the KKK at prayer. When talking of the "institutional racism" that the report claimed to be so rife in the church, it insisted: "The time for lament at such treatment is over . . . The time for action has now come."

What would that action look like? Well, certain remnants of the Anglican style remained, and so there were calls for the identifying of "workstreams" that might in turn report to a commission. These streams, covering every aspect of the church, would publish a final report to note "the continuing impact of institutional racism both within the society and the Church."

Otherwise, the report called for several things. Including quotas, obviously. Henceforth, there should be "one UKME [UK Minority Ethnic] clergy elected from each region." Something called "programme cohorts" should have a minimum of 30 percent UKME participation "in order to build up pipeline supply." And in happy bureaucratese, the document said that the church should develop an "online module for anti-racist learning programme." All short lists must include "at least one appointable UKME candidate," and where this did not occur, the "recruiter" should provide "valid, publishable reasons for failure."

Since there are almost five thousand nominally Church of England schools across the country, the report recommends that all its primary and secondary schools work "to develop a broad RE curriculum with specific reference to the promotion of racial justice." They must all mark "Black History Month, celebrate diverse saints and models (modern Anglican Saints/Martyrs)." And the church's theology, too, must change. The curriculum for ordinands must include participation in "an introductory Black Theology module." They must "diversify the curriculum," "produce a workable plan for increasing racial diversity," and "formally adopt Racial Justice Sunday in February of each year." All this will be overseen by the creation of a "Racial Justice Unit," to be funded in these cash-strapped times "for a five-year fixed-term basis in the first instance."

Why does the C of E behave like this? It is not as though other religions look around at their congregations and ask why they are not more diverse. Nor do other religions seem intent on chasing their existing adherents away. Yet the C of E does do this, in spite of the fact that it is not as though the church is absolutely chockablock with people wishing to join it. Nevertheless, the church continues to try to force a new demographic and belief upon itself. Its report said that those ordinands who do make it through must be forced to examine "the underlying theological assumptions that shapes racial justice such as Eurocentrism, Christendom and White normativity." The report stressed the need to "decolonize Theology, Ecclesiology and possibly examine official teachings of the Church that follows prejudicial theological value system." And, of course, it argued for going forward by once again going backward to the issue of slavery. It must again "acknowledge, repent and take decisive action to address the shameful history and legacy of the C of E's involvement in the historic transatlantic slave trade." At the start of the 2020 BLM protests, a statue of the seventeenth-century British philanthropist and slave-trade investor Edward Colston had been toppled from its plinth in the city of Bristol and pushed into the harbor. The C of E claimed that "the BLM movement and in particular the dumping of the Colston statue in Bristol docks shed new light and brought needed urgency to the C of E's consideration of its own contested heritage." The report makes it clear that the church is going to have to bring down monuments and statues that disturb the modern mind, for "our churches should be welcoming spaces for all, and we must deal with any part of the church building that may cause pain or offense."

In conclusion, the church itself must change. One "barrier to inclusion" for people from "UKME backgrounds" has been the challenge of "cultural assimilation" into the church, "where there is perceived to be little or no room for cultural expression outside of a normative culture which is predominantly white, middle class." Apparently, there is an "expectation upon UKME communities to abandon their own cultural heritage and current expression in favor of traditional host approaches." And so, the archbishops' report concludes, it would seem to be easier all round if the host chose to abandon its own heritage, working alongside "BLM and other interest groups" to facilitate change. This must include the taking down of statues and monuments that were audited as being on the wrong side of any historical divides, leading to a vision of overstretched clergy being expected to scour their churches for errant statues.[40]

One of the strangest things about reading documents such as these is that they show an institution that has fallen for the most negative possible interpretation of itself. The Anglican Communion is a naturally diverse community, binding together forty-one provinces from places across the globe. Many of the Church of England's most vibrant (perhaps its only vibrant) churches are in Africa. And when I have spent time with the Christian communities there, in countries such as Nigeria, I have never seen them subjected to racism from white people. I have only seen deeply sincere believers in a gospel that missionaries from the churches of Europe once brought to them. Now the institutions that once taught that gospel are busily preaching a different gospel. They are telling the world that they are racist and that they must change. It is a tale that, as another former C of E bishop, Michael Nazir-Ali, has pointed out, proclaims the church's faith in critical race theory, rather than in Christ.

As Nazir-Ali said, there is no need for the church to fall for this new religion. For it has a very fine story of its own to tell.

The Christian faith has an uncommonly long tradition of opposition to slavery. St. Bathilda was a former slave herself who campaigned for the abolition of slavery in the seventh century. St. Anselm outlawed slavery in 1102, while archbishop of Canterbury. William Wilberforce and the Clapham Sect spent all their energies and resources fighting to bring an end to the practice, inspired in this vision by their Christian faith. In the twentieth century, clergy had worked with Gandhi in his campaign for independence for India. And extraordinary clergymen such as Bishop Colin Winter and Bishop Trevor Huddleston campaigned against apartheid in South Africa. But all these women and men were forgotten by a church intent only on searching for the bad. As Nazir-Ali asked, "Why not stop actively seeking darkness" and instead "look at the light?" Why throw out the message of Christ for a message "based on Marxist ideas of exploitation?"[41] But the voice of this wise former bishop was ignored. In the Church of England and other denominations across the West, the old religion worked hard to divest itself of its own traditions and seemed intent on making the old faith nothing but yet another imitation of the new one.

Woke Episcopalianism

In the United States, the Episcopal Church followed precisely the same pattern. In January 2021, the Episcopal Church published a "racial audit" of itself that cost $1.2 million to perform. It covered the years 2018–20, and like their counterparts across the Atlantic, the Episcopalians pronounced themselves guilty from the outset: "The goal of this research has not been to determine whether or not systemic racism exists in the Episcopal Church, but rather to examine its effects and the dynamics by which it is maintained in the church structure. It was critical to approach this objective with openness, rather than starting with pre-existing assumptions and conclusions. To this end, we have employed the guiding tools of grounded theory and the theoretical framework of critical race theory."

The Episcopalians defined CRT as follows: "[CRT] is a social and theoretical framework that understands race as a lens through which to seek understanding of the world. It insists, like critical theory at large, that social problems are created by structures and institutions, rather than by individuals. Numerous scholars have contributed to the work of critical race theory, including Derrick Bell, Kimberlé Crenshaw, Richard Delgado, and others."

Of course, none of this should have come as much of a surprise to anyone watching the church leadership in recent years. In a recent book recommendation on his website, the Episcopal bishop of New York said his diocesan book study would be Ibram X. Kendi's *How to Be an Antiracist*. Bishop Dietsche promised that Kendi tackles "the deep currents of racism in our society and institutions," including what the bishop called "the intractability of white supremacy." "Unacknowledged racist assumptions infect every institution and system, and my heart and mind, and yours too," said the bishop, before concluding, "Reading this book convicted me, but made me grateful."[42]

It is against this background of wanting to find themselves guilty that the Episcopal Church approached its race audit. And the results showed that the clergy had swallowed wholesale the new gospel of Kendi-ism. Over 77 percent of the leadership defined racism as "a combination of racial prejudice or discrimination, a system that grants power to one social group." They did not define it as an intention to harm one group or an outcome that harms one group. They defined it as a system of power, which is much harder to see or fix without tearing that whole system down.

The audit's own evidence showed no difference between the treatment of white leadership and "BIPOC" (black, indigenous, people of color) leadership in the church. Both reported almost exactly the same levels of "respect" with which they felt they were treated. But some of the quotations used in the survey were alarming to say the least.

Noting only the race and status of the respondents, the audit quoted a white church leader saying, "The Episcopal Church has to stop being so white." A "person of color" in the church's leadership is quoted saying, "There's war. We're in the middle of a war, and I don't know why people don't seem to be behaving as if we should be . . . We're gearing up for a fight for our very existence, Black people in this country. We have a Black head of the Church, but the institution is institutionalized."

Inevitably the audit also came to the now traditional conclusions. One of the barriers for dealing with the church's "systemic racism" is people "becoming defensive" when systemic racism "is named as a problem." Here is DiAngelo-ism at work: the best way for the church to be not racist is for it to be unbothered when it is accused of institutional racism. Elsewhere it concludes that all answers must in-volve a "multifaceted approach" that should include the "reparation and redistribution of wealth." Though it warns that this should be attempted without exacerbating "the problems of racism and white dominant culture."

The work ahead for the Episcopalians sounds amazingly grueling. But they keep stressing that they are up for it. "Fully engaged leaders with a deep grasp of systemic racism" apparently must stress "the need to embrace the fact that anti-racism work is never done once and for all." There is going to have to be a "long-haul." But as the "recommendations" section says, there is much to do. The church must develop an "antiracist leadership," it must think about "inter-sectionality" and confront the "leverages of power." Most important is to "continue to educate all-white or predominantly white congre-gations about racialization and about the story/history of white-ness." It is also clear that "the Episcopal Church in its anti-racism resources ought to shift the language in order to reflect both the ways white people are privileged and diminished by white supremacy cul-ture and racist systems." Reparations, meanwhile, should continue to be encouraged "on the local level as well." In the meantime, the church can "design effective interventions for communities at dif-ferent points along the labyrinth or in anti-racism language along the spectrum from exclusive club to anti-racist organization. Anti-racism work and racial healing cannot be a cookie cutter approach and requires dynamic, agile, and multiple points of entry."[43]

Like the Church of England, the Episcopal Church in the United States has seen a vertiginous fall-off in its congregations in recent years. Like the Church of England, its pews are not just emptying but also growing older. Like the church across the Atlantic, it spent much of 2020–21 with its doors literally shut to its remaining flock. And like the Church of England, it chose this precise moment to berate its remaining congregation for being too white supremacist, claim that they were members of a communion which was "institutionally racist," and suggest that the answer to all of the church's considerable range of problems lay in lecturing its remaining congregations about racism.

The old gospel can barely be discerned in all of this. But the new gospel most certainly can be. Someday, it may be all there is left.

Catholicism

Some people might say that this is just what the remains of the Church of England and the Episcopalian Church might be expected to do and that there are other, more serious, churches that would not stoop to the same fashionable standards. Yet even the church that prides itself on being the one least likely to bend to, or shift with, the times—the Roman Catholic Church—is just as capable of caving in to the new religion of the current era. In June 2020, the Catholic chaplain of the Massachusetts Institute of Technology—Reverend Daniel Patrick Moloney—sent out a cautionary email to the Catholic community at the university warning them, at the height of the protests, that George Floyd's killing may have had nothing to do with racism. He also questioned Floyd's character, given his previous convictions for violence. He said that while Floyd should not have been killed by the police officer, Floyd himself "had not lived a virtuous life." He wrote: "Most people in the country have framed this as an act of racism. I don't think we know that." Speaking of police violence, Moloney warned against seeing racism as a major problem in the American police. Again, "I don't think we know that," he wrote. The police "deal with dangerous and bad people all the time, and that often hardens them," he said.

Inevitably, the message was leaked out and the mob came after him. A small number of people in the MIT community expressed hurt at the contents of the email. A vice president and dean for student life said that "the message from Father Moloney was deeply disturbing." She accused Moloney of "devaluing and disparaging George Floyd's character" and of failing to acknowledge "systemic racism." And the Catholic Church decided to give in to the new gospel. The Archdiocese of Boston swiftly distanced itself from the comments, and Moloney issued an apology for the hurt he had caused. The archdiocese also asked Moloney to resign his position with immediate effect.[44]

CONSEQUENCES

Perhaps it is inevitable that when the churches have such a view of themselves and their own history, people will take them at their word. What should someone with no knowledge of the churches make of institutions that say such things about themselves? An ever-increasing percentage of people have no experience of the Church of England, the Episcopalian Church, or any other church. When such institutions announce that they are institutionally racist and riven with bigotry, an outsider with no knowledge of them is likely to believe them. Why should they not? After all, who would say such things about themselves unless they were true? You have to know such institutions very well to know that they are not what their leaders say they are: to know that most clergy spend their lives devoting themselves to their flock, helping the poor, and doing good works. For people who have no experience of these institutions, there is no reason not to view them through the demonic lens through which they present themselves. And it is perhaps inevitable that, in time, that mix of ignorance and presumption of guilt will have consequences.

In July 2021, when Canada was going through another orgy of statue toppling, one of the proximate causes that month was a strange moral panic that had taken hold in the country. The Canadian media had recently begun to report that numerous graves had been found near residential schools run by the Catholic Church in areas with First Nations communities in them. On the evidence of one unverified report, based on ground penetration radar that was inconclusive, it was claimed that hundreds of unmarked graves existed. The media in Canada and then around the world claimed that the "mass graves" contained the bodies of children, with the strong implication that they were Indigenous children and the follow-on implication that they had been deliberately murdered by the Catholic Church. No bodies were found, and nothing had even been excavated. It was not clear that they were all children or that they were not in individual graves formerly marked by wooden crosses. Canadians already knew from a Truth and Reconciliation Commission that thousands of students had died of diseases such as tuberculosis at these crowded schools.

People started to burn down churches in Canada. Within a single week, almost thirty were torched or otherwise assaulted. The fact that many of the churches burned down were built by First Nations people did not detain those who had jumped on the anti–Canadian churches bandwagon. The then head of the British Columbia Civil Liberties Association took to Twitter to say, "Burn it all down."[45] Caitlin Urquhart, a former volunteer at the Newfoundland Canadian Bar Association Branch, said the same thing. A radio host demanded "Burn the churches down." A Canadian law professor described the burnings as "resistance to extreme and systemic injustice."[46] And Prime Minister Justin Trudeau's top advisor and friend Gerald Butts said that while burning churches was not advisable, it "may be understandable."[47] In no time, a story had gone from a claim of a discovery of graves, to a story of mass graves, to a story of children deliberately murdered by the Catholic Church and buried in mass graves, to Canadians actually burning down churches because they had become convinced that the churches had orchestrated the deliberate and organized mass murder of children. Because of course the churches would. Because the churches are racist like everything else.

RATIONALISM

Still, even if the churches and all philosophy are regarded as racist, there can still be one other hope for the Western mind. One final refuge that still exists, and which might be assumed to be sacrosanct:

simple logic and provable fact. We may not know our history, or not be confident of our history, or that our history was good. We may not be at all confident that the philosophical or theological roots of the West are not irredeemably corrupted by racism and its attendant sins. But there is at least the sanctuary of science, of math, of provable, verifiable fact. And on this ground perhaps something can be saved. Countries and churches may tremble, and histories may change, but the building blocks of logic, science, and math may still be relied upon. We may be sure of nothing else, but we may be certain that the Western traditions in these areas at least may continue. Once again, the hope is forlorn.

One by one, the sense-making organs of the scientific community and other parts of the STEM world have fallen to the same one-note dogma of the time. The medical community was one of the first to fall into it. In the immediate aftermath of the George Floyd killing, public gatherings were still banned in most countries, because of coronavirus restrictions. Governments had instituted such bans on the advice of the medical professionals. But as soon as the BLM protests began, more than a thousand medical professionals in the United States signed a petition calling for them to be allowed to go ahead because "opposition to racism" is "vital to the public health."[48] As far as public health concerns went, the one thing that trumped even the coronavirus was racism.

As the coronavirus crisis was going on, the lead journal of the medical world, *The Lancet*, ran a piece titled "Racism Is the Public Health Crisis."[49] The publication also published an "antiracism pledge," professing that "racism is a public health emergency of global concern. Anti-racism is a struggle all of us must join." *The Lancet* promised to "educate ourselves about racism," "pledge our solidarity with the Black Lives Matter movement," and "turn that pledge into concrete actions in our own work."[50] Other scientific journals have submitted to the same standard. In May 2021, *Nature* said in an editorial that the first anniversary of the death of George Floyd was a reminder to the journal that "systemic racism in science" exists and that the staff of *Nature* had to recognize "our part in it." And not just their own part, but the part of science as a whole in perpetuating racism. As *Nature* said, "Tackling systemic racism requires the system of science to change."[51] One of the few concrete suggestions that the journal came up with was to ensure that "antiracism is embedded" within all scientific organizations and that such work "wins recognition and promotion." According to *Nature*, "Too often, conventional metrics—citations, publication, profits—reward those in positions of power, rather than helping to shift the balance of power."

There is a lot in that. For instance, what is wrong with citations in scientific research? Is it better to have citations or not to have citations? The purpose of citations has generally been to provide evidence that the assertions contained are reliable and true. But if a scientific publication decides that such evidence is as good as an absence of evidence or actually worse than an absence of evidence, then out goes one of the building blocks of the scientific method. Besides, why is it the task of a scientific journal to shift the balance of power? Why is its aim not simply to publish the best and most important research, whoever comes up with it and whoever it benefits?

It is at such times that one particularly conservative critique that used to exist in the culture wars is shown to be woefully inadequate. Conservatives used to joke that the wildest fringes of academic thought had boundaries that would be asserted naturally. These commentators claimed that ideas such as CRT may well run like wildfire through the humanities but that even if this did happen, it did not matter overmuch. People were welcome to get themselves into debt studying for useless humanities degrees that educated them in non-disciplines. Because all the time, reality and the facts would continue to assert themselves in STEM subjects. These people asserted that while Theory, with a capital *T*, might work in lesbian dance theory classes, it would halt at the borders of the hard sciences and mathematics. It would stop at the doors of engineering, because at some point the bridges had to stay up.

Yet that claim—that hope—turns out to have been wildly optimistic. There turns out to be no reason why the tide that has rushed through everything else should halt at the borders of STEM.

If you wanted to kick away the remaining building blocks on which everything else is built, then kicking away the block of mathematical certainty is a pretty good way to do it. It is a similar trick to kicking away the idea that there is any such fixed thing as men and women. It sows confusion without making anything else remotely clearer. But if you wish to simply disorient or demoralize people, then it is a good place to kick at. That is precisely what has been done in recent years with the development of "equitable maths." This is the idea that math itself is problematic. The argument goes that math is elitist, privileged, and of course inherently racist. How can a system that owes its origins to several civilizations and was refined in the West in the last millennia be seen as systematically racist?

One way of doing this is to rely on scholars who have spent recent decades trying to define a whole set of aspirational ideas as inherently white supremacist and then attempting to anathematize them out of the field of education. For instance, Kenneth Jones and Tema Okun's *Dismantling Racism: A Workbook for Social Change Groups* has been used by a lot of people in the field of education since its first publication in 2001. That work identified a number of "norms and standards" that it claimed were "damaging" because "they promote white supremacy thinking." The authors claimed that these norms were damaging both to people of color and to white people. The characteristics selected as being especially damaging included "perfectionism," "worship of the written word," "sense of urgency," "individualism," and "objectivity." According to Jones and Okun, the idea that there is only one right way to do something in education is white supremacist. Instead, they recommend that "when working with communities from a different culture," educators should be clear that "you have some learning to do about the community's ways of doing" things. They also criticize white people for "valuing 'logic' over emotion."[52]

All of this is fairly disastrous just as theory. But trying to put it into practice is catastrophic. Take, for instance, a guide for teachers published twenty years after Jones and Okun's work. *Equitable Maths* describes itself as "a pathway to equitable math instruction" intended as a resource to give guidance to teachers of "Black, LatinX and Multilingual students" in America between grades 6 and 8. It cites Jones and Okun at the beginning of its first section, which is on "dismantling racism in mathematics instruction." It accepts and develops their definition of white supremacy and sees white supremacy as running throughout mathematics. As a result, and citing Kendi (obviously), it urges teachers to identify what it means to be "an antiracist math educator." What it apparently means is supporting students "to reclaim their mathematical ancestry," by seeking to "honor and acknowledge the mathematical knowledge of students of color, even if it shows up unconventionally." Again and again, the teaching guide gives ways to "dismantle the culture of white supremacy that exists within the math classroom."[53] Again and again, it seeks to do so by advocating that teachers presume that black, Latinx, and multilingual students already have some special knowledge of math that is hard or impossible for white people to appreciate or access. Worse, it presumes that nonwhite students find normal math hard or impossible to appreciate or access.

As ever, this mania has not been limited to America. The same ideas have spilled out everywhere. Ontario's Grade 9 Destreamed math curriculum, taught in Toronto's public schools, has tried to weed out "Eurocentric mathematical knowledges" and replace them with "a decolonial, antiracist approach to mathematics education." This emerges in small details, such as removing the credit we give to a Greek mathematician by replacing the "Pythagorean Theorem" with the term "side-length relationship for right triangles." But it emerges in large details too. For instance, it insists that contrary to the Eurocentric approach, "In an anti-racist and anti-discriminatory environment, teachers know that there is more than one way to develop a solution, and students are exposed to multiple ways of knowing and encouraged to explore multiple ways of finding answers." This includes "Indigenous pedagogical approaches" that emphasize "holistic, experiential learning" and the use of "collaborative and engaging activities" that show "respect for the diverse and multiple ways of knowing that are relevant to and reflective of students' lived experiences."[54]

But what exactly are these other ways of knowing? What might they look like? One example of what "antiracist" math might look like emerged, like so much else, in the summer of 2020. During those months, several math people in the teaching profession attempted to "deconstruct" one of the foundations of mathematics, indeed of logic itself—namely, the fact that two plus two equals four. According to these educators, the statement is not true. While two plus two can equal four, it can also allegedly add up to other numbers, including five. For some reason, perhaps to do with absolutely everything being caught up in a culture war, a crowd of people swiftly latched onto the claim. Others claimed that it was obvious that 2+2 cannot equal 4 and gave a variety of reasons. These included, but were not limited to, claims that 2+2=4 is part of a "hegemonic narrative," that the people who make such narratives should not get to decide what is true, that 2+2 should equal whatever people want it to equal, and that making such a definitive statement excludes other ways of knowing.

As the movement gathered force, one PhD candidate took to social media to declare that "the idea of 2+2 equalling 4 is cultural and because of western imperialism/colonization, we think of it as the only way of knowing." An "ethnic studies math teacher" at Washington State University called on people to attack the "haters" by proving that there are ways to make 2+2 equal 5.[55] Soon a biostatistics PhD at Harvard was trying to help out by saying that numbers are "quantitative measures" and "abstractions of real underlying things in the universe and it's important to keep track of this when we use numbers to model the real world."[56] Which cleared things up. Scores of other people, notably math teachers, took to social media to try to help out. Some people described the idea of 2+2 equaling 4 as a "simplification of reality." But the main aim of the activist teachers was clear: to sock it to the white supremacists by proving that 2+2 does not equal 4.[57]

It is possible that none of these activists had read George Orwell's most famous book. Or it is possible that they had read it years before, forgotten it, dismissed it as a work of another dead white male or—likeliest of all—assumed that its contents did not apply to them. But the whole 2+2=4 debate was especially instructive because in *1984* there is a resonant passage where Orwell writes that "in the end the Party would announce that two and two made five, and you would have to believe it. It was inevitable that they should make that claim sooner or later: the logic of their position demanded it. Not merely the validity of experience, but the very existence of external reality was tacitly denied by their philosophy."[58]

Too late, the bioethics PhD at Harvard who had leaped into the 2+2=5 case came to recognize the link to Orwell. When he was informed of it, he ended up describing it as "unfortunate."[59]

It is possible to dismiss all of this as simply a set of culture warriors battling each other in the public square without much in the way of real-world repercussions. But such an interpretation would be utterly wrong. The drive to make math when done correctly into a symbol of white supremacy means that standards in the subject, as in any and all other subjects, will be lowered or expunged altogether. What other possibilities are there, when everything that is provable is doubted and everything that can be tested is turned into part of the problem? The consequences of this are now spilling out at schools across America and the rest of the West.

Across America, there are now precisely such attempts to alter or eliminate the admissions system, ridding the system of selective admissions and moving to a system of lottery-based admissions. This is based on the belief that selection favors specific racial groups and that in order to achieve equity, the system must be disrupted.[60] One of those pushing for this in her district is San Francisco public school commissioner Alison Collins, who argued in 2020 that "when we talk about merit, meritocracy and especially meritocracy based on standardized testing, I'm just gonna say it. In this day and age we cannot mince words. Those are racist systems. If you're gonna say that merit is, like, fair—it's the antithesis of fair and it's the antithesis of just."[61]

Ibram X. Kendi is also against standardized testing in schools. People may be unsurprised to learn what accusation Kendi levels against standardized testing. In 2019, he said, "I'll say it again and again: Standardized tests have become the most effective racist weapon ever devised to objectively degrade Black minds and legally exclude their bodies."[62] This is not a fringe idea. Randi Weingarten, the president of the American Federation of Teachers, has said, "Standardized testing doesn't help kids learn, and it doesn't help teachers teach. We need to measure what matters."[63] And what exactly is it that matters? We are never told.

Of course, the consequences of the war on standardized testing can be easily foreseen. Thomas Jefferson High School for Science and Technology in Alexandria, Virginia, is not only struggling with its problematic name. It has also been struggling in recent years to change its admissions policy in order to be less selective. As it happens, the school has already undergone a significant shift in its makeup. Twenty years ago, 70 percent of the school's students were white. By 2020, 79 percent were minority ethnic, mostly from families of immigrant Asian origin. White students accounted for only 19 percent of the students that year. The failure to create any significant shift in the black admissions during this period was inevitably put down to systemic racism. And so, in the wake of the George Floyd murder, there was a move to introduce a lottery admissions policy, which was objected to by a large proportion of the school's parents. Those in favor of the policy said that they sought to have a school population that more closely mirrored the national population. But even if the policy was followed through, it would only have marginally altered the share of black and Hispanic students at the school. What it would have done is a number of other things.

It would have meant a forced increase in the number of white students at the school (by roughly an extra 25 percent) and a forced decrease in the number of Asian students (by roughly an extra 20 percent).[64]

As other schools and colleges across the country struggle with the same problem, from New York to California, they continue to find themselves facing the same conundrum. If the problem in everything is racism and the answer to everything is to disrupt the racist system, it appears to produce only two verifiable outcomes: a lowering of standards in the name of antiracism and a rise in the need for racist policies in order to deal with a problem that is always said to be racism. The war against standardized testing, like the war against religion, philosophy, and everything else in the West, does not erase racial differences. It foghorns them.

INTERLUDE:
GRATITUDE

Toward the end of *The Brothers Karamazov*, Dostoyevsky writes a chapter of pure terror. Earlier in the novel, one of the brothers—Ivan—has laid out his own deeply conflicted views on the nature of mankind, God, and the devil. As the novel develops, Ivan's mental state deteriorates. Those around him seem to believe that he is slipping into delirium tremens, usually associated with alcohol withdrawal. But the cause of Ivan's fear is left unclear and unexplained. His younger brother, Alyosha, only realizes how bad things are when he meets his brother one evening by a lamppost and says something that causes Ivan to grip him and begin to tremble. "You have been in my room!" Ivan accuses his brother. "You have been in my room at night, when he came." Alyosha misunderstands who he is talking about. Ivan howls at him, "Do you know about his visits to me? How did you find out?"[1] Later, when questioning the man who he thinks has killed his father, Ivan becomes seized with fear that this unnamed person is once again present in the room. He begins hastily looking in the corners for him.[2]

Eventually the reader is allowed to be there when Ivan is visited by the devil, who is sitting in his rooms, dressed like a Russian gentleman, using French phrases and clearly from "the class of former lily-fingered landowners who flourished in the days of serfdom."

Apparently the two have conversed before, but whether the devil is part of Ivan's consciousness or is actually before him is left unclear. The devil says that he wishes to be agreeable but that he is misunderstood—a "slandered" man. He philosophizes but complains that people do not want to hear from him. And then Dostoyevsky gives his devil a passing observation that only such a genius as he could throw in so casually. The devil explains, "My best emotions, such as gratitude, for example, are formally forbidden me solely on account of my social position."[3]

Why should "gratitude" be an emotion that is denied to the devil? Dostoyevsky leaves this unanswered. But it is worth reflecting on.

For acts of deconstruction and destruction can be performed with extraordinary ease. Such ease that they might as well be the habits of the devil. A great building such as a church or a cathedral can take decades—even centuries—to build. But it can be burned to the ground or otherwise brought down in an afternoon. Similarly, the most delicate canvas or work of art can be the product of years of craft and labor, and it can be destroyed in a moment. The human body is the same. I once read a particular detail of the genocide in Rwanda in 1994. A gang of Hutus had been at their work and among the people they macheted that day was a Tutsi doctor. As his brains spilled out onto the roadside, one of his killers mocked the idea that these were meant to be the brains of a doctor. How did his learning look now?

All the years of education and learning, all the knowledge and experience in that head was destroyed in a moment by people who had achieved none of those things.

It is one of the saddest realizations we have as a species: not just that everything is transitory but that everything—particularly everything we love and into which love has been poured—is fragile. And that just as the line between civilization and barbarism is paper-thin, so it is a miracle that anything at all survives, given the fragility of all things plus the evil and carelessness of which men are capable.

What is it that drives that evil? Many things, without doubt. But one of them identified by several of the great philosophers is resentment (or "ressentiment"). That sentiment is one of the greatest drivers for people who want to destroy: blaming someone else for having something you believe you deserved more.

Among those who have been interested in the question of *ressentiment* was Friedrich Nietzsche. It is alarming how specifically he diagnoses the type. At one point, he writes that any psychologist who wishes to study the subject must recognize that "this plant thrives best amongst anarchists and anti-Semites today, so it flowers like it always has done, in secret, like a violet but with a different scent. And just as like always gives rise to like, it will come as no surprise to find attempts coming once more from these circles, as so often before to sanctify *revenge* with the term *justice*—as though justice were fundamentally simply a further development of the feeling of having been wronged—and belatedly to legitimize with revenge emotional *reactions* in general, one and all."[4]

For Nietzsche, one of the dangers of the men of ressentiment is that they will achieve their ultimate form of revenge, which is to turn happy people into unhappy people like themselves—to shove their misery into the faces of the happy so that in due course the happy "start to be ashamed of their happiness and perhaps say to one another: 'It's a disgrace to be happy! *There is too much misery!*'" This is something that must be averted, for the sick, says Nietzsche, must not make the healthy sick too, or make the healthy "confuse themselves with the sick."[5] He returns to the subject again and again, as though circling to get exactly to the root of the thing he is attempting to diagnose. Eventually he makes the central insight, which is that ressentiment is at its heart a yearning for revenge motivated by a desire to "*anaesthetize pain through emotion*" (italics Nietzsche's own). One needs "the wildest possible emotion," he says, in order to arouse oneself to the crucial claim of the resentful person: "Someone or other must be to blame that I feel ill."[6]

What answer is there to this devastating situation? Only one that Nietzsche can see. The men of ressentiment rip at wounds that have closed and open scars "and make themselves bleed to death from scars long-since healed." Such people may drag down their friends, family, children, and everyone else around them, says Nietzsche. And the only answer is that someone must stand over the person (an "ascetic priest" in Nietzsche's telling) and say the most difficult thing. Which is that they are quite right. It is true. "Somebody must be to blame: but you yourself are this somebody, you yourself alone are to blame for it, *you yourself alone are to blame for yourself.*" Nietzsche recognizes that this is difficult, but if this was to be said, then if nothing else, one thing at least might be accomplished, which is that "the direction of *ressentiment*" could be "*changed.*"[7]

Others responded to Nietzsche's insights—notably Max Scheler and Helmut Schoeck. They added to it by noting that resentment relies always on playing A off against B. In particular, where A is praised solely and wholly in order to denigrate and devalue B.[8] In all matters, whether to do with money, sex, or anything else, no man feels that the scales are weighted in his favor. And so just as the men of resentment talk about "justice" while meaning "revenge," so it is that something is disguised within their talk of "equality." For anyone who talks of "equality" will find an inbuilt problem. Only a person who "fears he *will lose*" will demand equality as a "universal principle." It is a speculation, says Schoeck, "on a falling market.

"For it is a law according to which people can only be equal in respect of those characteristics having the *least value.* 'Equality' as a purely rational idea can never stimulate desire, will or emotion. But resentment, in whose eyes the higher values never find favor, conceals its nature in the demand for 'equality.' In reality it wants nothing less than the destruction of all those who embody those higher values which arouse its anger."[9]

This is another deeply pertinent insight. For all talk of "equality," like the talk of "justice," presents itself in one light—not least a disinterested light, as though its proponents only want an abstract thing and hardly notice whether or not this thing will ever benefit themselves. But very often it is no such thing. A set of far more fundamental issues are working themselves out.

In other words, it may be worth recognizing what we are up against when we hear the critics of the West today. For just as we are not up against justice but rather up against vengeance, so we are not truly up only against proponents of equality but also against those who hold a pathological desire for destruction.

An only vaguely milder version of this has existed in plain sight for decades. That is the obsession that started in the academy and then spread elsewhere that is given over to the veneration of "deconstruction." This is the process by which everything from the past can be picked over, picked apart, and eventually destroyed. It can find no way of building. It can only find a way of endlessly pulling apart. So a novel by Jane Austen is taken apart until a delicate work of fiction is turned instead into nothing more than another piece of guilty residue from a discredited civilization. What has been achieved in this? Nothing but a process of destruction.

Those who have made a career out of this find a number of things in their favor. One is the fact that their task is potentially endless, as the possible subjects appear limitless. It is a career for life for the deconstructionists. But still nothing is created or even produced at the end of this process. The only possible demand at the endpoint of deconstruction is to deconstruct some more. And it seems possible to pull apart and find cause for resentment endlessly. Certainly, that is the hope of the deconstructionists, who now scour the world of art and look for symbols of rape, male dominance, privilege, racism, and much more.[10] And of course they find things to occupy their time.

For you might easily look at a painting and ask what errant thoughts might have been behind it. You might also ask what labor went into it and whether any forced or unpaid labor was involved in it. You might look at the paint colors and question the origins of the pigments, whether they were legitimately or sustainably acquired. You might ask what pay the apprentices in the artist's studio received and whether everyone had been adequately compensated by their superior to produce this work for a man of even greater power. You might pull its subjects apart, and "interrogate" its meanings in the light of things that have come after it. You might see all manner of things. You might lament the lack of representation of any kind. Or you might step back and see the *Madonna of the Rocks* by Leonardo da Vinci, the *Annunciation* by Sandro Botticelli, or any number of other works of art stretching back across centuries of creation by the masters.

It is the same with buildings. You might look at the great cathedrals and other monuments of Europe and ask who carried all these stones or winched them up, whether they were appropriately paid for their labor and whether the conditions at the time were consistent with modern standards of worker safety. You might ask why people of only one skin color appear to be represented in the monuments or why people only of European background appear to be mentioned on them. You may even ask whether the act of building a structure to a particular God, in the name of a particular religion or denomination, is not in some way exclusive, even exclusionary. You might ask where the money for these great structures came from, whether that money was honestly acquired or whether some portion of the money was taken illegitimately from the poor, the needy, or even from other countries and peoples who had no say in where these finances went. You could do all these things and more. Or you could stand back and admire the Sainte-Chapelle in Paris, the Cappella Sansevero in Naples, the Duomo in Florence, or tens of thousands of cathedrals, churches, chapels, and other monuments. Why should we not simply stand back and credit our good fortune to have inherited these things and enjoy the great good fortune of being able to live among them?

These are a gift from humans to all humankind.

The reason is that what we have seen in recent decades in the West has been a grand project of deconstruction and destruction fueled by resentment and revenge. In this process, the West has been settled on as "the evil one" in the global search for blame. Obviously, many people inside the West have found it comforting to settle into this mindset as well. The men of resentment have had an easy time pointing to things that the West has done, pointing to bills unpaid and outrages forgotten or insufficiently atoned for. Such people have enjoyed reopening ancient sores and claiming to feel hurt for wounds and wrongs done long before they themselves were ever alive. They have felt contentment through opening up these old wounds and demanding that people pity them afresh as though they themselves were the victims. Because to do so is to place themselves at the center of all things, to expect recompense forever, and never to have to look to themselves to address anything—even if it is something they could only address themselves.

Such people have nothing to say about themselves, or about anyone outside of the West, because to do so might lead them to change the direction in which their resentment is funneled. It might in fact cause them to finally turn their gaze on themselves. If the West is not responsible for all ills in the world, in its past and in the past and present of others, then other actors must be held responsible. And some people would have to look to themselves to explain their lack of outcomes, achievements, and more. They would have to look into the causes of their discontents and see that at least one of them is themselves. How much easier it is to keep claiming that another party—and a vast, historic party at that—is responsible for all the ills of the world and of their own lives.

In recent decades, the sick have indeed infected the healthy and dragged them down into a demented discourse of their own invention. They have pulled almost everyone around them into the zero-sum discussion that insists that the history of the West is a history of patriarchal oppression, sexism, racism, transphobia, homophobia, larceny, and much more. These people take an interest in other societies solely in order to play them off against the West. They are interested in native tribes solely in order to try to demonstrate how bankrupt the West is. And they are interested in every other civilization in no serious sense. They do not learn the languages of other civilizations or study their cultures in any depth—certainly to nothing like the extent that the much-derided "Orientalists" and others from the Western past did. But they praise any culture so long as it is not Western solely and simply in order to denigrate and devalue the West. As a result, they reach their final end argument, which is to demand why anyone should admire or wish to continue a civilization that has done so much wrong and had such bigotry and hatred built in throughout its history.

Of course, there are many responses that can be made to this. And there are also some answers. For if someone offered me this litany of wrongs of the West, I could reply most easily in a few words. Paris. That is one that I would select early. Venice, I might say next. Rome is not nothing. Nor is Florence a dump. In fact, just to stay with cities, surely Vienna, Prague, Madrid, Lisbon, and Budapest count for something? What about New York or Chicago? The list could go on endlessly. You might linger on any one country for hours. But this points to a fact that is missing. For if you are to weigh a thing up, then you must not simply pile things up on one side of the scale. You must put something on the other side too. If you put the fact that the West has had racism in its history and leave the scale weighted only on that side, then of course you will come out with unbalanced judgments. And that is what has been allowed to happen. But must the good things not count for something? What about the great cathedral and university towns of the West: Oxford and Cambridge, Heidelberg and Regensburg, Ely and Salisbury, Bologna and Valencia?

Why is it possible to discuss the whole history and guilt of the West and not linger on these jewels even for a moment?

It is because the people of resentment are intent on forbidding the best emotions. What are those emotions? The most important, without doubt, is gratitude. The reason Dostoyevsky's devil cannot feel gratitude is that only a person intent on great evil would be denied, or deny themselves, this crucial human attribute. Without an ability to feel gratitude, all of human life and human experience is a marketplace of blame, where people tear up the landscape of the past and present hoping to find other people to blame and upon whom they can transfer their frustrations. Without gratitude, the prevailing attitudes of life are blame and resentment. Because if you do not feel any gratitude for anything that has been passed on to you, then all you can feel is bitterness over what you have not got. Bitterness that everything did not turn out better or more exactly to your liking—whatever that "liking" might be. Without some sense of gratitude, it is impossible to get anything into any proper order.

For of course it is possible to lament what did not come to you or did not happen for you. That process could be endless, and everybody on earth could play it. The more important task of life is to recognize what you do not have while being grateful for what you do.

You might regard it as a terrible thing that not everybody in the Western past always held views wholly in accordance with the social and moral values that we happen to adhere to in the 2020s. You might deride that fact or otherwise pick over it. But it makes no sense to do so unless you also recognize, for instance, that to live in the West in this time is to enjoy a piece of historical good fortune unlike almost any good fortune in history. You might feel some regret that things happened in the eighteenth century that people are not proud of today. But you might balance that out by feeling some gratitude to be part of a civilization in which all human life came to be regarded as sacred, in which people are regarded as being endowed with innate dignity, in which peace is the normal state of affairs and where wrongs done in the current day can be remedied through the application of the law. I have been to many parts of the world where some or all of these things are missing: where life is able to be ended with exceptional brutality and with no recourse to any courts or other system of justice. I have visited many countries where peace is the exception not the norm and where young people who want to make a difference in their society have absolutely no chance of ever doing so. The world is full of countries, outside the West, where the things that people in the West take for granted are ideas that seem centuries in the future, if they are conceivable at all. Places that, unlike the West, are not interested in openness to the world and are not remotely concerned with self-criticism, progress, or any other form of betterment.

People who have the good fortune to live in the West are not just the inheritors of comparatively good economic fortune. They have inherited a form of government, justice, and law for which they ought to feel profound gratitude. It may not always be perfect, but it is better by far than any of the alternatives on offer. And when it comes to what we in the West have inherited all around us, this must count as one of the greatest gifts, if not the greatest gift, that any civilization has left for those who came after. A gift not just in liberal order and beautiful cities and landscapes but in artistic achievement, cultural inheritance, and a wealth of examples of how to live. Examples never exceeded anywhere on earth.

And we do not defend these things because they are created by white people. Any more than we would wish to defend Thomas Jefferson or David Hume simply because they were white males. Such people, ideas, buildings, and cities of the West are worthy of respect not because they are the product of white people but because they are the inheritance of all mankind. It is possible today to fixate on the identity of these people and to demand that we "tear this all down." Or, more moderately, that we tear some of it down. But a saner, more reasonable approach would be to look at what we have inherited that is good and try to build on top of it.

In the last year of his life, the English philosopher Roger Scruton underwent a set of trials and misfortunes inflicted upon him by others. Perhaps distracted by these trials, he discovered too late that a cancer had grown inside him and would end his life in not much more than six months. The last thing he wrote was a reflection on that year of his life—what he had been through and all the terrible things that had happened to him. But he said, and they were the last words he published before his death, "Coming close to death you begin to know what life means, and what it means is gratitude."[11]

There are many attitudes that we all take in our lives, some of which dominate at one point in our lives and recede in another. But a life lived without gratitude is not a life properly lived. It is a life that is lived off-kilter: one in which, incapable of realizing what you have to be thankful for, you are left with nothing but your resentments and can be contented by nothing but revenge.

CHAPTER 4

CULTURE

In the freezing January of 1928, a young British artist could be found in the basement of London's Tate Gallery, repainting his first major commission. Rex Whistler was just twenty-one when he was chosen to design and paint a mural that would cover all four walls of the long refreshment room of the gallery. The result was titled *In Pursuit of Rare Meats*, a fantasy portrayal of the "Duke of Epicurania" and his court heading out to find morsels across an imaginary land. At the mural's unveiling in December 1927, George Bernard Shaw gave one of the speeches. The socialist playwright managed to upset the artist's mother, first, by mentioning Whistler's more famous American namesake (no relation) and, second, by implying that Rex, who was not from a wealthy family, was not a gentleman.

That aside, the launch was a triumph. The fantastical, idyllic, occasionally macabre scenes with which Whistler had covered the walls were packed with what would become his signature touches. Great trompe l'oeil columns around the doorways and windows, great lakes and seas with mermaids, and a landscape scattered with deserted arcadian temples in an expanse of rolling countryside. Throughout this land, strange figures feasted, chased, preened, hobbled, and charged. At one end was a portion of an idyllic city, at another a unicorn escaping the notice of a party of strange characters in a wood. The work took Whistler and his assistant Nan West a grueling eighteen months, and Whistler was paid five pounds a week. He turned down invitations and postponed visits to his closest friends to get the vast work finished. That was the origin of Shaw's "joke"—that Whistler had been paid by the week and therefore was like a plumber who came in with his bag of tools. Still, *The Times* and other newspapers praised the work from the moment of its unveiling. "The most amusing room in Europe" was one of the titles given to it by the press.

There was a heavy snowfall that winter, followed by a sudden thaw, and in January the river Thames burst its banks. On the night of January 6, the filthy water of the river poured through into the lower ground floor of the Tate and all through the just unveiled room. When the waters receded, the artist went in, accompanied by a friend, to inspect the damage. The river had left a line of scum eight feet above the floor. "The whole room is completely wrecked," Whistler wrote in a letter. The canvas had peeled off in places, the floors and furnishings were ruined. "Well," the artist said, as he stood in the ruins of his work, "at least the mermaids came into their own."[1] The room was closed to the public again, and Whistler immediately set about the desultory work of redoing his first major work.

I have always found there to be something deeply touching about the character as well as the work of Rex Whistler. He was astoundingly talented, had more technical ability than almost anyone of his generation, and possessed an invention and ease that made everything he painted instantly recognizable. He was also loved by everyone who knew him or even just met him—men and women alike. He worked exceptionally hard at his vocation, had a number of unreciprocated passions for women from a different social class than his own, and was just beginning to master the art of oil painting when World War II broke out.

Whistler volunteered to join up straightaway. And while he could have got a comparatively cushy job as a war artist, he seemed to feel that wouldn't be right and instead joined up with the Welsh Guards, eventually training to become a tank commander. Throughout his years of training, he continued to paint, amusing his regiment with specially painted murals and cartoons, and continuing to design stage sets and book designs, among other work, all through those terrible years. For Christmas 1941, he designed the cover of *The Listener* magazine. The image is of St. George defeating the dragon, atop a pile of skulls, surrounded by a motif of bayonets, books, musical instruments, and the theatrical masks of comedy and tragedy. In the winter of 1943–44, while doing final training with his tank battalion in the south of England, he designed the stage sets for *Le Spectre de la Rose* starring Margot Fonteyn in London. The war-exhausted audiences reportedly sighed with delight when the curtain first went up.

A few months later, the artist was on his way to Normandy, France. Whistler's tank crew engaged the Nazi enemy in what was then the largest solely British tank battle of the war. As Whistler attempted to dash from one of his tanks to another, he was killed by enemy fire. It was his first day of action. He was just thirty-nine.

Almost eighty years later, in December 2020, it was announced that the Tate was expected to permanently close the Whistler restaurant. The decision followed a set of complaints two years earlier about the mural. A member of the board who was also chair of the gallery's Ethics Committee, one Moya Greene, looked into the complaints, and after leading a thorough investigation into what was on the walls of the gallery, she reported back to her fellow trustees. The committee members were, she said, "unequivocal in their view that the imagery of the work is offensive." Worse, she reported, "the offense is compounded by the use of the room as a restaurant."[2] By the time the committee reported, the restaurant had already been closed because of COVID, but even when the galleries reopened, the condemned restaurant did not.

The problem the ethics committee had found was that Whistler's mural, unveiled a century earlier, had depictions of non-Europeans. The depiction of Chinese people in one tiny corner of the mural was deemed to portray the Chinese in a "stereotypical" way. Worse was that in one of the strange hunting parties, a woman in a frilly frock appears to be dragging a black child, who must be a slave, and hauling him off against his will. It is one of several disturbing scenes in the mural. What, if anything, was Whistler trying to say through such tiny details (none of the guilty characters in question is more than a couple of inches high)? A reasonable interpretation is that even in arcadia there is cruelty and suffering, as well as Epicureanism and delight. It is a typical touch. There was always a worm in Whistler's arcadias. In a later mural, he painted himself into a corner of the room dressed as a street sweep. In the Tate mural, there is a tiny white boy drowning in one corner, while at the highest point of a cliff, Whistler places an urn with the initials "D.A.W.," a reference to his older brother Denny, who had died in childhood. For decades, all of this was accepted as part of the work. As late as the early 2010s, when the Tate carried out a much-needed cleaning of the mural, no concerns were raised about it. Indeed, the complex restoration project was reported on by the BBC and others with no hint of any problem. Only a decade ago, the room still delighted and amused. When the restaurant reopened in 2013, those who praised it included the *Guardian*'s restaurant critic, who noted the immersive "fairground ride" and "sylvan beauty" of Whistler's fantasy, while also praising the excellence of the restaurant's wine list.[3]

It was just five years later that the Tate first received complaints about the Whistler mural. These seem all to have come from an Instagram account called The White Pube. When this account first noticed the Whistler mural, it also noted that the restaurant website quoted the *Guardian* reviewer's praise of the wine list. The White Pube put these two together, fulminating, "How do these rich white people still choose to go there to drink from 'the capital's finest wine cellars' with some choice slavery in the background? Tate you are all deranged." The authors of that post were one Gabrielle de la Puente and Zarina Muhammad.

Back then, the museum had responded to this intolerable pressure from one Instagram account by trying to contextualize the minor fig-

ures in the mural. The text the Tate came up with to post online and
display by the mural noted that the painting was one of Whistler's
most important works but declared that it did indeed contain a number of scenes that were "unacceptable." It described the scenes as
imperialist (as though a Duke of Epicurania ever had ridden across
the land) and continued: "These depictions demonstrate attitudes to
racial identity prevalent in Britain in the 1920s. The weakening of
the British Empire around this time paradoxically prompted cultural
expressions of the superiority of the 'British race.'"

In time, the specialist and national media were all onto it, with
one site lamenting that for years tourists had been "clinking china"
alongside "a massive mural that depicts child slavery."[4] Of course,
if any tea drinkers were worried about that, then they'd just have
to wait and see some of the themes that would confront them in
the galleries above their heads. Soon an online petition was got up.
This carefully selected the two tiny images, blew them up to a fuller
size, and put them on either side of a carefully selected photo of a
group of white people of a certain age looking satisfied after finishing a meal in the restaurant. The petition was titled "Remove the
Racist and Harmful *Pursuit of Rare Meats* Mural at Tate Britain's
Rex Whistler." It continued in similarly strident tones. "Tate Britain
allowing this overtly racist painting to remain for diners' enjoyment
is not acceptable. Changes need to be made in either removing the
painting from the restaurant or removing the restaurant from mural
room itself—there simply should not be a dining experience open
in this modern and multicultural Britain, where all races are not re-
spected." Incensed signatories claimed that so long as the Tate held
on to this mural, the institution was showing that it was not committed to racial justice.[5]

As the petition began to get more and more signatures, the Tate
seemed to think it was on the run. By the time that some hundreds
of people had signed, a spokesperson for the gallery announced that
"Tate has been open and transparent about the deeply problematic
racist imagery in the Rex Whistler mural." And the gallery insisted

that the interpretation text now on the wall alongside the mural was part of the gallery's efforts to confront the "racist and imperialist attitudes in the 1920s and today." A spokesperson for the Tate announced that their work in "confronting" such histories went hand in hand, "with championing a more inclusive story of British art and identity today."[6]

Nevertheless, when the Tate Ethics Committee reported back in 2020, they were dismissive of the gallery's initial efforts. They unequivocally condemned the mural, insisted that the gallery had not dealt with the situation adequately, and concluded that the only possible options were for the room to be closed or for the mural to be removed. At the time of writing, the Tate is preparing for an external consultation on the mural's fate. In the meantime, the room remains closed to the public.

Of course, the more you look into the matter, the clearer it becomes that the assault on the Whistler mural is a textbook case of a modern mobbing by extreme activists. The Instagram account White Pube, which started the pressure on the Tate, has been described by no less an expert than *Vogue* as "the self-styled cowboy critics shaking up the arts establishment." The account is run by people who claim that the arts in Britain are dominated by white middle-class people. As well they might be in a country that is still majority white. But the White Pube cowboys are after more than just increasing access or representation in the arts. One of their posts written in June 2020 states, "Fuck the Police, Fuck the State, Fuck the Tate: Riots and Reform."[7] Which, with the exception of one clause, is bog-standard revolutionary fare. But it is still not entirely commonplace for the chant of "Fuck the police" to be followed by "Fuck the Tate," or indeed to "fuck" any other art collection. But this is the fare that White Pube deals in. And their small support base eggs them on. As one of their supporters wrote after White Pube had got the Whistler mural in their sights, "Never knew there was a basement restaurant, let alone a white supremacist basement restaurant."

Perhaps it is unsurprising that once this anti-Whistler mural campaign gained traction, some politicians sought to join in. One such was Diane Abbott, the Labour MP who just four months earlier had been shadow home secretary. When the campaign was at its height, Abbott tweeted: "I have eaten in Rex Whistler restaurant at Tate Britain. Had no idea famous mural had repellent images of black slaves. Museum management need to move the restaurant. Nobody should be eating surrounded by imagery of black slaves." The post was accompanied by two incriminating images, one incidentally from a different painting. Abbott finished this off with the hashtag "#BlackLivesMatter."[8]

What is more interesting even than the ill will of these instigators is how far they were able to run. For what is most telling about the Whistler mural affair is not that shrill and overmegaphoned voices made their voices heard. Nor that a work of art should suffer such a stratospheric context collapse. Rather it is that the trustees of the Tate—whose job is to safeguard a historic national collection—should instead have stood judgment over a work in its care and misrepresented it so obscenely. Because of them, "the most amusing room in Europe" turned in a matter of months into a "white-supremacist" restaurant that celebrated slavery.

What might they have done instead? They might have said that the characters being complained about were the tiniest imaginable details in a work positively bursting with details. They might have pointed out that art galleries such as the Tate are absolutely chock-full of artistic details that might be considered disturbing. The Renaissance galleries are packed with crucifixions and martyrdoms. Most galleries have significant numbers of nude or seminude bodies. There are generally a few rapes. And the modern galleries (not least the exhibitions for the finalists of the Turner Prize, which the Tate hosts each year) display things that Whistler would never have imagined in his worst nightmares.

The trustees might have bothered to resist as ahistorical and anti-artistic the imposition of George Floyd onto a delicate and whimsical work of art created a century earlier. And they might have pointed out that a work of art and a political manifesto are different things. That just as a novel that mentions slavery does not mean that the novelist is celebrating slavery, so a work of art depicting something evil does not mean that the artist is somehow urging for it to happen. Yet the Tate's trustees did none of these things. Instead, they accepted that the steamroller of modern political fashion had every right to crush a work in their care. They effectively conceded the appalling claim that Rex Whistler was some kind of proslavery, pro-empire, racist, white supremacist. And since Whistler does not make the news very often, and was killed before he could leave any direct descendants to defend him, such an outsize and outlandish claim has a chance of sticking. So it is that eighty years after he gave his life fighting Nazism, Whistler now stands besmirched by the gallery he spent months toiling away for.

Watching Rex Whistler getting put through the vengeful spin cycle of this is somehow worse than watching some other cases. His art was never political. And was never meant to have to prove itself by such willfully hostile modern lights.

RACIST LITERATURE

Unfortunately, the cycle that Whistler was put through is not one that only he has gone through. In the last few years, almost every great figure in the history of Western art has been put through the exact same process. Always at the hands of people who range from the semi-informed to the uninformed. Always subjected to the same coarse form of attack. And almost always responded to by people in charge of some of our great cultural institutions—alleged guardians of the heritage—who run up the white flag of surrender the moment the first shot is fired by people who are clearly bad actors.

Nearly everything in literary history has now been subjected to the same, dulling, remorseless, Kendi-ish maltreatment. Universities that have announced that their curriculums are going to be "decolonized" or "diversified" always fall into the same remorseless groove. In his 1977 work *Marxism and Literature*, Raymond Williams infamously declared that in the far-reaching cultural revolution to come, it would be necessary for everything to go—all the acquisitions of civilization, including literature itself. Even Williams's most devoted followers had trouble with this suggestion, not least because nearly all of them held university chairs in the study of literature. But in his hope for a future where all literature would be swept out of the way, leaving a memory only of the present, he seems now to have been ahead of his time.

In January 2021, academics in the English department at the University of Leicester were given two pieces of good news. The first was that a round of redundancies could be expected. The second was that the department was henceforth going to provide a "decolonized" curriculum that would be dedicated to "diversity." Faculty were told that this meant that medieval literature would stop being taught and the teaching of early modern literature would be reduced. So out would go *Beowulf* and the works of Geoffrey Chaucer and in would come what? The university insisted that Shakespeare was safe, but President and Vice Chancellor Professor Nishan Canagarajah said that it was necessary to change the course in order to be "sustainable" and to "compete on a global level." What this meant in principle was that students would study a chronological span of English literature "from Shakespeare to Bernadine Evaristo." Such courses would allow a chronological study of literature with modules on "race, ethnicity, sexuality and diversity, a decolonized curriculum," and so on.[9] Perhaps people should have been grateful that Shakespeare could still get a look-in. But only a short while later, it looked as if the Bard of Stratford-upon-Avon might be for the chop—or at least for the severe cutting—in one of the places that was meant to uphold, celebrate, and sustain his legacy.

In May 2021, Shakespeare's Globe Theatre in London announced that it, too, was seeking to become "anti-racist" and intending to "decolonize" Shakespeare. The theatre on the south side of the Thames is near the site of the playwright's original playhouse and was reconstructed at enormous expense in the 1990s. Audiences were meant to be treated to seeing Shakespeare's work there in the setting for which he originally wrote the works, and for years tourists and locals alike rejoiced in the opportunity. But nothing is safe from the precepts of CRT. And the Globe's "anti-racist" seminars dedicated to trying to "decolonize" Shakespeare's plays appear to have unfolded in the usual manner.

Experts claimed that Shakespeare's plays are "problematic." Which they may well be. But these experts meant the term only in the same dull and reductive tenor in which everything else in the era plays. The crack squad of Shakespeare scholars who the Globe unleashed included one who first complained that in *A Midsummer Night's Dream* the character Lysander says at one point "Who would not trade a raven for a dove?" and then complained that this meant that Shakespeare associated whiteness with beauty and blackness with ugliness. Others claimed that Shakespeare used terms such as "fair" to denote someone good. And meanwhile one Dr. Vanessa Corredera from Andrew University in Michigan claimed that all of Shakespeare's plays are "race plays" and contain "racialized dynamics." By Dr. Corredera's standards, it was clear that Shakespeare is a very sloppy writer. Talking about *A Midsummer Night's Dream*, she said, "In context with other plays and even the Sonnets, this language is all over the place, this language of dark and light . . . these are racializing elements."[10]

It is an interesting claim this, by a professor of English literature, that Shakespeare's "language is all over the place." Before the recent, racialized revolt, scholars of English had generally admired Shakespeare's way with words. But it takes a course of "decolonizing" and an "anti-racism" agenda to turn even that around, and for a place that is meant to protect the legacy of Shakespeare to commission and then respectfully listen to scholars whose own words and scholarship are so fantastically hostile and inept toward him. Inevitably, the Globe denied that it was assaulting Shakespeare and claimed that his reputation was safe. But there were already signs, which they should have been aware of, that this was not so.

Only months earlier, the *School Library Journal* had run a debate on whether Shakespeare's works should still be taught in American classrooms. According to one expert, Shakespeare's works are "full of problematic, outdated ideas, with plenty of misogyny, racism, homophobia, classism, anti-Semitism and misogynoir." She concluded that educators in America are "coming to the conclusion that it's time for Shakespeare to be set aside and deemphasized to make room for modern, diverse and inclusive voices." A former Washington State public school teacher meanwhile said that she had already eliminated Shakespeare from her classroom in order to "stray from centering the narrative of white, cisgender, heterosexual men. Eliminating Shakespeare was a step I could easily take to work toward that."

Another teacher, a head of English at a high school in Michigan, said that teachers must "challenge the whiteness" of the claim that Shakespeare's works are "universal."

In response to these and other outlandish claims, Ayanna Thompson, a professor of English at Arizona State University and the president of the Shakespeare Association of America, said that teachers should continue to teach Shakespeare but should do so alongside more diverse writers. Such as Toni Morrison. This was suggested like a plea bargain, and as though no one had taught any black writer before and that lovers of Shakespeare needed to put in some type of mitigating plea if their idol was going to be allowed to remain.[11]

The more this goes on, the harder it is to find any author who is deemed to pass any muster whatsoever. A Massachusetts school was one of those to ban Homer, deeming *The Odyssey* as just one part of a canon of texts by dead white men that were problematic.[12] In such judgments, you see the whole canon of English literature being not reinterpreted but simply deemed inadmissible. Students are told that all literature before the present day was abhorrent and are then ordered to have extra portions of Toni Morrison instead.

But at least Shakespeare was being assailed through an illiterate assault on his works. Other writers were not so lucky. In fact, at the same time, other writers were being blacklisted not for anything they had ever written or said but for ancestors who they could never even have met.

In the antiracist stampede of 2020, the British Library announced that it "had made a commitment to its staff and its users that it will become an actively anti-racist organization, and will take all the necessary steps required to make this promise a reality." As one part of this great commitment, the Library announced that it was working to create a list of authors who were found to have any connection to the slave trade or colonialism. As it was forming this blacklist of authors, news of some of the names that had been put on it were published online by the Library. The initial list contained the names of three hundred guilty parties, including Oscar Wilde, Lord Byron, and George Orwell. The Library explained that "some items now at the British Library, previously owned by particular figures cited on these pages, are associated with wealth obtained from enslaved people or through colonial violence. Curators in the Printed Heritage Collections team have undertaken some research to identify these, as part of an ongoing work to interpret and document the provenance and history of the printed collections under our care."[13] These "curators" made many early discoveries from their research. One such was that the author Rudyard Kipling was guilty of having made the British Empire "a central theme" in his literary output.

Clearly only the best researchers are hired at the British Library. One of these, the chief librarian, Liz Jolly, used the moment to publicly announce that "racism is the creation of white people."[14]

Elsewhere, the Library said that although the poet Samuel Taylor Coleridge had expressed antislavery views himself and had recorded these views in his poetry, he was on the blacklist nonetheless because he was recorded as having a nephew who lived in Barbados and worked closely with estates where there were slaves. The sins of the father is a familiar problem, but the sins of the people known to the nephew is a new form of associative guilt.

Still the blacklist became more ridiculous. Because one of the people on it—to the surprise of many—was the former Poet Laureate Ted Hughes. Hughes was born in 1930, some years after the slave trade was ended and at too young an age to have any significant effect on the last days of empire. He died in 1998. Yet still the British Library added him to its dossier of wrongdoers.

The reason was that the sleuths who are employed at taxpayer expense claimed they had found that one of Hughes's ancestors, Nicholas Ferrar, was "deeply involved" with the London Virginia Company, which helped to set up colonies in North America. Of course, there was no claim that Hughes had any connection with Ferrar, because he was born in 1592, and even the British Library's research squad had worked out that they could not smear Hughes by direct link. Nevertheless, they insisted that he was one of those who fitted their blacklist criteria of being a person with "connections to slavery" or someone who had "profit[ed] from slavery or colonialism." The Library's researchers had clearly not done any research into the extent to which Hughes might have benefited from this ancestor. He was born and brought up in a poor part of Yorkshire. His father ran a tobacco shop, and Hughes made it to Cambridge University on a scholarship, making his career and what money he did from his own work.

On this occasion, there was a short and sharp intervention from some of the few remaining adults in the room. First some actual, real-life researchers not employed by the Library did the most basic, cursory work. They pointed out that aside from the absurdity of trying to damn Hughes by association with a man alive in the time of Shakespeare, there were other distinct problems with the Library's claim. For it transpired that Nicholas Ferrar had died without children, so even if Ted Hughes was related to him, it could not have been as a direct descendant. They also pointed out that Nicholas Ferrar was actually the author of a pamphlet attacking slavery before the British slave trade had even begun.

The Library smeared one of the twentieth century's great poets by connecting him to a nonrelation who had died centuries earlier and was opposed to the slave trade.

It was not an optimal start for the British Library's project, and the estate of Ted Hughes clearly stepped in to demand an unqualified apology, which was forthcoming. The Library announced that it wished to apologize to Mrs. Carol Hughes and to family members and friends, "owing to a reference included in the spreadsheet to a distant ancestor . . . which we withdraw unreservedly." The Library promised not to repeat the accusation and apologized for the distress caused. Hughes's widow welcomed the apology while lamenting the Library's "highly misleading comments."[15]

There are several reminders in this affair. One is that the people who claim to know what they are talking about do not. They are mostly ignorant, sloppy, and less than half-informed. The other is that the slightest firm pushback can bring about a reversal. So why does this not happen more often? Why is it that the same language, ideas, assertions, and dogmatisms are able to run through everything? For that is what they have done. It doesn't matter how delicate or profound the subject, how frivolous or deep it might be. Everything is inspected under the same remorseless light. And everything comes out looking equally and eternally guilty.

RACIST GARDENING

Sometimes it is great literature. At other times it can be something as light and apparently carefree as gardening. In March 2021, it was Kew Gardens that came under the spotlight. That was when the head of the largest botanic gardens in Britain gave an interview to *The Guardian* to "hit back" at claims that the publicly funded gardens he managed had been "growing woke." The cause of the complaints had been the recent publication of a ten-year manifesto that had recently appeared, which said that the five key priorities for Kew in the next decade included having conversations about its links to imperialism and colonialism. Kew obviously, predictably, said that it intended to "decolonize" and acknowledge its "exploitative and racist legacies." Richard Deverell, formerly of the BBC, chose to hit back at criticisms of this agenda and did so in strident terms. So in the pages of *The Guardian*, he announced that it was no longer possible to stay silent.

"We are at a fork in the road moment," Deverell said, with great conviction. The outpouring of feeling around the world at the death of George Floyd meant that long-standing injustices had to be faced up to. Kew could not and would not stand aside in this great reckoning. "Like so many other organizations, parts of Kew's history shamefully draw from a legacy that has deep roots in colonialism and racism," said Deverell. "Much of Kew's work in the 19th century focused on the movement of valuable plants around the British empire for agriculture and trade, which of course means that some key figures in our past and items still in our collections are linked to colonialism." The Kew botanist Sophie Richards, who is of Caribbean heritage, agreed with him. "We shouldn't forget," she said, "that plants were central to the running of the British empire."

But what does it mean, practically, to "decolonize" a garden? Mr. Deverell had part of an answer. "For more than 260 years, scientists from Kew have explored every corner of the world documenting the rich diversity of plants and fungi. We were beacons of discovery and science, but also beacons of privilege and exploitation," he said. He also added that "there is no acceptable neutral position on this subject; to stay silent is to be complicit. Each of us needs to step up to tackle injustices in our society." Yet what is the head of a botanical garden to do?

The one concrete idea Deverell seemed to have at this "fork in the road" moment was to change the display boards and descriptions. For instance, the mention of sugar and rubber plants would be changed to "reflect their links to slavery and colonialism." Elsewhere, he claimed that the gardens had been loose with their descriptive language in the past. They had referred to certain plants as having been "discovered" at certain times. The eagle-eyed Deverell was quick to point out that many of these plants had been known about by Indigenous communities for years before Western botanists and explorers came across them. Which indeed they may have been. But they were still "discovered" by the people who found them there and brought them to a wider audience that has been able to appreciate them ever since. Casting directors "discover" movie stars and your friends "discover" a great restaurant across town. There need not be anything sinister about such a description. To quibble with it is to try to satisfy a grandiose claim with a piece of pedantry. But that seemed to be all Mr. Deverell had in his armory. His other main suggestion was to make sure that "people do not feel intimidated by the Victorian wrought iron gates of Kew." As though there were friendly wrought-iron gates and unfriendly wrought-iron gates, and it is necessary to land on the right side of this divide, as all others.

Nor was Kew the only such culprit. Indeed, the world of gardening turned out to be as resentful and desiring of offense as every other realm of society. Kew had recently released a gardening podcast called "Dirt on Our Hands: Overcoming Botany's Hidden Legacy of Inequality." In it, the BBC broadcaster James Wong had set out to explore the inequality and racism that lie behind "the seemingly democratic and wholesome world of plants." Unsurprisingly, it turned out to be as seethingly racist as everything else.

According to Wong (who is half Malaysian), somebody at the Chelsea Flower Show once complimented him on his "wonderful English." On other occasions, visitors to the horticultural display had, he said, assumed that he would only be interested in tropical gardens. Another garden historian and presenter of the BBC's *Gardener's World*, Advolly Richmond, claimed that she often gets "double takes" because "sometimes I am the only black face in many, many situations to do with gardens and gardening."[16] Wong took to the pages of *The Guardian* to say that the great joy of the natural world is that it can "transcend gender, class, race, sexuality and political persuasions." And yet, he insisted, in a piece titled "Weeding Out Horticulture's Race Problem," it would come as a surprise to many people "how much of a systemic problem racism is within the seemingly friendly, mild-mannered world" of horticulture.[17] Though of course readers of *The Guardian* would most likely not have been surprised at all by the deceptively friendly face of horticulture. In fact, the bigotry seething behind the mild-mannered facade would most likely have been just what lefty readers had been primed to see around every corner.

For in the November after the death of George Floyd, Wong had already taken to the paper to argue in favor of the politicization of gardening. As the headline read, "Other Arts Are Political, Why Not Gardening?" Wong attacked people he had overheard at the Hampton Court flower show five years earlier who had complained that a horticultural installation that was inspired by "the issues facing displaced people around the world" was bringing politics into gardening. The complaint was quite wrong, he said. Since everything should be politicized, why should gardening not be? Examples of low bigotries in the world of gardening included that words such as "native" and "heritage" were used as bywords for "better."[18] Later, on social media, Wong reacted to a professor of cities and landscape who asserted that "gardens are denied their political agency because they too often reveal uncomfortable politics."[19] Wong asserted, even more baldly, that British gardening has "racism baked into its DNA." On this occasion, his evidence was that presenting a planting concept once to a roomful of "100% white" people, someone said that they should use "native wildflowers." The idea of "native" wildflowers was, he said, "not just historically fucked" but "predicated on often unconscious ideas of what and who does not 'belong' in the UK." "This is the kind of exhausting shit you have to go through everyday if you work in UK horticulture."[20]

All this certainly spoke to the *Guardian*'s view. In an editorial supporting the head of Kew Gardens, the paper concluded that the ties of rhododendrons and flowering magnolia at Kew should not distract the visitor. The botanical gardens "are not just green spaces for exercise and diversion." They were places that had been used for "botanical research" and an "appeal to science," yet were "far from apolitical." Such gardens came from an elitist Western pursuit for the "exotic" often collected "with economic purposes in mind." The "white men" who did this had an agenda. As the paper's headline blared, "The Guardian View on Botanical Gardens: Inextricably Linked to Empire."[21] Like everything else, you might say.

While Britain was waging war on the rhododendrons, in Canada emphasis fell on the unsuspecting lawns. In September 2020, John Douglas (a history professor at Thompson Rivers University in Kamloops) gained national attention when he argued the urgent case for decolonizing Canada's lawns. According to Professor Douglas, the lawn is "a statement of control over nature." Which it is, of course. But in the current era, it is not enough to observe that. The sprinklers of anti-Western hostility must also be turned on. So Professor Douglas could be found arguing that all this attempt to dam water, plant lawns, flatten landscapes, and "find a non-indigenous species of plant" to put in it was yet another example of a now familiar pattern.

"A backyard with a big lawn is like a classroom for colonialism," he explained.

Others joined in this game. According to Dan Kraus, a senior conservation biologist at the Nature Conservancy of Canada, a lawn—like a nation—should be "diverse." "It is a cultural thing," he has said. "There is this interesting comparison like, valuing diversity versus sameness." He believes that future generations may look back at non–culturally diverse lawns in bafflement, and say, "Why did you do that?"[22] Which is possible. Or, alternatively, future generations may look back at Mr. Kraus and feel another bafflement entirely.

RACIST MUSIC

Because one of the things that has made the West is its openness to ideas and influences. The history of the West is a history of gathering knowledge wherever it could be found. A history of collecting plants, ideas, languages, and styles. Not in order to subjugate or steal them but to learn from them.

Nevertheless, there is now not a realm of life and culture so delicate or so sacrosanct that this era's omnipresent, omnirelevant ideology—asserting precisely the opposite of that tradition of openness—cannot sweep through it. Always with the same remorseless dogmatism with which it sweeps across everything else. In the post-Floyd summer of 2020, classical music was one of the surprising targets. Though this had been building for some while. In 2015, the *Oxford Handbook* series saw fit to add a new title to its catalog: *The Oxford Handbook of Social Justice in Music Education.* Among the suggestions of this book were that music competitions ought to end and be replaced by drawing attention to economic inequality, that music ought to be about politics, that music education in North America is a "part of an obvious agenda of cultural Whiteness and that the posture that performers adopt on stage is racist." It argued that cultural changes mean that we should stop taking musical notation seriously, that political activism is the highest form of education, and that to fight existing power structures, we should seek not just to teach hip-hop but to "be" hip-hop.[23] Whatever that means. At any rate, precisely how hip-hop can a white man hope to be? Without getting into trouble?

In any case, the activists' sights had been set for some years in preparation for the move against American orchestras that occurred in the summer of 2020. An issue that had been going around for years—that of the demographic makeup of audiences and performers—was once again brought out as a cultural battering ram.

For decades, orchestras and other classical music groups had been working to increase the numbers of female players and ethnic minority players in their ranks. As a result of a long debate, one of the tools that many orchestras came up with was to institute a process of "blind auditions." The idea was of course to ensure that any interview panel deciding on a particular player's competency would not be influenced by the visual giveaway of whether the person was female or from an ethnic minority. For years, this was deemed to be a progressive move, and many people partially attribute the rise in minority representation in orchestras to it. In 2016, one of the trombonists in the orchestra at the Metropolitan Opera, Weston Sprott (who also teaches at the Juilliard School), came out forcefully for blind auditions. "In my experience," he said, "I have been the winner of numerous auditions where a screen was present from start to finish, but I have never won a professional audition where the screen came down. If you're serious about diversifying your ensemble, the first of many steps is to raise the screen and let your ears (not your eyes) guide your artistic convictions. Diversity will follow."[24]

But then in 2020, you could almost hear the gearbox crunch as the principles of the process were suddenly reversed. All of a sudden, blind auditions were the problem. As the *New York Times* blared in a headline during July 2020, "To Make Orchestras More Diverse, End Blind Auditions." For that month's consensus was that if orchestras were to be more diverse, then rather than ignore race or give everybody the same chance by having blind auditions, they should instead be made to take into account "race, gender and other factors." While the paper acknowledged that blind auditions had been "transformative" in increasing the number of female players in orchestras, it claimed that there was "not enough" change in the racial makeup of orchestras. "The status quo is not working," said the paper. "Blind auditions are no longer tenable," and while the policy had been "well-intentioned," it had now allegedly "impeded diversity."

There may be a number of reasons for underrepresentation in orchestras. For instance, it is possible that there are simply not enough young black Americans being trained up as classical performers. Whatever the reasons for that, one solution would be to increase classical music aid across the American schooling system, especially in black-majority schools. But as is the case so often, this would be too big an issue to address. Whereas beating up on orchestra boards for not having enough (black) players in their orchestra is a relatively cost-free exercise. The argument for incremental change, which had been one argument in classical music circles for years, was suddenly deemed to be part of the problem.

According to the *New York Times*' chief classical music critic, "Slow and steady change is no longer fast enough."[25]

Still, this suggested that the problem was easy to solve. Either to raise the screens or to bring them down. But even on this, no one can agree. Anthony McGill, the principal clarinetist for the New York Philharmonic, who happens to be black, says, "I don't know what the right answers are." And it is noticeable that in a follow-up piece titled "Black Artists on How to Change Classical Music," the *New York Times* could not find a single black musician who supported the idea of stopping blind auditions.[26] The National Alliance for Audition Support (an initiative designed to increase representation in American orchestras) claims that "aspects of our audition/tenure processes continue to contribute to the legacy of systemic racism that has existed in our country since before the very first orchestra was founded." It says that "training in anti-racism, implicit bias and group communication skills are imperative at all levels" of orchestral management and support. But its 2021 guidelines also call for screens to be up throughout all stages of the audition process, as well as insist on no screening of resumes.[27] Whether pro- or antiscreening, all of this has one thing in common. It is presented under one unarguable premise: that classical music is a "white-dominated field," as the *New York Times* said, and must therefore be transformed.

The point began to be made endlessly. In July, it was the opera's turn. "Opera can no longer ignore its race problem," claimed the *New York Times*. On the very same day, the *Washington Post* decided to go with: "That sound you're hearing is classical music's long overdue reckoning with racism." This prominent piece asserted that "systemic racism . . . runs like rot through the structures of the classical music world." It claimed that institutions must "correct the imbalances that keep the classical stage so habitually tilted and tinted white." As an example, the *Post* presented the Kennedy Center, which had recently arranged a Zoom call with community arts leaders in which the center's vice president, Marc Bamuthi Joseph, stressed the center's desire to commission "anti-racism works." For as he said, the center's goal is to "make anti-racism systemic."[28] What happened to the goal of such a center simply being to perform the best work possible? After all, there is nothing wrong with white people being in an audience, any more than there is anything wrong with white people being in a congregation. If there are not enough black people in a particular gathering, it doesn't make the gathering wrong. It may just not appeal to everyone, and it should be possible to make some peace with that, or affect it, without insisting that the cause must be "racism."

Yet the same juggernaut goes through everything. The Baltimore Symphony Orchestra asserts in its 2021 charter that "diversity, racial equity, and inclusion are strategic imperatives to the success of the BSO's second century." Furthermore, it says: "We believe it to be inherently within the BSO's mission to celebrate the arts and reject systemic racism in all its forms. We recognize that the legacy of white privilege persists across our entire organization and we pledge to transform this institution in partnership with our musicians, administrative staff, patrons, and community."[29]

In the last two years, this same trend has swept through every part of the musical world. In the dash not to remain on the wrong side of a stampede, there has been a constant drive to find more black composers from the past and present. At least one major baroque ensemble in America has found itself caught in this trap. Because of course the music it plays is all by dead white composers. Still, its board is demanding that this baroque ensemble play new music in order that it can play music by black composers. If people thought it was hard to find the required number of black composers working today, wait till they try to find black composers willing to compose in a baroque idiom. In other cases, orchestras have already begun to part ways with music directors and others not willing to fire existing players and replace them with black players. In at least one case in the United

States, the victim of the resulting purge has been a musician of Asian origin. Meaning that in the name of increasing ethnic minority representation, the institution has eased out an existing musician from a minority. Because while few black artists need help reaching the top of the world's pop charts, it has been decided that they do need to be pushed to the top of the baroque music scene.

Perhaps it is inevitable in a world in which everything else is racist that even the fundamentals of music would be branded in the same light. In the last generation, there has been an increasing drive at the top universities in the Western world to drop the very idea of musical notation because of its allegedly elitist, white, and Western connotations. At universities including Stanford, Harvard, and Yale, there has been an ongoing debate over what demands they should make of those reading music. Should students be expected to learn about the canon of Western music? Should they even be expected to learn the Western system of musical notation, given that it is just one form of musical notation and Western at that? Should the study of music demand any prior musical literacy at all?

The problem is in most ways a new one. Earlier generations of ethnomusicologists tended to assume that Western music notation was a useful tool for understanding non-Western musical traditions. It is only in recent years that this assumption has been called into question. And, of course, there is an interesting question here. For what are people to do and how are they to understand any musical system at all unless they use some notation system? Very few cultural systems in the world have developed a sophisticated system of notation that accurately captures the two necessary elements of pitch and time. The Western system developed an ability to notate pitch from as early as the ninth century. The notation of rhythm became possible from around the twelfth century. And by the fourteenth century, Europe had developed a system of notation not far off from the modern system.

The Chinese have a system, and one has been developed in India. But neither is capable of doing what the Western system of notation can do. And there is a perfectly easy means by which to demonstrate this fact: which is that Western ethnomusicologists can with a very considerable degree of accuracy capture the music of India, China, and almost every other musical tradition. While the same cannot be said the other way around. While India and China have their own systems of notation, it is not the case that if you played a symphony by Mahler to Indian or Chinese musicologists, they would be able to write it down in their notation system and then perform the symphony back for you while reading from their notation system. The results would not sound even remotely the same. Indeed, the results would bear almost no resemblance to what had first been heard.

The French-Israeli ethnomusicologist Simha Arom has devoted his life to the study of the complex music of Africa. In his works such as *Polyphonies et polyrythmies instrumentales d'Afrique Centrale* (1985), Arom analyzes and notates the sophisticated polyphonic and polyrhythmic music of Africa. His work includes notation of the highly complex techniques of Central African music—a tradition that the composer György Ligeti, who learned from Arom's work, described as opening the door to "a new way of thinking about polyphony, one which is equally rich as or . . . even richer than the European tradition."[30] Yet much as Ligeti and other composers gained from this knowledge, the transit remains one-way. Although Arom was able to capture the complex music of Central Africa while using the Western system of notation, no African system exists that could notate and then even approximately replicate a piano concerto by Beethoven. This is not a value judgment. It is simply a matter of fact, and just one reason why the Western system of notation can be said to be of far greater utility than is any other existing system of notation and therefore—if for no other reason—worth studying.

Any reasonable analysis of the facts would recognize the truth of the situation discussed above. And yet to mention it is not just controversial but contentious, particularly in the West. Not because it is untrue but because it is inconvenient to some wider ideological purview. The fact that the system under assault from academics and others happens to be the system that is most effective stops seeming perverse once you understand that the reason it is under assault is not that it is the most effective system.

The reason it is under assault is simply that it is Western.

It is not as though this assault is happening in obscure quarters. Indeed, this land grab by certain scholars is happening at Oxford University, among many other places. In March 2021, professors of the music faculty were shown a new set of proposals that said that "arising from international Black Lives Matter demonstrations, the Faculty Board proposed making changes to enhance the diversity of the undergraduate curriculum." Why should the music faculty of Oxford University feel impelled to make any changes because of the BLM movement? Only for the same reason that everyone else is expected to.

Among the highlights of the music faculty's deliberations was one professor's branding musical notation itself as a "colonialist representational system." Elsewhere, professors were told that the current undergraduate course demonstrated "complicity in white supremacy" and focused too much on "white European music from the slave period." By which the professors meant the era of Mozart and Beethoven. A faculty member who decides on which courses should form the degree complained that the course's "white hegemony" had to be addressed. It was also claimed that teaching musical literacy in a notation system that had not "shaken off its connection to its colonial past" would be a "slap in the face" for certain students.

Skills such as learning to play a keyboard instrument or learning to conduct orchestras should apparently no longer be part of the course because the relevant repertoire "structurally centers white European music," causing "students of color great distress."

Naturally, it was also complained of that the majority of teachers in these relevant specialisms are "white men." Finally, it was said that the "structure of our curriculum supports white supremacy" not only because of the "almost all-white faculty" but because it was giving "privilege to white musics." One suggestion for alternative courses was that Oxford University should introduce new courses in pop music and popular culture. One example of a potential area of study being "Artists Demanding Trump Stop Using Their Songs."[31]

As though to show that there is always another circle in the inferno, within weeks of that announcement, it was the turn of the Royal Academy of Music to announce what it was planning to do in reaction to the death of George Floyd. According to the academy, it was now necessary to look at everything in a new light, including its world-renowned collection of twenty-two thousand rare instruments. According to a spokesperson for the institution, which was founded in 1822, there was an ongoing commitment "to making our curriculum more diverse." But it was also necessary to take the opportunity "to view the collection, which has been built up over two centuries, through a decolonization lens."

Who, or what, might be the victims of this cull? All that seemed to be known was that the academy had links with George Frideric Handel, previously best known for writing *The Messiah* but now better known for having invested in a company that owned slaves. Elsewhere, it seemed that several ivory keyboards might need to be "decolonized."[32] Nobody knows what was going through the mind of George Floyd during the last terrible minutes of his life. But it might have surprised him to learn that his death could lead to a purge of historic harpsichords at one of London's premier music conservatories.

And the problem for so much of the era is that the political assertions do have practical consequences. It is not just that theoretical discussions occur in music faculty discussion meetings. It is that the same rebarbative, retributive worldview is run with everywhere. Eventually everything becomes viewed through the same negative, hostile light, even in the arts, where works created in a spirit of generosity, sincerity, and tribute are now labeled as works of "appropriation" or "colonialism."

CULTURAL APPROPRIATION

In her *New York Times* best seller *So You Want to Talk about Race*, Ijeoma Oluo tried to define what cultural appropriation actually is. She takes several runs at it.

> At its core, cultural appropriation is about ownership of one's culture, and since culture is defined both collectively and individually, the definition and sentiment about cultural appropriation changes with one's identification and sentiment about aspects of their culture.

Perhaps aware that this sentence does not make matters completely clear, Oluo has the grace to say that there is an explanation for this. The sentence may sound "really complicated" but "that's because it is." And this, she suggests, may be one reason that "cultural appropriation has been a difficult concept for many." Yet again she tries to simplify it, and in yet another run—printed in bold this time—she informs us that: "We can broadly define the concept of cultural appropriation as the adoption or exploitation of another culture by a more dominant culture."[33] Examples that Oluo gives include the wearing of Indian headdresses "as casual fashion," certain Halloween costumes, and white people's rapping. When it comes to whether or not white people ought to be able to rap, Oluo says that legally they should be allowed to do so. The law should not prohibit it. But, she says, "whether you 'can' or 'should' do something is a different matter."[34]

According to critics such as Oluo, white people's "taking" culture that is not theirs is wrong for two main reasons. The first is that they cannot know or share the roots of the culture that they are appropriating and that it hurts people who have been born into that culture to see others attempt to absorb it without feeling their pain. The second is that white people who appropriate other cultures apparently go on to make money from their appropriations, often unfairly. So when a white rapper makes money from a record deal, for instance, they are earning money that has effectively been stolen from a nonwhite person who could have done the same task at least as well, if not better.

Of course, a number of problems arise from such assertions. Not the least of them is that such assertions presume that cultural pain is constant, unending, and unshareable. More prosaically, they present a range of practical problems. For instance, is it permissible to engage in the culture of another group so long as you do not excel at it? If you are bad at engaging in that culture, then how bad does it have to be before it is insulting? And how good does it have to be before this engagement starts to constitute a threat? What are people to do if they are partly of the tradition in question but not wholly so? If only one of their parents, or one of their grandparents, happens to be of the tradition that they would like to engage with?

One demonstration that those who make assertions such as these have not really thought about the consequences of their claims can be seen in the fact that their examples are so consistently flippant. Once again, Oluo claims that cultural appropriation is "the product of a society that prefers its culture cloaked in whiteness" and a society that "only respects culture cloaked in whiteness."[35] The examples she gives of this are people's wearing feathered headdresses to Coachella and "white college kids wearing dreadlocks." Oluo wrestles with herself slightly over whether people should be allowed to borrow from other cultures but concludes that "marginalized cultures" must be heard. "And if that means your conscience won't allow you to dress as a geisha for Halloween, know that even then, in the grand scheme of things—you are not the victim."[36]

Yet the grand scheme of things appears to be the last thing on the mind of those who talk of appropriation. Very few people would go to the wall for the right to wear a Native American headdress to Coachella or to dress as a geisha for Halloween. Indeed, the obsession with Halloween costumes in US discussions of cultural appropriation displays not just immaturity but a deliberate unwillingness to confront the serious, sincere, and profound exchanges that actually distinguish the history not just of Western art and culture but of world culture. By focusing on costumes or hair braids, the opponents of cultural appropriation make the job too easy for themselves. And they ignore—whether through malice or ignorance—the much bigger questions that loom up behind.

CULTURAL ADMIRATION

For the history of Western culture is not a story of cultural appropriation. It is far more accurate to describe it as a story of cultural *admiration*. For centuries, European artists and composers looked around the world not with detestation but with admiration, even veneration. They wanted to look at everything that the world outside had to offer. And when they "appropriated" aspects of the culture of a group other than the group they happened to have been born into, they did so not out of a desire to monetize the results, or to steal the pain of other people, but as a way to understand the human condition and reflect it in all its richness.

Take one of the great oratorios of the twentieth century. Even as Michael Tippett was writing it in the 1930s and 1940s, his *A Child of Our Time* was in an idiom that was out of fashion. The great oratorios of the nineteenth century were big beasts, remote from what Tippett then saw as the urgent political cataclysm of his day. But he was spurred to write one of his greatest works by an urgent recent event.

In November 1938, a young Jewish man called Herschel Grynszpan assassinated a German diplomat in Paris. The Nazis immediately used this as a pretext for what became known in Germany as Kristallnacht, with Jewish homes and Jewish-owned businesses systematically destroyed with state coordination. As news drifted out from the continent, the young, radically left-wing, and pacifist composer in England began imagining a musical response to the growing violence and racial discrimination engulfing the continent. And as he contemplated a musical response to a world that was beginning to turn "on its dark side," he was gifted a magnificent idea.

Sometime early in 1939, Tippett heard a broadcast on the radio in England that included a number of African American spirituals, then known as Negro spirituals. Such spirituals were fairly popular at the time and already performed with some frequency. But this particular performance moved Tippett greatly. He had known a number of the spirituals since his school days during World War I and had most likely heard a concert of spirituals while he was a student at the Royal College of Music in 1925. But this performance struck a profound chord, and he instantly sought out the black writer James Weldon Johnson's two-volume edition of spirituals. From there, Tippett conceived the idea of interspersing these spirituals at crucial moments within his oratorio, much as Bach includes Lutheran chorales during his Passions. So at climactic moments of this modern oratorio, Tippett included "Steal Away," "Nobody Knows the Trouble I See, Lord," "Go Down, Moses," "Oh, By and By," and finally and perhaps most movingly, at the very end of the work, "Deep River." The chorus and soloists sing, "I shall know my shadow and my light" and then after the difficult, contorted harmonic passages that accompany it, the performers all finally fall into the deep balm of this great spiritual. "Deep river, my home is over Jordan. Deep river, Lord, I want to cross over into campground. That land where all is peace."[37]

The spirituals from A Child of Our Time were such a success that the composer eventually did a separate arrangement of them that got performed as often, if not more often, than the oratorio itself did. Their popularity helped make Tippett's pacifist oratorio his most performed work, one that has moved audiences around the world for generations. Tippett himself attended performances around the world, including a multiracial performance in the Cathedral of Lusaka, in Zambia, before the country's president. Several of the era's great sopranos, including Faye Robinson and Jessye Norman, distinguished the work through their performances of it. In 1966, Tippett went to conduct a performance at a school in Baltimore and was, as his biographer has written, "delighted to find the choir a mixture of black and white singers." It was performances such as these, in the country that had gifted him the spirituals, that he felt most moved by. A friend of his related that on at least one occasion when the work was performed in America: "Of course all the audience started to sing the spirituals, and it made him weep apparently. Almost makes me weep to see him telling me."[38] Just as Bach's congregations would have known the chorales in the Passions, here was the place where the songs had come from and to the joy of the composer, the audience joined in with them as their own. Nothing Tippett ever wrote in the decades afterward, even his *Third Symphony*, which in its text quotes directly from the words of Martin Luther King Jr., ever gained the emotional and popular appeal of that great work of World War II.

Yet in recent years, all this, like everything else, has come to be portrayed in a different light. As early as 2000, there were people complaining that Tippett had no right to use spirituals from a tradition he did not belong to. At the time of a performance in Los Angeles by the Los Angeles Philharmonic, several musicologists complained that the inclusion of the spirituals was "worrisome." Though sincerely intended, they can seem, one critic claimed, like "cultural appropriation." Today's world, they complained, did not properly acknowledge the contribution of African American music in the Western canon. And the conductor Roger Norrington joined in, claiming that there was a risk that Tippett was "turning spirituals into early-afternoon tea." Which is a generalizing claim to make in itself.[39] In America, proposed performances of the work have been stopped as students have complained about cultural appropriation and even the simple fact that the spirituals were known in their day as "Negro spirituals." While that term may not be acceptable today, it was simply the term of the day, and stripped of all context or even an attempt at understanding, it seems that this great work now stands as yet another casualty of campaigners and others willfully trying not to understand the context or intent of the work.

At the time Tippett was writing, the very performance of the spirituals he used would have been banned in Nazi Germany, which would have forbidden them as *Negermusik*. But at the very moment that this would have been the case in Germany, an English composer raised up that very same art and gave it a platform for the whole world to admire and share in. It is commonly said that if someone is going to use the music of a different culture, then they should at least encourage the people from that culture to perform their own music. But how many presumptions are bound up in that? If no African or African American is available to sing the spiritual, should it go unsung? And why if you wish to promote or protect a particular cultural expression would you go after precisely the people trying to bring that culture to a wider audience? Of all people, why go after them?

There is something not just sad but shameful about an era trying so hard not to admire, appreciate, or even just understand the hopes and dreams of earlier days. As though everybody who dreamed or created before the present must be found to have slipped up somewhere and then be cast aside for good.

CULTURAL APPROBATION

But that is just one of the problems of the ravenous expression of opprobrium now known as "cultural appropriation." For the idea, spun off so mean-spiritedly from the American academy, does not simply claim that artists and others must "stay in their lane," it surveys the vast savannah of past creativity and sees it in a light that is solely negative. It looks to Western art and attempts to see it as a history of illegitimate acquisition and theft. What it resolutely fails to do is to recognize the spirit not just of generosity but of deep tribute that the history of Western art has always expressed when it met non-Western traditions.

It is exceptionally easy to claim that Western artists—like Western explorers, soldiers, and botanists—merely saw the world outside of Europe as a place to artistically rape and pillage. What it refuses to recognize is that almost none of the work now interpreted in this light was created with such a mean or meaningless intent. For many centuries, the history of painting in Europe was slow to pick up outside techniques simply because artists, like everyone else, were unaware of cultures that were then beyond their known world. But when painters, composers, and other artists did find their way outward from Europe, it was with a wonder and a respect that bears no resemblance to the spirit in which their actions are now commonly interpreted.

From the late eighteenth and early nineteenth centuries, painters such as Jean-Auguste-Dominique Ingres and Eugène Delacroix were fascinated by the world of North Africa. "Exoticism" was not something they had contempt for. It was something they were passionately interested in and inspired by. Paintings such as Ingres's *Odalisque* and Delacroix's *Women of Algiers* (both now in the Louvre) are not robberies from North Africa. They are an extension of a long history in Western art of wanting to find out about everything, including what had previously been unknown. In the time of Leonardo da Vinci, human anatomy was a type of unknown country. In later centuries, people became more aware of parts of the world and cultures that the peoples and artists of Europe were then only just discovering. And not only did they want to keep discovering, and finding out, but whenever they did, the greatest of them were always deeply receptive to what they found. In fact, in the history of Western art, it might be said that it has always been those artists who have kept striding and striving to find out and incorporate everything in the known world who changed the world of art.

Those who sealed themselves off willfully from everything that was out there fell into a kind of cul-de-sac of creation.

But those who kept looking outward kept developing and learning and paying tribute. When Henri de Toulouse-Lautrec discovered Japanese lithography, not only did it transform his own art but through his art it trickled through all the artistic movements of which he was such an influential part. Many cultures around the world have tried to protect and cordon off what they have, believing outside influence to be a negative thing. Yet Western art has constantly sought to go in another direction, opening itself up to the world and seeking to learn from it.

The same process applied in architecture, where travelers from Europe went out and brought back ideas from the places they had seen. The architecture of many of the cities of the Mediterranean, in particular, owe a huge amount to the Orient. But across the West, there are buildings that reflect the insatiable appetite of architects to be, as one recent book describes it, in "dialogue" with architecture from the Middle and Far East.[40]

But nowhere is this so pronounced as in the world of music. Of course, for centuries the ability to travel was limited even for the very wealthy. But the great composers of European history always kept their ears open for new musical styles, influences, and forms. One of the great composers of the late Renaissance, Orlando di Lasso (born circa 1532), was widely traveled for his time. And as well as composing some of the greatest Mass settings of the Renaissance era, he had a quick ear for picking up other styles. Exotic and comic songs were picked up by him, most likely through his travels in Italy, where he would have been able to pick up parts of the Moorish traditions that had made it that far. It is argued that the troubadour tradition of love songs drew on a Moorish tradition that most likely came up to Europe through Spain before making its way to France, where it was developed. Other forms, such as the passacaglia, appear to have started in similar ways. They may even have come from South America, where they would have been brought back by Portuguese travelers. Once found, they were admired and became part of the fashion and the culture that had stumbled on them.

For centuries, this pattern continued. The great composers of the classical era, including Mozart and Haydn, found Turkish influences that would have come to them through the Hapsburg empire. Canonical masterpieces such as *The Magic Flute* have aspects of Turkish style in them. This was no insult or theft by Mozart, simply an expression of the same ravenous appetite for new sounds and ideas that all great composers have. It was an appetite that developed and expanded as the ability of Western composers to learn and travel grew.

In the nineteenth and twentieth centuries, the great composers of Europe began to explore as far afield as they could. Claude Debussy found himself absorbed in the art and sound world of Japan. Without that interaction, it is impossible to see how Debussy would have written many of his late piano works, among others. As the twentieth century developed, this fascination with the world beyond Europe grew. And though today, thanks to the influence of Edward Said over almost every discipline, this is seen as somehow sinister, there was nothing sinister about it. It was as a demonstration of European cosmopolitanism that great composers kept wanting to look beyond their own traditions and expand them.

In the summer of 1908, a friend of Gustav Mahler's who was staying with him in Toblach heard the great composer and conductor express interest in China and its music. When the friend returned to Vienna, he went to a shop and bought a phonograph cylinder of Chinese music, which had actually been recorded in China. That summer was among the saddest and hardest of the composer's life. Mahler was mourning the death of his young daughter Maria, and to save himself, he threw himself into his work. As well as working on his ninth symphony, he worked on a manuscript that became *Das Lied von der Erde* (*The Song of the Earth*). For his text, he drew on a volume called *Die chinesische Flöte*, which was a set of translations of Chinese poetry from the Tang dynasty by the poet Hans Bethge. These words prompted one of Mahler's greatest masterpieces, a symphony of songs in which the composer speaks of the fleeting nature of joy, the fickleness of life, and the deep solace of eternity.[41]

But Mahler was not alone in this. The Vienna of his day was filled
with composers and artists ravenous to find new sources of inspiration outside of Europe. At the same time as Mahler was writing,
another composer-conductor was rivaling him in the concert hall,
as well as in the affections of Alma Mahler. Like his more famous
contemporary, Alexander von Zemlinsky looked elsewhere for the
source of his inspiration. His greatest work, the *Lyric Symphony* of
1923, in many ways resembles the lieder-symphony form of Mahler's
great work. But for his text, Zemlinsky looked to India and landed on
the poetry known as *The Gardener* by the great Bengali poet Rabindranath Tagore, who was an almost exact contemporary of Zemlinsky's. The combination of Tagore's ravishing words and Zemlinsky's
music (not least the love message "Du bist mein Eigen" [You are my
own]) made such an impression at the time that it found its way into
a work by another composer of the era, Alban Berg, who quoted
from it in his own *Lyric Suite*.

Of course, Vienna in the early twentieth century was an unusually
fertile place, intellectually and culturally. But although the internationally searching nature of its artists might have been exceptionally
developed, it was not unique. As the twentieth century progressed,
more and more artists and composers managed to acquaint themselves with other traditions and venerate them.

The English composer Gustav Holst may be best known for his orchestral suite *The Planets*. But his work is shot through by his fascination with the culture of India. In the late 1890s, Holst went to the
reading room of the British Museum to read the fifth-century works
of the poet Kālidāsa known as the *Rigveda*, especially the work
known as *Meghadāta* (*The Cloud Messenger*), as well as the great
Hindu epics *Rāmāyana* and *Mahābhārata*. The composer, who was
then in his twenties and scratching a living as a trombonist, found
the translations awkward. So in addition to his busy work schedule,
he decided to study Sanskrit. Through doing so, he managed to make
his own translations from the Sanskrit to compose such major works

as his *Choral Hymns from the Rig Veda, The Cloud Messenger,* and his opera *Savitri.*

This hunger to discover didn't belong to any one nation or group of people in the nineteenth and twentieth centuries. It wasn't just British composers or German composers who wanted to foray into everything the world had to offer. It was a Western habit. It was something that composers and artists in each country did for themselves as they looked to see where to take their art and how to communicate more fully in their chosen language. The greatest French composer of the late twentieth century, Olivier Messiaen, was one of the most innovative composers of any era. And in part it was because he kept his ears open for sounds wherever he heard them, whether in the natural world or in the world of man-made music. It has been recognized for decades that the research and work Messiaen did on Indian music, especially its highly complex rhythmic structures, was central to the technique of his musical language.

Messiaen made his studies of Indian music in Paris in the 1930s, and the results can be seen from as early as the visionary *Quartet for the End of Time,* which he composed and first performed alongside fellow prisoners while in a German prisoner-of-war camp in 1941. All his life, the rhythms of India stayed with him. He saw the musical discoveries of India not as something that should stay in India but as something to be shared by him and any other artist who valued them with anyone in the world who would listen. Perhaps a final example could suffice.

In the early twentieth century, there was an increasing interest in the music of the Far East. Musicians including the composer Percy Grainger transcribed Balinese music from a gramophone record and attempted to capture its sonorities with a percussion ensemble. But it was the Canadian-born composer and ethnomusicologist Colin McPhee who took the study further. McPhee had lived in Bali during the 1930s and had both studied the gamelan and attempted to transcribe its complex rhythmic structures. His transcriptions included a work for two pianos called *Balinese Ceremonial Music*. And while he dreamed of a synthesis of Western and Balinese music, it was another composer who would accomplish that. On McPhee's return to America, he found a fellow performer in the form of Benjamin Britten. They performed the *Balinese Ceremonial Music* together in a concert on Long Island in 1941. The music had a profound effect on the young composer.[42]

Over a decade later, in the mid-1950s, Britten was considering which way to turn after finishing his masterpiece *The Turn of the Screw*. During a world tour, performing and conducting, he managed to include a stay on Bali. It was a profound and crucial visit for the composer. While on the island, he had the opportunity to listen to live gamelan music for the first time. He wrote to the daughter of Gustav Holst, Imogen Holst, from Ubud, Bali, in January 1956. "The music is fantastically rich," he told her, "melodically, rhythmically, texture (such orchestration!!) and above all formally. It is a remarkable culture. We are lucky in being taken around everywhere by an intelligent Dutch musicologist, married to a Balinese, who knows all musicians—so we go to rehearsals, find out about and visit cremations, trance dances, shadow plays—a bewildering richness. At last I'm beginning to catch on to the technique, but it's about as complicated as Schoenberg."[43]

Britten told other friends of his wish that he could send them a photo of a gamelan: "They are fantastic, most complicated and beautiful and they are everywhere . . . the air is always full of the sound of gongs, drums, and metallophones!"[44] While on the island, he took care to compile what he could in the way of live sketches of performances he heard. He even arranged to have tape recordings made of the gamelan music. What his memories, his own sketches, and the recordings he took all added up to was an infusion of new ideas and a whole new sound world that Britten brought into some of his most important scores from immediately after the Bali trip and right through to the end of his life. The first major work that reflected his new passion was his score for the ballet *The Prince of the*

Pagodas, the only full ballet score he ever wrote and one that to this day stands out, as the late conductor and composer Oliver Knussen (who recorded the full score) once said, because it is so generous. It is unadulteratedly lush, with none of the slither of steel that can run through many of the composer's works.

In it, he made all sorts of innovations in the orchestra. He used Western tom-toms doubled with cello pizzicato to try to re-create the sounds of the double-headed kendang drum's sonority, with one passage directly quoting from the Peliatan gamelan's recording of *Kapi Radja*. It was a whole new sound world, and once he was in it, Britten never completely left it. It became part of his own musical imagination. His "church parables" from the 1960s, *Curlew River* and *The Burning Fiery Furnace*, are filled with sounds and ideas that Britten got from his immersion in the sound world of Bali. And the last opera he ever wrote, *Death in Venice* (1973), is filled with the sounds he heard two decades earlier. Again, he tries to find sounds in the orchestra that will capture the sounds of the East. He uses Western piccolos, sometimes doubled with harmonics on the strings, to try to capture the sound of the bamboo suling flute. He incorporates into the score a fusion of Western and Eastern techniques. There are rhythmic passages that clearly come from the world of the gamelan. But perhaps most moving in what Britten is doing in this last great work is that he juxtaposes the terse, ungenerous music that accompanies Gustav von Aschenbach in his Germanic monologues with this ravishing sound world that it also opens up to him. The two styles are brought together in the piece, but there is no doubt over where Britten shows the generous, creative springs of art as coming from.

I could go on, almost endlessly. But even if we just stayed with the examples cited above, could it really be honest to lambaste the art of the West for being parochial or limiting? The very question now has a "damned if you do, damned if you don't" quality. For if a culture is to be condemned as insular, parochial, and limited if it is inward-looking, yet lambasted for cultural appropriation if it is outward-looking, then what exactly is a culture to do? In such a situation, it would appear that an unfair, indeed hostile, trap has been set up. One in which Western culture can be simultaneously attacked for its insularity and lambasted for not being insular enough.

The term "cultural appropriation" has had a very free run. Perhaps it is time that it is finally pushed back against. For the history of Western art and Western culture cannot be best understood by interpreting it as some act of grand theft. Much more accurate is to understand the history of Western culture—especially as the centuries have progressed—as being a history of admiration, interest in, and praise for other cultures.

And that gets to something absolutely central to the misunderstanding in the guiding anti-Western ethos of our time. Either you can see your cultural inheritance as only for yourself and others who happen to be born inside the same borders or culture. Or you can see it as something that you would want to share. This is, or can be, a two-way street. For just as the history of Western art has been filled with respect for other cultures, so on occasion this habit has been reciprocated. In parts of Asia, there is a thriving classical music scene. Not just in orchestras and other ensembles playing classical music but in composers and other musicians who admire the Western tradition and work within it, giving it their own particular twists and additions along the way. Composers such as Toru Takemitsu from Japan and Tan Dun from China composed or compose still in a way that is recognizably that of classical European culture. And although they have critics, no serious critical movement in the West has attacked, let alone insulted and defamed, these composers for working in that tradition. No school of Western thought is attempting to prevent Japanese or Chinese composers who write works for the symphony orchestra from doing so. There is no movement on the campuses or in the studios of the West insisting that European music should be for European peoples only and that the use of the idioms, styles, or instruments of Western music is some kind of theft or appropriation. By and large, any and all additions to the canons of Western art are welcomed, and if there are gaps that exist, then these are gaps that practitioners are actively seeking to fill.

In Abu Dhabi, there is a now a magnificent new Louvre containing artifacts from the Paris museum alongside newly acquired and newly created artworks from around the world. To visit it is to be reminded of the fact that although there are obviously specific cultures and cultural movements, there is no reason why culture should be regarded as having borders that cannot be traversed. On the contrary, the whole history of culture is one of sharing, borrowing, imitating, and admiring. Who would have it any other way? Only, it seems, a movement almost entirely centered in the West itself that believes—or claims to believe—that the West alone should not be admired and must not be allowed to admire in turn. This belief is not just factually wrong. It is morally wrong: an error that not only would rob the West of its own culture but would rob the rest of the world of sharing in it.

CONCLUSION

In 2021, America went through a sudden and steep learning curve on CRT. Thanks to a small group of campaigners and a number of news outlets, suddenly everybody in the country seemed to know about CRT, or at least was talking about it. Parents and teachers across America began to blow the whistle about what was being taught in American schools. Employees revealed what was happening in American corporations. And in time, even the government agencies, including the American military, were revealed to be mired in the same game.

That June, General Milley, the chairman of the Joint Chiefs of Staff, testified before Congress and was asked by one representative about reports that the US Military Academy at West Point had been teaching a course involving CRT. A guest lecturer was even reported to have given an address at West Point that included a section on "white rage." This was that month's addition to the phrase book of terms intended to "problematize," or rather pathologize, the existence of white people. In response to this query, General Milley did not back down. He defended the study of CRT at West Point, saying, among other things: "I want to understand white rage. And I'm white."[1] CRT seemed to have washed through every echelon of public life in America.

Large chunks of America, not least American parents, did not like the sound of this. They did not like it when they discovered that their children were being talked about, and to, in highly racialized terms. At school board meetings across the country, parents began to object to a curriculum that was teaching their children that being on time, giving correct answers in math, and more was "hidden racism." And not just white parents. Large numbers of black parents and parents of other racial minorities had the courage and fury to stand up and object to this sort of division. From being a fringe academic theory only a couple of decades earlier, CRT was suddenly being talked about not just by talk show hosts but at school board meetings across the country.

It was an important moment. What had happened at Grace Church School in Manhattan, where a teacher had recognized that "problematizing whiteness" meant problematizing white children, began to happen all over the country. Again and again, parents were discovering that whatever "problematizing whiteness" meant in theory, in practice it was itself highly problematic. Kimberlé Crenshaw and other proponents of CRT appeared not to have prepared for this fact. CRT was experiencing its first encounter with the general public, and the encounter was not proving to be a success.

And so at this stage, the proponents of the theory fell back onto a number of deflecting moves. The first was to claim that what was going on was an entirely invented hysteria and that the people who were now talking about CRT had simply created a new enemy to rail at that was in fact no more than a figment of their imagination— predominantly the imagination of the American right. *Time* magazine was among those to claim that "Critical Race Theory is simply the latest bogeyman,"[2] while *Inside Higher Ed* called it a "bizarre hysteria" created by "wealthy right-wing and libertarian donors."[3] In the *New York Times*, Michelle Goldberg claimed that the CRT term itself "has become unmoored from any fixed meaning." She went on to argue that she was "highly skeptical" of the idea that CRT was being taught in American schools, and proceeded to argue that in any case "antiracist education" isn't "radically leftist" but simply "elementary."[4] *The Guardian* summed it up by claiming that what was going on was a "Critical Race Theory panic."[5] These writers tried to claim that critics of CRT were simply trying to stop the teaching of slavery, Jim Crow laws, and anything else negative in the American past.

This overlapped with a second move that was also deployed. Which was the pretense—practiced by Joy Reid of MSNBC, among others, on her evening show—not only that CRT was not being taught in American schools but that, in any case, CRT was not what critics said it was. At one and the same time, people such as Reid argued, CRT was both too complex for ordinary people to understand and an exceptionally obvious demand for social justice. To boost these claims, and settle the matter once and for all, Reid invited Kimberlé Crenshaw onto her show. Crediting her with having come up with the term "critical race theory" and revering her for having done so, Reid allowed Crenshaw to make several claims. One of which was that the backlash against CRT was an effort "to reverse the racial reckoning unlike anything we've seen in our lifetime."[6] So at one and the same time, CRT did not exist, was not being taught, was being taught (and that was a good thing), and was also too complex for most mortals to understand (although we should praise those who invented such a clear and necessary theory).

These contradictory claims drew a certain amount of criticism. One of those who led that criticism was Christopher Rufo of the Manhattan Institute, who had recently emerged as one of the leading voices opposed to CRT being spread in educational and other institutions across America. Rufo called out Reid for her confused claims, in particular for her softball interview with Crenshaw. Eventually Reid rose to the bait. She invited Rufo onto her show but then refused to let him speak. Instead, she pretended, among other things, that whereas there was no such thing as "critical race theory" (or that if there was, he did not understand it), there certainly was a thing called "critical Rufo theory." So having prevented him from saying a single line without interruption, she congratulated him on inventing a bogeyman idea that she now pretended didn't exist and sent him on his way.

Rufo soon became the punching bag for others who wanted to play the same game. But such moments of potential inflection are important. And the most interesting exchange that occurred at this corner of the debate came when Rufo was interviewed on the Black News Channel by Marc Lamont Hill. As it happened, I had met Lamont Hill myself, some years ago on a stage in Doha. On that occasion, I had tried to persuade the other panelists beforehand that whatever disagreements we might have about the West onstage that night, we should all agree to say at least something critical about the de facto caste system or other human rights violations that existed in the country that was hosting us.

Needless to say, Lamont Hill did not join me in saying anything remotely critical about our Qatari hosts, though he happily railed away about American racism for them.

So I knew the form and watched with interest. But Lamont Hill is no fool, and when he interviewed Rufo, he had a devastating question up his sleeve. The question was this: "If I were to say to you now, Christopher, 'What do you like about being white?' what would you say?" Rufo is also no fool, and he knew that he had just been led onto an unbelievably dangerous, potentially career-ending, land mine. At first, he laughed nervously and struggled for an answer: "It's such an amorphous term, it's like a census term," he said. But Lamont Hill pushed, asking Rufo to "indulge him" for a moment. After all, as Lamont Hill said, "If you were to ask me some things I like about being black, I could talk about cultural norms, I could talk about tradition, I could talk about the kind of commonalities I feel around the diaspora, if I were to ask you—particularly if you are saying whiteness is a thing that is being constructed as negative and shouldn't be—name something positive that you like about being white."

Rufo tried to swerve once more by saying that a lot of public schools are claiming that things like timeliness, rationality, objectivity, and the Enlightenment are being ascribed to a white identity and that this is wrong, and they should be ascribed to all human beings. Lamont Hill said this was a strawman and reiterated that these were all negative things being ascribed to being white, while he was asking for something that was positive about being white. Rufo laughed and said, "Again I don't buy into the framework that the world can be reduced into these metaphysical categories of whiteness and blackness. I think that's wrong. I think we should look at people as individuals. I think we should celebrate different people's different accomplishments . . . I reject that categorization. I think of myself as an individual human being with my own capabilities, and I would hope that we could both judge each other as individuals and come to common values on that basis."[7]

Inevitably enough, Lamont Hill concluded that the ability to see yourself in this fashion was yet another example of white privilege.

The reason the exchange was so interesting was that Lamont Hill knew exactly what he was doing. He knew that he was leading Rufo onto the most dangerous possible territory—both for him personally and for white people as a whole. If there are things that are bad about being white, then there must be things that are good about being white. What are they? There are in fact a number of ways this question might be answered—ugly though it is to even ask it. But a ducking of this issue most likely cannot go on interminably.

The first way to answer it is to try to take the path that Rufo tried to take. That is to say—basically, I do not want to see color. I do not want to see people primarily through the prism of their skin pigmentation. I think that skin color is essentially uninteresting and unimportant, and we should leave it at that. This is a perfectly respectable answer to give, and it is about the only answer that is survivable if asked such a question in any public forum today.

The second way to answer it would be to step a little further along the same road as that: which is to say that effectively what is described as "white culture" is in fact no more than a part of a universal culture. And that whereas some black people and people of other races might decide to cut themselves off from allowing other people to join their party, white people should take a different route. That what is called "whiteness" is something that can be open to all people. And that whereas the traditions and cultural norms of black Americans may try to be kept back solely for the enjoyment of other black people, white culture should not be identified in such a way and should almost be a synonym for something that is open to all. So in an era that wishes to identify people along tribal lines, "whiteness" becomes a convening body for people of any background or skin color who wish to engage themselves in an ongoing tradition known in shorthand as the Western tradition.

Both of these are the softest options and eminently respectable. But there is a third option, which Lamont Hill must have known could be possible to tease out, and which he almost certainly knew that his interlocutor would not say. For this is the currently unacceptable answer. The nuclear answer. That answer to someone asking what is good about being white might go along something like the following lines:

"I don't especially think of myself as being white and don't particularly want to be cornered into thinking in such terms. But if you are going to corner me, then let me give you an answer to the best of my ability.

"The good things about being white include being born into a tradition that has given the world a disproportionate number, if not most, of the things that the world currently benefits from. The list of things that white people have done may include many bad things, as with all peoples. But the good things are not small in number. They include almost every medical advancement that the world now enjoys. They include almost every scientific advancement that the world now benefits from. No meaningful breakthrough in either of these areas has come for many centuries from anywhere in Africa or from any Native American tribe. No First Nation wisdom ever delivered a vaccine or a cure for cancer.

"White people founded most of the world's oldest and longest-established educational institutions. They led the world in the invention and promotion of the written word. Almost alone among any peoples it was white people who—for good and for ill—took an interest in other cultures beyond their own, and not only learned from these cultures but revived some of them. Indeed, they have taken such an interest in other peoples that they have searched for lost and dead civilizations as well as living ones to understand what these lost peoples did, in an attempt to learn what they knew. This is not the case with most other peoples. No Aboriginal tribe helped make any advance in understanding the lost languages of the Indian subcontinent, Babylon, or ancient Egypt. The curiosity appears to have gone almost entirely one way. In historical terms, it seems to be as unusual as the self-reflection, the self-criticism, and indeed the search for self-improvement that marks out Western culture.

"White Western peoples happen to have also developed all the world's most successful means of commerce, including the free flow of capital. This system of free market capitalism has lifted more than one billion people out of extreme poverty just in the twenty-first century thus far. It did not originate in Africa or China, although people in those places benefited from it. It originated in the West. So did numerous other things that make the lives of people around the world immeasurably better.

"It is Western people who developed the principle of representative government, of the people, by the people, for the people. It is the Western world that developed the principles and practice of political liberty, of freedom of thought and conscience, of freedom of speech and expression. It evolved the principles of what we now call 'civil rights,' rights that do not exist in much of the world, whether their peoples yearn for them or not. They were developed and are sustained in the West, which though it may often fail in its aspirations, nevertheless tends to them.

"All this is before you even get onto the cultural achievements that the West has gifted the world. The Mathura sculptures excavated at Jamalpur Tila are works of exceptional refinement, but no sculptor ever surpassed Bernini or Michelangelo. Baghdad in the eighth century produced scholars of note, but no one ever produced another Leonardo da Vinci. There have been artistic flourishings around the world, but none so intense or productive as that which emerged around just a few square miles of Florence from the fourteenth century onward. Of course, there have been great music and culture produced from many civilizations, but it is the music of the West as well as its philosophy, art, literature, poetry, and drama that have reached such heights that the world wants to participate in them. Outside China, Chinese culture is a matter for scholars and aficionados of Chinese culture. Whereas the culture created by white people in the West belongs to the world, and a disproportionate swath of the world wants to be a part of it.

"When you ask what the West has produced, I am reminded of the groups of professors assigned to agree on what should be sent in a space pod into orbit in outer space to be discovered by another race, if any such there be. When it came to agreeing on what one musical piece might be sent to represent that part of human accomplishment one of the professors said, 'Well, obviously, it will be Bach's Mass in B Minor.' 'No,' averred another. 'To send the B Minor Mass would look like showing off.' To talk about the history of Western accomplishments is to be put at great risk of showing off. Do we stay just with buildings, or cities, or laws, or great men and women? How do we restrict the list that we put up as a preliminary offer?

"Of course, you may dispute some of these details, or you may dispute whole swathes of it, think its tone is wrong, does not show enough humility or self-deprecation. You may even say that this understated homily sounds 'triumphalist' or otherwise in bad taste. But what cannot be disputed is the most devastating proof of all, which is the simple matter of footfall: a footfall that is entirely one-directional. For there is, even today, no serious movement of peoples in the world struggling to get into modern China. For all its financial prowess, the world does not wish to move to that country. It does want to move to America and will go to extraordinary lengths—even the risk of life—to reach that goal. Similarly, there is no serious global effort to break into any of the countries of Africa. Indeed, a third of sub-Saharan Africans polled in the last decade said that they wanted to move. Where they want to move is clear.

"The migrant ships across the Mediterranean go only in one direction—north. The people-smuggling gangs' boats do not—halfway across the Mediterranean—meet white Europeans heading south, desperate to escape France, Spain, or Italy in order to enjoy the freedoms and opportunities of Africa. No significant number of people wishes to participate in life among the tribes of Africa or the Middle East. There is no mass movement of people wishing to live with the social norms of the Aboriginals or assimilate into the lifestyle of the Inuit, whether those groups would allow them in or not. Despite everything that is said against it, America is still the world's number one destination for migrants worldwide. And the next most desirable countries for people wanting to move are Canada, Germany, France, Australia, and the United Kingdom.[8] The West must have done something right for this to be the case.

"So if you ask me what is good about being white, what white people have brought to the world, or what white people might be proud of, this might constitute the mere beginnings of a list of accomplishments from which to start. And while we are at it, one final thing. This culture that it is now so fashionable to deprecate, and which people across the West have been encouraged and incentivized to deprecate, remains the only culture in the world that not only tolerates but encourages such a dialogue against itself. It is the only culture that actually rewards its critics. And there is one final oddity here worth noting. For the countries and cultures about which the worst things are now said are also the only countries demonstrably capable of producing the governing class unlike all of the others.

"It is not possible today for a non-Indian to rise to the top of Indian politics. If a white person moved to Bangladesh, they would not be able to become a cabinet minister. If a white Westerner moved to China, neither they nor the next generation of their family nor the one after that would be able to break through the layers of government and become supreme leader in due course. It is America that has twice elected a black president—the son of a father from Kenya. It is America whose current vice president is the daughter of immigrants from India and Jamaica. It is the cabinet of the United Kingdom that includes the children of immigrants from Kenya, Tanzania, Pakistan, Uganda, and Ghana and an immigrant who was born in India. The cabinets of countries across Africa and Asia do not reciprocate this diversity, but it is no matter. The West is happy to accept the benefits this brings, even if others are not."

This would have been one way for Rufo to answer that question. But it is understandable that he did not. For at present, such a truthful answer remains at the very edges of permissible sayability. And into the silence left by the impossibility of saying what is true, anything and everything can roam. When white people have to be ashamed of the culture that has produced them, almost anything can happen. And that is the situation into which we have slipped.

I had a very wise friend who died during the COVID pandemic, a distinguished Indian-born economist called Deepak Lal. In his later years, Deepak used to chortle unstoppably when discussing the latest idiocies afflicting the universities in America and other institutions in the West to which he had devoted most of his working life. "Everybody claims that after the age of Christianity, we are going to enter an age of atheism," he once said to me. "Whereas it is perfectly clear that we are entering an age of polytheism. Everybody has their own gods now." It is true. After the central religious and cultural stories of the West were taken out of the culture, and people were encouraged to turn on their own past, the culture became entirely hollowed out. It is amazing how flimsy and empty the ideas are that can flood in to fill their place. In the place of a history or tradition, we got instead the talk of "values" only, as though those values came from nowhere or could be invented afresh. In the name of great openness, we became close-minded, and in the name of progress, we absorbed ideas that turned out to be highly regressive. The result is a great melee. A great search for meaning by people who have been blinded from the outset by the people who were meant to have given them sight. Even Deepak might have been surprised at how self-hobbled the West now is: how willing it now is to prostrate itself before any tradition so long as it is not its own.

To take just one example, in 2021, the State Board of Education in California approved a model curriculum in Ethnic Studies that included prayers to the Aztec gods. The "affirmations, chants and energizers" were meant to "bring the class together" and "build unity around ethnic studies principles and values, and reinvigorate the class." These prayers included the "In Lak Ech Affirmation," an Aztec prayer calling on Tezkatlipoka, Quetzalkoatl, Huitzilopochtli, Xipe Totek, and Hunab Ku. Twenty times the names of these Aztec gods are invoked as they are asked to help provide such things as "strength that allows us to transform and renew." Since the model curriculum is provided to almost eleven thousand schools in the California area, this should count as a goodish number of invocations per day for any deity. And had the relevant Aztec gods indeed existed, then they might have been surprised to have been called from their slumber in the 2020s by students in the California area.

And the students in turn might have been surprised by what they summoned up. The claps and chants to Tezkatlipoka were meant to request that the god enable the students to be "warriors" for "social justice." Back in the day, the Aztecs went a step further than that. For Tezkatlipoka was traditionally worshipped with both human sacrifices and great feats of cannibalism. The California students might also have been surprised that while their prayers to Huitzilopochtli asked the god for "healing epistemologies" and "a revolutionary spirit," back in the day, the Aztecs used to celebrate this god as a god of war, in whose honor they performed hundreds of thousands of human sacrifices.[9]

One might like to presume that the California State Board of Education has no idea what it is doing. Worse is to consider, even for a moment, that it does.

In the absence of anything else, the only public ethic in the West that people are encouraged to unite around is opposition toward it-self. And this now takes increasingly ugly and divisive forms. The summer of 2021 saw the release of the US census carried out the previous year. Among other things, it showed a decline in the white population. "Number of White People Falls for First Time" was how the *Washington Post* announced the fact.[10] This was when Jimmy Fallon's studio whooped about the decline of white people and the comedian laughed along with them. And you have to stop for a moment to wonder about that. Turn it any other way around and see how ugly it is. "For the first time in American history the number of black people went down." Cue applause and cheers. Or imagine the majority populations in China, Japan, India, or any other country outside the West whooping and cheering about their own demographic decline. If you do so, you get some sense of how demented and self-hating the West had become in this current era.

On matters big and small, comic and tragic, this self-loathing runs on. There is now almost nothing that cannot be run through it. The attack on inanimate objects might have reached a pinnacle in the summer of 2021, when the University of Wisconsin removed a forty-two-ton rock that had been accused of racism by a couple of students. People could get the same treatment. When a white woman disappeared in Wyoming, and before her body was discovered, there was national interest in the case. Joy Reid of MSNBC dismissed this as "missing white woman syndrome."[11] Just the latest pseudomedical pathologizing of anyone who was white, a pathologizing that had seen the invention of "white fragility," "white tears," "white rage," and more. In the same month, a "Black National Anthem" made its first appearance at an NFL game. Before the kickoff in the game between the Dallas Cowboys and Tampa Bay Buccaneers, the ballad "Lift Every Voice and Sing" was played. Suddenly Americans were told that this song—written in 1900 by James Weldon Johnson—better represented black Americans than did "The Star-Spangled Banner." Talk of a nation split apart along racial lines began to sound like a lot more than just talk.

Through this whole period, there have been daily examples of demented behavior and permissible bigotry. But there have also been occasional moments of light from brave individuals who have stepped forward and said that they will not see their society turned against itself and groups within it pitched against each other afresh. People such as Jodi Shaw, a self-described "lifelong liberal" who quit her job at Smith College, in Massachusetts, over diversity and inclusion initiatives, which, she said, had created a "racially hostile environment." Staff struggle sessions had consistently berated white staff members, and in her resignation statement, Shaw said, "I ask that Smith College stop reducing my personhood to a racial category. Stop telling me what I must think and feel about myself. Stop presuming to know who I am or what my culture is based upon my skin color. Stop asking me to project stereotypes and assumptions onto others based on their skin color." The college offered her a "generous settlement" that would have "required confidentiality," but Shaw turned it down, saying that the "importance of telling the truth" was greater.[12]

Sadly, cases such as Shaw's get attention because they remain relatively rare. While a few people stood up and said they would not countenance the ongoing assault on majority populations in the West, too many others went along with it, playing along with the newly imposed rules and language of the people who insisted that the West and the people of the West had nothing good to be said for them. Those who had appointed themselves referee were disproportionately feted. In 2021, Ibram X. Kendi was the recipient of a MacArthur "genius" fellowship. Other people who had joined the bandwagon were likewise, if rarely more munificently, rewarded. Yet while everyone in the private sector, public sector, and entertainment industries in particular fell over themselves to prove their antiracist credentials, nothing could prove enough for Robin DiAngelo, the Miss Whiplash of antiracism, and her cohorts. In 2021, she had a new book out called *Nice Racism*, in which she scolded the white population afresh. According to DiAngelo, young people "who actually have cross-racial friendships tend to have relationships that are conditional. Their friends of color must tolerate constant racist teasing or be dismissed as angry and 'not fun' and then abandoned." How exactly DiAngelo had access to such omniscient knowledge was never made plain. But it did lead her to conclude, "So no, I don't think the younger generation is less racist than the older ones."[13]

Anyone else might conclude from this that the game that DiAngelo, Kendi, and others are inviting people to participate in is unwinnable. It is never possible to be antiracist enough for these people, and it seems fair to conclude that they are unfair actors. Even demonstrable, quantifiable, observable improvements are dismissed as though they mean nothing at all. Millennials are as bad as Jim Crow. Generation Z are quite as bad as the slaveholders. Even if the ambition is to have an absolute equality of outcomes in our societies, there doesn't appear to be any serious reflection on how these theories are practically going to help us reach that state.

One hopeful sign could be discerned in the fact that whenever people got a taste of what these antiracist policies meant in practice, the experience stung those it touched. In September 2021, the English Touring Opera said that it had dropped half of its orchestral players. The reason given was that it needed to prioritize "increased diversity in the orchestra" in line with the "firm guidance of the Arts Council."[14] Perhaps on paper diversity quotas looked splendid. In practice, it meant finding musicians who had worked for you for years and struggled through the lockdowns of COVID only then to be fired because of the color of their skin. If the anti-Western "diversity" mantras were ugly in theory, they were uglier still in practice. And they were being enacted in almost every forum in the culture, more or less publicly, every single day.

Still, it is the question that waits after this conclusion that is more pertinent. When you are invited to play an unwinnable game, a thought will inevitably pop into your head: even if this game could be won, would it be a game worth winning?

In recent years, Americans and other people in the West have fallen over themselves to prove that they are not what their critics say that they are. They try to prove that they are not racist, homophobic, misogynistic, and more, and hope that it is understood that while their history may have included racism, racism was not by any means the sole point of their history. Governments, individuals, sports teams, awards ceremonies, and all cultural institutions have bent over themselves to demonstrate their diversity. They have gone out of their way to increase their enrollment and recruitment of people who are not white. They have tried to make sure not just that minority groups are represented in every walk of life but that they are overrepresented. So that there is actually more visibility in the public eye than there is in the public as a whole. The aim has behind it a presumption that if exact representation or overrepresentation is achieved, then something great will happen. And while it is true that a society that allows its most talented people to rise as seamlessly as possible can be advantaged, there is no evidence that a society thrives by developing the racial and cultural obsessions that the West has now developed.

While there may be sectors that benefit from looking like the public (the government, the police, and perhaps customer services being among the most obvious examples), should the same apply to every realm of life? Must a firm of architects be as diverse as possible? A fire department? A musical ensemble? Or a basketball team? Would any of these areas be improved if absolutely accurate representation were really the goal? If overrepresentation is not a problem, is there any point at which it becomes one? At the end of all of this, while the West mires itself in this ever-greater self-inflicted sclerosis, does the West beat China? Does it even stand a chance? Is the game that our entire culture has dedicated itself to even a game worth playing?

This is the question that hovers over all of this. Occasional glimpses of the price to be paid if the answer is no keep poking through. It is not theoretical. Today the West faces challenges without and threats within. But no greater threat exists than that which comes from people inside the West intent on pulling apart the fabric of our societies, piece by piece. By assaulting the majority populations in these countries. By saying that our histories are entirely reprehensible and have nothing good to be said about them. By claiming that everything in our past that has led up to our present is irredeemably riddled with sin and that while these same sins have beset every society in history, the debtor should knock at only one door. And most importantly by those who pretend that a civilization that has given more to the world in knowledge, understanding, and culture than any other in history somehow has nothing whatsoever to be said for it. What is anyone to say or do in the face of such myopic, omnipresent hatred?

We have, it seems to me, only a couple of options. They are options that remain the same today as they have always been. One is to fight and defend our own history along clear but exclusionary lines. The steam building for this backlash is already starting to become visible. It would consist of a brutal but logical calibration. If people decide that they have contempt for our ancestors, then we will have contempt for theirs. There is, after all, no reason why everybody in the West should agree to remain stuck forever in the position of a masochist with no safe word. More likely is that a growing number of people will come to reject the whole game. They might reply with the following calibration. If you do not respect my past, then why should I respect yours? If you do not respect my culture, then why should I respect yours? If you do not respect my forebears, then why should I respect yours? And if you do not like what my society has produced, then why should I agree to your having a place in it? This way lies an awful amount of pain. It also concludes inevitably in conflict, solvable only by force. It is an option much to be avoided.

Unfortunately, there are plenty of people of all colors and political sides who seem intent on pushing us into that place. British academic and race-baiter Kehinde Andrews recently claimed that the whole system in the West needs to be overturned. What does he mean by this? In his own words, "I mean simply revolution. I'm not going to lie. This is a revolutionary argument. We need to do something different. We need to overturn. You cannot just rely on these institutions because they are actually the problem. You can't separate racism from capitalism, so we need to do something else. There is no other solution than revolution."[15]

Fortunately, there are also wiser voices around. One of them is the American writer Thomas Chatterton Williams. In his recent memoir, *Self-Portrait in Black and White*, Williams writes: "One way or another, we are going to have to figure out how to make our multi-ethnic realities work, and one of the great intellectual projects facing us—in America and abroad—will be to develop a vision of ourselves strong and supple enough both to acknowledge the lingering importance of inherited group identities while also attenuating, rather than reinforcing, the extent to which such identities are able to define us."[16]

Where Kendi, Coates, and others look out at the world and seem intent on ensuring that nothing and no one is ever given any benefit of the doubt, Williams is rightly startled by this "inflexibility and lack of generosity."[17] And where these people hold themselves out as antiracists, Williams acknowledges what so many people can see but too few have said. Which is that:

> the most shocking aspect of today's mainstream antiracist discourse is the extent to which it mirrors ideas of race—specifically the specialness of whiteness—that white supremacist thinkers cherish. "Woke" antiracism proceeds from the premise that race is *real*—if not biological, then socially constructed and therefore equally if not more significant still—putting it in sync with toxic presumptions of white supremacism that would also like to insist on the fundamentality of racial difference. Working toward opposing conclusions, racists and many antiracists alike eagerly reduce people to abstract color categories, all the while feeding off of and legitimizing each other, while any of us searching for gray areas and common ground get devoured twice.[18]

It may seem today that there are more people on the side of Kendi and DiAngelo than there are on the side of Williams. But history

is on Williams's side. And not just in the presumptuous, too often
heard claim that the future will bear him out. But in the sense that
the recent and distant past already does so. Glenn Loury, Adrian
Piper, Henry Louis Gates Jr., and many others have made a similar point, and like a growing number of others, Williams marshals
them to his side. For all have understood that the best of human
knowledge and culture must be transferable and understandable
across racial and social lines. Otherwise, we decide that some things
must be cordoned off, offered to, and appreciated by only certain
racial or ethnic groups. That way lies a replay of all the worst
things of the past. Replayed in the guise of opposition to just such a
replay.

People growing up in the West today remain among the luckiest
people in human history. But luck is not an entirely abstract thing,
and nor is it a complete lottery. Societies are not simply lucky. As
Branch Rickey famously said, "Luck is the residue of design." We in
the West are lucky because men and women before us worked hard
to make it so and performed feats extraordinary and mundane to
see that luck was what we got. A luck that much of the world still
wants to take a part in. Of course, there are divisions. But as Henry
Louis Gates Jr. said, the only way to transcend the divisions is to
forge "a civic culture that respects both differences and commonalities." And the only way this can be done "is through education that
seeks to comprehend the diversity of human culture." And to recognize that "any human being sufficiently curious and motivated can
fully possess another culture, no matter how 'alien' it may appear
to be."[19]

Much of the world can see this. Too few people in the West today
apparently can. But they can learn to see it and be encouraged to see
it. And encouraged at the same time to realize that the culture, history, and people they have been taught to disdain and deplore have
handed them riches that are enough for a whole lifetime. People always did question what the purpose of things is. They do so now

as much, if not more, than ever. And today when people ask where meaning can be found, they should be encouraged to look at what is all around them and just beneath their feet. If they look properly, and with some forgotten humility, they might recognize that what they have is more than luck. It is all that they will ever need.

ACKNOWLEDGMENTS

I would like to thank everybody at HarperCollins who has made this book possible. In particular, my editors, Eric Nelson in the US and Oli Malcolm and Joel Simons in the UK. I would also like to thank my agent, Matthew Hamilton of the Hamilton Agency. Other than that, I must simply thank—without naming them—all those friends, colleagues, and enemies with whom I have argued out these issues for many years.

NOTES

INTRODUCTION

1. Ibram X. Kendi, *How to Be an Antiracist* (New York: One World, 2019), p. 85.
2. Lyell Asher, "How Ed Schools Became a Menace to Higher Education," *Quillette*, March 6, 2019.
3. Exec. Order No. 13985, "Advancing Racial Equity and Support for Underserved Communities through the Federal Government," The White House, January 20, 2021.

CHAPTER 1: RACE

1. Episode 1,500 of *The Tonight Show*, NBC, August 12, 2021.
2. Derrick Bell, *And We Are Not Saved: The Elusive Quest for Racial Justice* (New York: Basic Books, 1987), p. 159.
3. Richard Delgado and Jean Stefancic, *Critical Race Theory: An Introduction* (New York: New York University Press, 2001), pp. 2–3.
4. See Eduardo Bonilla-Silva, *Racism without Racists: Color-blind Racism and the Persistence of Racial Inequality in the United States* (Lanham, MD: Rowman & Littlefield, 2003).
5. See esp. Michel Foucault, *Discipline and Punish: The Birth of the Prison* (New York: Pantheon, 1977).
6. Michael Moore, *Stupid White Men* (New York: ReganBooks, 2001), pp. 58–59.
7. Dr. Thomas Sowell, "Random Thoughts," *Creators*, July 24, 2012, www.creators.com/read/thomas-sowell/07/12/random-thoughts-12-07-24.

8. Robin DiAngelo, *White Fragility: Why It's So Hard for White People to Talk about Racism* (Boston: Beacon Press, 2018), p. xi.
9. DiAngelo, p. ix.
10. DiAngelo, p. xii.
11. DiAngelo, p. xiii.
12. DiAngelo, p. 91.
13. DiAngelo, p. 11.
14. DiAngelo, pp.149–50.
15. Robin DiAngelo on *Amanpour & Company* in 2018. Broadcast again on PBS on June 13, 2020.
16. Sheryl Gay Stolberg and Marjorie Connelly, "Obama Is Nudging Views on Race, a Survey Finds," *New York Times*, April 27, 2009.
17. Associated Press, "Polls Show Sour Views of Race Relations in Trump's America," July 16, 2019.
18. See, for instance, Sharon M. Chubbuck, "Whiteness Enacted, Whiteness Disrupted: The Complexity of Personal Congruence," *American Educational Research Journal* 41, no. 2 (Summer 2004): pp. 301–33.
19. Cristina Beltran, "To Understand Trump's Support, We Must Think in Terms of Multiracial Whiteness," *Washington Post*, January 15, 2021.
20. See Skeptic Research Center, "How Informed Are Americans about Race and Policing?" Research Report CUPES-007, February 20, 2021.
21. See the *Washington Post*'s database of fatal shootings by on-duty police officers: www.washingtonpost.com/graphics/investigations/police-shootings-database/.
22. Susan Goldberg's June 2021 letter to subscribers of *National Geographic*.
23. "Is the West Fundamentally Racist? With Kehinde Andrews and Jeremy Black," *Intelligence Squared*, April 8, 2021, www.intelligencesquared.com/events/is-the-west-fundamentally-racist-with-kehinde-andrews-and-jeremy-black/.
24. Griffin Leeds, "Everyone Mistook a Priest for a KKK Member," *The Tab*, April 5, 2016.
25. J. K. Trotter, "That KKK Robe Sighting at Oberlin Was Probably Just a Student Wearing a Blanket," *The Atlantic*, March 5, 2013.
26. "University of Missouri Students Report Threats; Police Quell KKK Rumors," *CNN*, November 12, 2015.
27. DBK Admin, "UMD Police Are Investigating Plastic Wrap Resembling Noose Found Near Campus," *Diamondback*, June 27, 2017, https://dbknews.com/0999/12/31/arc-gcbl54bhjfcp3kmxqfyqjuwgsu/; see also Malik (@mwalterrs), Twitter, June 27, 2017.
28. "MSU Student Finds Noose Hanging outside Dorm Room," WLNS-TV (Michigan), October 4, 2017.
29. "Student Reports Being Accosted; Racial Slurs Used," Vincennes University, March 26, 2018, www.vinu.edu/en/web/external-relations/b/student-reports

-being-accosted-racial-slurs-used; "Alleged Hate Crime Now Being Called False Reporting," *Vincennes Sun-Commercial*, March 29, 2018.

30. Sarah Silverman (@SarahKSilverman), Twitter, February 12, 2017.
31. "A Former NFL Player Is Accused of Destroying His Business to Make It Look like a Hate Crime Burglary," CNN, September 15, 2019, www.cnn.com/2019 /09/14/us/former-nfl-athlete-hate-crime-business-trnd/index.html.
32. "Kamala Harris: Violent Attack on Empire Star Is 'Attempted Modern Day Lynching,'" The Hill, January 29, 2019.
33. *The Late Show with Stephen Colbert*, February 1, 2019.
34. Adam Rutherford, "How to Argue with a Racist," The Voltaire Lecture, Humanists UK, May 24, 2019, YouTube video, www.youtube.com/watch?v=cYf -xNsIb2I.
35. Ibram X. Kendi, *Antiracist Baby* (New York: Penguin, 2020).
36. See Christopher F. Rufo (@realchrisrufo) at https://mobile.twitter.com/real chrisrufo/status/1366820252252733446.
37. Kendi, *How to Be an Antiracist*, p. 44.
38. Kendi, p. 47.
39. Kendi, p. 19.
40. Kendi, pp. 142–43.
41. Martin Sekkat, *How to Be an Antiracist Family: 25 Inspiring Tales about Racism to Read Together with the Kids* (Martin Sekkat, 2020).
42. Otegha Uwagba, *Whites: On Race and Other Falsehoods* (London: 4th Estate, 2020), p. 37.
43. Uwagba, pp. 38–39.
44. See the statement (posted by abigail_heringer) at www.instagram.com/p/CL LAuiwpzB_/?igshid=6yyor2fhsrcd.
45. "In an Emotional Finale, Bachelor Matt James Breaks up with the Winner over Racially Insensitive Social Media Posts," *Washington Post*, March 15, 2021.
46. "Chris Harrison Exits 'Bachelor' Franchise; Rose Withers on 19-Year Run as Host after Racism Controversy," *Deadline*, June 8, 2021.
47. "Anita Rani: My 'Brown Face' Could Have Stopped Me Reaching Strictly Come Dancing Final," *The Telegraph*, July 27, 2021.
48. "I'll Take 'White Supremacist Hand Gestures' for $1,000," *New York Times*, May 16, 2021.
49. Christopher F. Rufo, "Failure Factory," *City Journal*, February 23, 2021.
50. Christopher F. Rufo, "Woke Elementary," *City Journal*, January 13, 2021; Christopher F. Rufo, "Revenge of the Gods," *City Journal*, March 10, 2021.
51. Christopher F. Rufo, "Teaching Hate," *City Journal*, December 18, 2020.
52. Selim Algar and Kate Sheehy, "NYC Public School Asks Parents to 'Reflect' on Their 'Whiteness,'" *New York Post*, February 16, 2021.
53. Susan Edelman, "Bronx Educator Claims She Was Fired after Sharing Holocaust Story, Refusing 'Wakanda' Salute," *New York Post*, February 20, 2021.

54. Paul Rossi, "I Refuse to Stand by While My Students Are Indoctrinated," Bari Weiss Substack, April 13, 2021, https://bariweiss.substack.com/p/i-refuse-to-stand-by-while-my-students.

55. "'Woke' Principal of Elite NYC School Caught Ripping 'Demonizing' Curriculum," *New York Post*, April 20, 2021.

56. "Anti-Racism at Harvard-Westlake School," July 24, 2020, https://www.hw.com/pdf/Anti-RacismatHarvard-Westlake.pdf.

57. Bari Weiss, "The Miseducation of America's Elites," *City Journal*, March 9, 2021

58. Vernellia Randall, "The Whitest Law School Rankings," Race, Racism and the Law, March 8, 2021, https://racism.org/2021-law-school-rankings?showall=1.

59. Christopher F. Rufo, "Obscene Federal 'Diversity Training' Scam Prospers—Even under Trump," *New York Post*, July 16, 2020.

60. https://mobile.twitter.com/realchrisrufo/status/1299379197253541888?lang=en.

61. https://mobile.twitter.com/realchrisrufo/status/1290410612867047424?lang=en.

62. See https://mobile.twitter.com/realchrisrufo/status/1293605747394150401.

63. Chrissy Clark, "Revealed: Whistleblower Docs Show 'Big 4' Firm's Massive 'Anti-Racist' Indoctrination," *Daily Wire*, March 4, 2021.

64. Joseph Simonson, "Cigna's Critical Race Theory Training: Don't Say 'Brown Bag Lunch' and Be Mindful of 'Religious Privilege,'" *Washington Examiner*, March 19, 2021,

65. Paul Bond, "After Coca-Cola Backlash, LinkedIn Removes Diversity Lesson Telling Employees to 'Be Less White,'" *Newsweek*, February 23, 2021.

66. "Fury as KPMG Boss Becomes 'Latest Victim of Cancel Culture' after Being Forced to Quit over Video Telling Well-Paid 'Woke' Staff They Are 'Lucky' and Should Not 'Moan' during Pandemic," *Mail Online*, February 12, 2021.

67. Christopher F. Rufo, "The Wokest Place on Earth," *City Journal*, May 7, 2021.

68. https://nypost.com/2021/05/13/disney-scrubs-anti-racism-training-after-backlash-report/.

69. Afua Hirsch, "If Coronavirus Doesn't Discriminate, How Come Black People Are Bearing the Brunt?," *The Guardian*, April 8, 2020; Ibram X. Kendi, "What the Racial Data Show," *The Atlantic*, April 6, 2020.

70. The CDC report that generated the controversy is here: www.cdc.gov/vaccines/acip/meetings/downloads/slides-2020-11/COVID-04-Dooling.pdf.

71. Abby Goodnough and Jan Hoffman, "The Elderly vs. Essential Workers: Who Should Get the Coronavirus Vaccine First?," *New York Times*, December 6, 2020.

72. See Harald Schmidt, PhD, Lawrence O. Gostin, JD, Michelle A. Williams, ScD, "Is It Lawful and Ethical to Prioritize Racial Minorities for COVID-19 Vaccines?," *Journal of the American Medical Association*, October 14, 2020.

73. Abby Goodnough and Jan Hoffman, "Frontline Workers and People over 74 Should Get Shots Next, C.D.C. Panel Says," *New York Times*, January 14, 2021, www.nytimes.com/2020/12/20/health/covid-vaccine-first-elderly-workers.html.

74. Natalie Colarossi, "Vermont Under Fire for Distributing COVID Vaccine Based on Race," *Newsweek*, April 2, 2021.

75. Bram Wispelwey and Michelle Morse, "An Antiracist Agenda for Medicine," *Boston Review*, March 17, 2021.

76. American Medical Association, "Organizational Strategic Plan to Embed Racial Justice and Advance Health Equity, 2021–2023," www.ama-assn.org/about/leadership/ama-s-strategic-plan-embed-racial-justice-and-advance-health-equity.

77. Maria Godoy, "Is It Time for a Race Reckoning in Kidney Medicine?," NPR, December 28, 2020.

78. Akinyemi Oni-Orisan, PharmD, PhD, Yusuph Mavura, MS, Yambazi Banda, PhD, Timothy A. Thornton, PhD, and Ronnie Sebro, MD, PhD, "Embracing Genetic Diversity to Improve Black Health," *New England Journal of Medicine*, March 25, 2021.

79. Jake Miller, "Anti-Racist Epidemiology," Harvard Medical School, February 10, 2021, https://hms.harvard.edu/news/anti-racist-epidemiology.

80. Roni Caryn Rabin, "Huge Racial Disparities Found in Deaths Linked to Pregnancy," *New York Times*, May 7, 2019.

81. Tina Hesman Saey, "DNA Databases Are Too White, so Genetics Doesn't Help Everyone. How Do We Fix That?" *Science News*, March 4, 2021.

82. Damon Young, "Whiteness Is a Pandemic," *The Root*, March 17, 2021.

83. "Editor of JAMA Leaves after Outcry over Colleague's Remarks," *New York Times*, June 2, 2021.

84. See Cheryl I. Harris, "Whiteness as Property," *Harvard Law Review* 106, no. 8 (June 10, 1993), https://harvardlawreview.org/1993/06/whiteness-as-property/.

85. Uwagba, *Whites*, pp. 84–86.

86. Aruna Khilanani, MD, MA, "The Psychopathic Problem of the White Mind," a talk at Yale's Child Study Center, April 6, 2021. After some criticism, the talk was subsequently taken off Yale's platform, but a copy of the recording can still be heard here: https://bariweiss.substack.com/p/the-psychopathic-problem-of-the-white.

87. Donald Moss, "On Having Whiteness," *Journal of the American Psychoanalytic Association*, May 27, 2021.

INTERLUDE: CHINA

1. "Our Man in China," Damon Albarn interview with Bryan Appleyard, *The Sunday Times*, August 24, 2008.

2. National Center for Health Statistics, "Provisional Drug Overdose Death

Counts," *Vital Statistics Rapid Release*, updated December 15, 2021, https://www.cdc.gov/nchs/nvss/vsrr/drug-overdose-data.htm.

3. See Francis Pike, "Did Chinese Fentanyl Kill Michael K. Williams?" *The Spectator*, September 8, 2021.

4. IMF Direction of Trade Statistics, *The Economist*: https://twitter.com/mcpli/status/1416739704804888584.

5. Stephen Rand, "Danny Alexander's Surprising Second Act—in Beijing," *The Article*, July 1, 2020.

6. Clive Hamilton and Mareike Ohlberg, *Hidden Hand: Exposing How the Chinese Communist Party Is Reshaping the World* (New York: One World, 2020), p. 106.

7. Hamilton and Ohlberg, pp. 35–36.

8. Clarissa Tan, "Britain Has Many Problems—Racism Isn't One of Them," *The Spectator*, February 15, 2014.

9. Remarks by Ambassador Linda Thomas-Greenfield at a UN General Assembly Commemorative Meeting for International Day for the Elimination of Racial Discrimination, New York, March 19, 2021.

10. Remarks by Ambassador Linda Thomas-Greenfield at the 30th Annual Summit of the National Action Network, April 14, 2021.

11. "China Urges Relevant Western Countries to Tackle Racial Discrimination," *XinhuaNet*, July 13, 2021, http://www.xinhuanet.com/english/2021-07/13/c_1310059138.htm.

12. Ben Westcott and Steven Jiang, "Foreign Countries That 'Bully' China Will Meet a 'Great Wall of Steel,' Says Xi during Communist Party Centenary," *CNN*, July 1, 2021.

13. Dennis Sewell, "The Second Time as Farce: The Crimes of Communism, Retro-Bolshevism and the Centenary of the 1917 Russian Revolution," New Culture Forum, June 2016.

14. "Nearly Two-Thirds of US Young Adults Unaware 6m Jews Killed in the Holocaust," *The Guardian*, September 16, 2020.

CHAPTER 2: HISTORY

1. https://bariweiss.substack.com/p/the-psychopathic-problem-of-the-white.

2. Jennifer Chambers, "1619 Project Reframing History of Slavery Draws Crowd to Ann Arbor," *Detroit News*, January 28, 2020.

3. "The #1619 Project: A Conversation Nikole Hannah-Jones & Jake Silverstein from the NY Times Magazine," Chicago Public Schools, October 8, 2019, YouTube video, www.youtube.com/watch?v=Y8Y9qJUeSQ4&t=2540s.

4. Robby Soave, "Yes, the 1619 Project Actually Suggests That Year Was America's True Founding, and Nikole Hannah-Jones Admits It," *Reason*, September 23, 2020.

5. Jake Silverstein, "On Recent Criticism of the 1619 Project," *New York Times*, October 16, 2020.

6. See Josh Blackman "Which Is It? 1619 or 1776?," *Reason*, October 10, 2020.

7. Matthew Desmond, "In Order to Understand the Brutality of American Capitalism, You Have to Start on the Plantation," *New York Times*, August 14, 2019.

8. Caitlin Rosenthal, *Accounting for Slavery: Masters and Management* (Cambridge, MA: Harvard University Press, 2018), p. xii.

9. See also Phillip W. Magness, "The Case for Retracting Matthew Desmond's 1619 Project Essay," American Institute for Economic Research, February 11, 2020.

10. Nikole Hannah-Jones, "America Wasn't a Democracy until Black Americans Made It One," *New York Times*, August 14, 2019.

11. "We Respond to the Historians Who Critiqued the 1619 Project," *New York Times Magazine*, December 20, 2019, www.nytimes.com/2019/12/20/magazine /we-respond-to-the-historians-who-critiqued-the-1619-project.html.

12. Tom Mackaman, "An Interview with Historian James Oakes on the New York Times' 1619 Project," *World Socialist Web Site*, November 18, 2019, www.wsws.org/en/articles/2019/11/18/oake-n18.html.

13. Nikole Hannah-Jones (@nhannahjones) Exchange with Wesley Yang (@ wesyang), Twitter, November 21–22, 2019; Elliot Kaufman, "The '1619 Project' Gets Schooled," *Wall Street Journal*, December 16, 2019.

14. Adam Serwer, "The Fight over the 1619 Project Is Not about the Facts," *The Atlantic*, December 23, 2019.

15. Charles Kesler, "Call Them the 1619 Riots," *New York Post*, June 19, 2020.

16. Nikole Hannah-Jones (@nhannahjones), Twitter, June 20, 2020.

17. Eric Kaufmann, "The Great Awakening and the Second American Revolution," *Quillette*, June 22, 2020.

18. Ja'Loni Owens, "Moving the Jefferson Statue Is Not Enough," *Hofstra Chronicle*, June 29, 2020.

19. Frantz Fanon, *The Wretched of the Earth*, trans. Constance Farrington (New York: Grove, 1963), p. 7.

20. Fanon, pp. 11–12.

21. Fanon, pp. 14, 19.

22. Fanon, p. 27.

23. Fanon, p. 43.

24. Fanon, pp. 102–3.

25. Fanon, p. 163.

26. Fanon, pp. 195–96.

27. Fanon, p. 313.

28. Edward Said, *Orientalism* (New York: Vintage, 1979), p. 204.

29. Said, p. 6.

30. Jane Austen, *Mansfield Park* (London: Oxford World Classics, 1990), p. 155.

31. Edward Said, *Culture and Imperialism* (New York: Vintage, 1994), p. 112.

32. *Will and Codicils of the Rt. Hon. Cecil John Rhodes* (Oxford: Oxford University Press, 1929), p. 12.

33. See www.rhodeshouse.ox.ac.uk/about/the-mandela-rhodes-foundation/.

34. "Oxford University's Racist and Violent Attitudes Are Unacceptable: Qwabe," YouTube video, January 11, 2016, https://www.youtube.com/watch?v=hur EgLq1dsk.

35. "RMF to Protest at Oriel following Rhodes Statue Petition," *Cherwell*, November 7, 2015.

36. Paul Maylam, *The Cult of Rhodes: Remembering an Imperialist in Africa* (Johannesburg: David Philip, 2005).

37. Felix Gross, *Rhodes of Africa* (Westport, CT: Praeger, 1957), Introduction, p. vi.

38. Olive Schreiner, *Trooper Peter Halket of Mashonaland* (London: T. Fisher Unwin, 1897), p. 37.

39. Gordon Le Sueur, *Cecil Rhodes: The Man and His Work* (London: John Murray, 1913), p. 159.

40. I am especially grateful to Madeline Briggs of *The Poor Print* for her piece "Misinformation in the Rhodes Campaign," January 22, 2016.

41. The article can still be read on Gilley's personal website as well as online at the website of the National Association of Scholars.

42. See full text at https://theconversation.com/ethics-and-empire-an-open-letter -from-oxford-scholars-89333.

43. "Oxford University Accused of Backing Apologists of British Colonialism," *The Guardian*, December 22, 2017.

44. Nigel Biggar, "Vile Abuse Is Now Tolerated in Our Universities," *The Times*, April 10, 2018.

45. Quoted by Nigel Biggar in "Don't Feel Guilty about Our Colonial History," *The Times*, November 30, 2017.

46. Michael Nazir-Ali, "The C of E Has Fallen for Anti-Christian Theories of Race," *The Spectator*, May 1, 2021.

47. *Hansard*, July 8, 1920.

48. "Oxford Student Doesn't Regret Making 'White Girl' Waitress Cry," *Metro*, May 19, 2016.

49. Deneesha Pillay, "'UCT Protests Have Nothing to Do with #FeesMustFall,' Says Student Attacked by Stick-Wielding Activist," *Times Live* (South Africa), September 22, 2016.

50. Elizabeth Redden, "Students Burn Artwork, Vehicles in Escalation of U Cape Town Protests," *Inside Higher Ed*, February 18, 2016.

51. Kendi, *How to Be an Antiracist*, p. 39.

52. Kehinde Andrews, "The Racial Consequences of Mr. Churchill," Churchill College, University of Cambridge, available online at www.youtube.com /watch?v=wermPu-oG5w&t=2820s.

53. See the *2018 Global Slavery Index* published by the Walk Free Foundation, www.globalslaveryindex.org/2018/findings/global-findings/.

54. See Michael Taylor, *The Interest: How the British Establishment Resisted the Abolition of Slavery* (London: Bodley Head, 2020), p. xvii.

55. "Essai sur les Moeurs," in Voltaire, *Œuvres complètes*, ed. Louis Moland, 52 vols. (Paris: Garnier, 1877–85), chap. 197, pp. 177–78.

56. See Anthony Sullivan, *Britain's War Against the Slave Trade: The Operations of the Royal Navy's West Africa Squadron, 1807–1867* (London: Frontline Books, 2020).

57. See "Nelson Letter a Forgery," The Nelson Society: https://nelson-society.com /nelson-letter-a-forgery/.

58. Priyamvada Gopal (@PriyamvadaGopal), "I resist urges to kneecap white men every day," Twitter, February 5, 2019, https://twitter.com/priyamvada gopal/status/1093141557597880321.

59. Andrews, "The Racial Consequences of Mr. Churchill."

60. Andrew Roberts and Zewditu Gebreyohanes, "'The Racial Consequences of Mr. Churchill': A Review," Policy Exchange, 2021.

61. See Geoffrey Wheatcroft, *Churchill's Shadow: An Astonishing Life and a Dangerous Legacy* (London: Bodley Head, 2021). See also the review by Andrew Roberts, "Churchill as Villain—but Is This a Character Assassination Too Far?," *The Spectator*, August 14, 2021.

62. Najib Jutt (@NajibJutt) on Twitter: https://twitter.com/NajibJutt/status /1405583305039245315.

63. See Nabila Ramdani, "Voltaire Spread Darkness, Not Enlightenment. France Should Stop Worshipping Him," *Foreign Policy*, August 31, 2020.

64. Richard Toye, *CNN*, June 10, 2020.

65. See Andrew Roberts, *Churchill: Walking with Destiny* (London: Allen Lane, 2018), pp. 785–89. See also Andrew Roberts and Zewditu Gebreyohanes, "'The Racial Consequences of Mr. Churchill': A Review," Policy Exchange, 2021.

66. https://nabbosa.medium.com/black-history-month-part-1-uk-history-f822f 953591c.

67. https://eminetra.co.uk/historian-backs-canterbury-cathedral-for-keeping -statues-with-slavery-links/280997/.

68. https://order-order.com/2021/02/11/watch-khans-statue-advisor-yells-at-queen -and-threatens-to-punch-security/.

69. "Robert Milligan: Slave Trader Statue Removed from Outside London Museum," *BBC*, June 9, 2020.

70. Reuters, "Cambridge College Removes Suspected Slave Plantation Bell from View," May 8, 2019.

71. Gareth Harris, "Debate Flares as British Museum Moves Bust of Slave-Owning Founder Hans Sloane," *Art Newspaper*, August 25, 2020.

72. See Nigel Biggar, "Whites and Wrongs," *The Critic*, March 18, 2021.

INTERLUDE: REPARATIONS

1. www.un.org/WCAR/durban.pdf.
2. Mark Steyn, "The Slyer Virus: The West's Anti-Westernism," in *The Survival of Culture: Permanent Values in a Virtual Age*, ed. Hilton Kramer and Roger Kimball (Chicago: Ivan R. Dee, 2002), p. 123.
3. Tom O'Connor, "North Korea Calls U.S. Country of 'Extreme Racists' after George Floyd Protests," *Newsweek*, June 4, 2020.
4. See Brian Reynolds Myers, *The Cleanest Race: How North Koreans See Themselves and Why It Matters* (New York: Melville House, 2010).
5. Ta-Nehisi-Coates, "The Case for Reparations," *The Atlantic*, June 2014.
6. "Ta-Nehisi-Coates Revisits the Case for Reparations," *New Yorker*, June 10, 2019.
7. "Remaking of the British State: For the Many, Not the Few," a report produced on behalf of the Labour Party by Sean Patrick Griffin, 2021.
8. "Biden Backs Studying Reparations as Congress Considers Bill," AP News, February 17, 2021.
9. Christine Tamir, "The Growing Diversity of Black America," *Pew Research*, March 25, 2021.
10. Chaim D. Kaufmann and Robert A. Pape, "Explaining Costly International Moral Action: Britain's Sixty-Year Campaign against the Atlantic Slave Trade," *International Organization* 53, no. 4 (Autumn 1999): pp. 631–68.
11. ReNews event, "Journalism and History: Is the Narrative Being Co-opted by an Ideological Agenda?," April 8, 2021.
12. Jeff Flynn-Paul, "The Myth of the 'Stolen Country,'" *The Spectator*, September 26, 2020.
13. June Sarpong, *The Power of Privilege: How White People Can Challenge Racism* (New York: Harper Collins, 2020), pp. 84–85.
14. Rachel Weiner, "Arlington Prosecutor Promises Data-Driven Reduction in Racial Disparities," *Washington Post*, April 24, 2021.
15. Evan Nicole Brown, "Will It Take a Clever Acronym to Stop Racially Motivated 911 Calls?," *New York Times*, July 24, 2020.

CHAPTER 3: RELIGION

1. "US Commander in Afghanistan Investigates 'Burning' of Qur'ans at Base," *The Guardian*, February 21, 2012.
2. Matthew Rosenberg and Julian E. Barnes, "A Bible Burning, a Russian News Agency and a Story Too Good to Check Out," *New York Times*, August 12, 2020.
3. John McWhorter, "The Virtue Signalers Won't Change the World," *The Atlantic*, December 23, 2018, www.theatlantic.com/ideas/archive/2018/12/why-third-wave-anti-racism-dead-end/578764/.
4. Peter Martyr d'Anghera, *De Orbe Novo, the Eight Decades of Peter Martyr*

      d'Anghera, book 2 (1516), trans. Francis Augustus MacNutt (1912 ed.).

5.   Michel de Montaigne, *The Complete Essays* (New York: Penguin, 2003), p. 231.

6.   Montaigne, p. 236.

7.   Jean-Jacques Rousseau, *A Discourse on Inequality* (New York: Penguin, 1984), p. 68.

8.   Claude Lévi-Strauss, *Tristes Tropiques* (London: Hutchinson, 1961), p. 389.

9.   Allan Hanson, "The Making of the Maori: Culture Invention and Its Logic," *American Anthropologist* 91, no. 4 (December 1989), pp. 890–902.

10. Roger Sandall, *The Culture Cult: Designer Tribalism and Other Essays* (Boulder, CO: Westview, 2001), pp. vii–ix.

11. Naomi Klein, *No Is Not Enough: Defeating the New Shock Politics* (London: Allen Lane, 2017), p. 266.

12. Klein, pp. 224–25.

13. Klein, pp. 225–26.

14. Craig Simpson, "Immanuel Kant's 'Racism' Will Be Taught Alongside His Philosophy after Demand from Students," *Daily Telegraph*, December 19, 2020.

15. Matthew A. Sears, "Aristotle, Father of Scientific Racism," *Washington Post*, April 6, 2018.

16. Eric Hobsbawm, "Barbarism: A User's Guide," *New Left Review* 206 (July–August 1994), pp. 44–54.

17. Nabila Ramdani, "Voltaire Spread Darkness, Not Enlightenment. France Should Stop Worshipping Him," *Foreign Policy*, August 31, 2020.

18. Andrew Valls, "'A Lousy Empirical Scientist': Reconsidering Hume's Racism," in *Race and Racism in Modern Philosophy*, ed. Andrew Valls (Ithaca, NY: Cornell University Press, 2005), pp. 128–29. See also Kendi, *How to Be an Antiracist*, p. 249.

19. Jane O'Grady, "'Who Are You to Say That?': On Free Speech and Wokeness," *The Article*, July 19, 2020.

20. "Edinburgh University Renames David Hume Tower over 'Racist' Views," *BBC News*, September 13, 2020.

21. Caitlin Hutchison, "David Hume: University of Edinburgh Launches Review of Buildings Linked to Slave Trade," *The Herald*, February 16, 2021.

22. See esp. Georgios Varouxakis, "John Stuart Mill on Race," *Utilitas* 10 (1998): pp. 17–32. See also Georgios Varouxakis, "Empire, Race, Euro-centrism: John Stuart Mill and His Critics," in *Utilitarianism and Empire*, ed. Bart Schultz and Georgios Varouxakis (Lanham, MD: Lexington Books, 2005), pp. 137–53.

23. See, for instance, Brent E. Kinser, *The American Civil War in the Shaping of British Democracy* (New York: Routledge, 2011).

24. See esp. Georgios Varouxakis, "'Negrophilist' Crusader: John Stuart Mill on the American Civil War and Reconstruction," *History of European Ideas* 39, no. 5 (2013): pp. 729–54.

25. John Stuart Mill, "Contest in America," in *The Collected Works of John Stu-*

art Mill, vol. 21, ed. John M. Robson (Toronto: University of Toronto Press, 1984), pp. 141–42.

26. "Is the West Fundamentally Racist?," www.youtube.com/watch?v=XNOlY DjbUqo.

27. Kendi, *How to Be an Antiracist*, pp. 31–32.

28. Thomas Jefferson to Marquis de Chastellux, June 7, 1785, https://founders .archives.gov/documents/Jefferson/01-08-02-0145.

29. Karl Marx to Friedrich Engels, July 30, 1862, *Marx and Engels Collected Works*, vol. 41 (London: Lawrence & Wishart, 1984), p. 388.

30. Marx to Engels, August 7, 1866, *Marx and Engels Collected Works*, vol. 42, p. 303.

31. Marx to Engels, May 10, 1861, *Marx and Engels Collected Works*, vol. 41, p. 285.

32. Karl Marx, "The Russian Menace to Europe," *New York Tribune*, April 7, 1853.

33. Karl Marx, "The Russian Loan," *New York Tribune*, January 4, 1856.

34. Karl Marx, "On the Jewish Question" (1843), in *Karl Marx: Selected Writings*, 2nd ed., ed. David McLellan (Oxford: Oxford University Press, 2000), pp. 66–69.

35. Karl Marx, "The Future Results of British Rule in India," *New York Daily Tribune*, August 8, 1853.

36. Karl Marx, *The Poverty of Philosophy* (1847)(Moscow: Progress Publishers, 1955), pp. 49–50.

37. James Miller, "Karl Marx: Prophet of the Present," *New York Times*, August 6, 2019.

38. Matthew Campbell, "French Philosopher Michel Foucault 'Abused Boys in Tunisia,'" *Sunday Times*, March 28, 2021.

39. "Church of England Is 'Deeply Institutionally Racist'—Welby," *BBC News*, February 12, 2020.

40. See references to leaked document in Douglas Murray, "The New Religion of the Church of England," *The Spectator*, March 20, 2021.

41. Michael Nazir-Ali, "The C of E Has Fallen for Anti-Christian Theories of Race," *The Spectator*, May 1, 2021.

42. www.episcopalnyreads1book.com/bishop-dietsche.

43. See www.episcopalchurch.org/wp-content/uploads/sites/2/2021/04/RR-Racial -Justice-Audit-Report_ENG.pdf.

44. Deirdre Fernandes, "MIT Catholic Chaplain Forced Out after Message on Floyd Killing and Protest," *Boston Globe*, June 16, 2020.

45. "Head of B.C. Civil Liberties Group Under Fire over 'Burn It All Down' Tweet," *Global News*, July 5, 2021, https://globalnews.ca/video/8003774 /head-of-b-c-civil-liberties-group-under-fire-over-burn-it-all-down -tweet.

46. Heidi Matthews (@Heidi_Matthews), *Twitter*, July 3, 2021.
47. Gerald Butts (@gmbutts), *Twitter*, July 6, 2021.
48. Mallory Simon "Over 1,000 Health Professionals Sign a Letter Saying, Don't Shut down Protests Using Coronavirus Concerns as an Excuse," *CNN*, June 5, 2020.
49. Kehinde Andrews, "Racism Is the Public Health Crisis," *The Lancet*, April 10, 2021.
50. See www.thelancet.com/racial-equality.
51. "Tackling Systemic Racism Requires the System of Science to Change," *Nature*, May 19, 2021.
52. "Dismantling Racism: A Workbook for Social Change Groups," Kenneth Jones and Tema Okun, ChangeWork, https://www.dismantlingracism.org/, 2001.
53. https://equitablemath.org/.
54. See Jason To (@Jason_To), *Twitter*, June 9, 2021.
55. Mel LiFlora (@melliflora), *Twitter*, August 1, 2020.
56. Kareem Carr (@Kareem Carr), *Twitter*, August 1, 2020.
57. See James Lindsay, "2+2 Never Equals 5," *New Discourses*, August 3, 2020.
58. George Orwell, *1984* (New York: Houghton Mifflin Harcourt, 1983), p. 76.
59. Kareem Carr, Twitter, August 5, 2020.
60. See, for instance, Sophie Bearman's (@stbearman) post: https://twitter.com/stbearman/status/1356649178026233857?s=20.
61. Alison Collins (@AliMCollins), Twitter, October 13, 2020.
62. Ibram X. Kendi (@DrIbram), Twitter, September 19, 2019.
63. Randi Weingarten (@rweingarten), Twitter, July 6, 2021.
64. See Asra Q. Nomani and Glenn Miller, "Rallying to Protect Admissions Standards at America's Best Public High School," *Quillette*, September 23, 2020.

INTERLUDE: GRATITUDE

1. Fyodor Dostoyevsky, *The Brothers Karamazov*, trans. David McDuff (New York: Penguin, 2003), p. 769.
2. Dostoyevsky, p. 797.
3. Dostoyevsky, p. 820.
4. Friedrich Nietzsche, *On the Genealogy of Morality*, trans. Carol Diethe (New York: Cambridge University Press, 2006), p. 48.
5. Nietzsche p. 91.
6. Nietzsche p. 93.
7. Nietzsche pp. 93–94.
8. See Max Scheler, *Ressentiment* (New York: Schocken, 1972), p. 68.
9. Helmut Schoeck, *Envy: A Theory of Social Behaviour* (Indianapolis: Liberty Fund, 1987), p. 282.

10. See Roger Kimball, *The Rape of the Masters: How Political Correctness Sabotages Art* (New York: Encounter, 2003).
11. Roger Scruton, "My 2019," *The Spectator*, December 21, 2019.

CHAPTER 4: CULTURE

1. See Laurence Whistler, *Laughter and the Urn: The Life of Rex Whistler* (London: Weidenfeld & Nicholson, 1985), p. 113. See also Hugh Cecil and Mirabel Cecil, *In Search of Rex Whistler: His Life and His Work* (London: Frances Lincoln, 2012), pp. 40–51.
2. "Rex Whistler's Tate Britain Restaurant Mural Is 'Offensive,' Ethics Committee Says, Threatening Closure," *Art Newspaper*, December 7, 2020.
3. Marina O'Loughlin, "Restaurant: Rex Whistler Restaurant, London SW1," *The Guardian*, December 21, 2013.
4. Kate Brown, "Tate Britain Has Responded to Backlash over a Mural of Enslaved Children at Its Restaurant with a Statement Acknowledging Its History," *Artnet News*, August 4, 2020.
5. See "Remove the Racist and Harmful 'Pursuit of Rare Meats' Mural at Tate Britain's Rex Whistler," Change.org, www.change.org/p/tate-britain-remove-the-racist-and-harmful-pursuit-of-rare-meats-mural-at-tate-britain-s-rex-whistler?redirect=false.
6. Brown, "Tate Britain Has Responded to Backlash over a Mural of Enslaved Children."
7. The White Pube, "Fuck the Police, Fuck the State, Fuck the Tate: Riots and Reform," June 14, 2020, www.thewhitepube.co.uk/riots.
8. Diane Abbott (@HackneyAbbott), Twitter, August 5, 2020, https://twitter.com/HackneyAbbott/status/1290920584994594818.
9. Craig Simpson, "Chaucer Courses to Be Replaced by Modules on Race and Sexuality under University of Leicester Plans," *The Telegraph*, January 20, 2021.
10. Craig Simpson, "Fair Is Foul for Shakespeare as His Texts Are Deemed 'Racially Problematic,'" *The Telegraph*, May 21, 2021.
11. Amanda MacGregor, "To Teach or Not to Teach? Is Shakespeare Still Relevant to Today's Students?," *School Library Journal*, January 4, 2021.
12. Meghan Cox Gurdon, "Even Homer Gets Mobbed," *Wall Street Journal*, December 27, 2020.
13. British Library, "Provenance Research for Books in the British Library," www.bl.uk/help/guide-to-provenance-research-with-printed-books#.
14. Craig Simpson, "Exclusive: British Library's Chief Librarian Claims 'Racism Is the Creation of White People,'" *Daily Telegraph*, August 29, 2020.
15. Jack Malvern and Lianne Kolirin, "British Library Sorry for Linking Poet Ted Hughes to Slave Trade," *The Times*, November 25, 2020.
16. Nazia Parveen, "Kew Gardens Director Hits Back at Claims It Is 'Growing Woke,'" *The Guardian*, March 18, 2021.

17. James Wong, "Weeding Out Horticulture's Race Problem," *The Guardian*, June 14, 2020.

18. James Wong, "Other Arts Are Political, Why Not Gardening?," *The Guardian*, November 29, 2020.

19. Ed Wall (@eddwall), Twitter, December 12, 2020.

20. James Wong (@Botanygeek), Twitter, December 12, 2020.

21. "The Guardian View on Botanical Gardens: Inextricably Linked to Empire," *The Guardian*, April 2, 2021.

22. Sierra Bein, "Is It Time to Decolonize Your Lawn?" *Globe and Mail*, September 5, 2020.

23. Cathy Benedict, Patrick Schmidt, Gary Spruce, and Paul Woodford, eds., *The Oxford Handbook of Social Justice in Music Education* (New York: Oxford University Press, 2015), pp. 69, 70, 194, 199, 305, 282, 416.

24. "Weston Sprott Lays His Cards on the Table," *International Musician*, July 6, 2016.

25. Anthony Tommasini, "To Make Orchestras More Diverse, End Blind Auditions," *New York Times*, July 16, 2020.

26. "Black Artists on How to Change Classical Music," *New York Times*, July 16, 2020.

27. *NAAS Recommended Audition and Tenure Guidelines*, January 15, 2021, https://static1.squarespace.com/static/602d7bac7cb8834f84ebcef0/t/60f1 e593a5d32b6e4ddb2409/1626465683788/NAAS+Recommended+ Audition+and+Tenure+Guidelines+v.+01.15.21+%28Watermarked%29 .pdf.

28. Michael Andor Brodeur, "That Sound You're Hearing Is Classical Music's Long Overdue Reckoning with Racism," *Washington Post*, July 16, 2020.

29. The Baltimore Symphony Orchestra, Charter of the DEI Committee of the Board of Directors, March 26, 2021.

30. See György Ligeti, foreword to *African Polyphony and Polyrhythm: Musical Structure and Methodology*, by Simha Arom (Cambridge: Cambridge University Press, 1991).

31. "Musical Notation Branded Colonialist by Oxford Professor Hoping to 'Decolonise' the Curriculum," *The Telegraph*, March 27, 2021.

32. Jonathan Ames, "Royal Academy of Music Set to Decolonise Collection," *The Times*, May 24, 2021.

33. Ijeoma Oluo, *So You Want to Talk about Race* (New York: Seal Press, 2018), pp. 139–40.

34. Oluo, p. 143.

35. Oluo, p. 144.

36. Oluo, p. 146.

37. See Oliver Soden, *Michael Tippett: The Biography* (London: Weidenfeld & Nicholson, 2019), p. 216.

38. Soden, p. 499.

39. Mark Swed, "Daring to Ask the Big Questions," *Los Angeles Times*, January 24, 2000.

40. See, for instance, Neil Jackson, *Japan and the West: An Architectural Dialogue* (London: Lund Humphries, 2019).

41. See Henry-Louis de La Grange, *Gustav Mahler: A New Life Cut Short (1907–1911)* (New York: Oxford University Press, 2008), pp. 211, 700.

42. Benjamin Britten, *Letters from a Life: Selected Letters and Diaries of Benjamin Britten, vol. 2, 1939–1945*, ed. Donald Mitchell and Philip Reed (Berkeley: University of California Press, 1991), pp. 921–27.

43. Benjamin Britten, *Letters from a Life: The Selected Letters of Benjamin Britten, vol. 4, 1952–1957*, ed. Philip Reed, Mervyn Cooke, and Donald Mitchell (Woodbridge: Boydell & Brewer, 2008), p. 385.

44. Britten, vol. 4, p. 388.

CONCLUSION

1. Alex Horton, "Top U.S. Military Leader: 'I Want to Understand White Rage. And I'm White,'" *Washington Post*, June 23, 2021.

2. Olivia B. Waxman, "'Critical Race Theory Is Simply the Latest Bogeyman.' Inside the Fight Over What Kids Learn about America's History," *Time*, June 24, 2021.

3. Isaac Kamola, "Where Does the Bizarre Hysteria about 'Critical Race Theory' Come From? Follow the Money!," *Inside Higher Ed*, June 3, 2021.

4. Michelle Goldberg, "The Maddening Critical Race Theory Debate," *New York Times*, June 28, 2021.

5. Julia Carrie Wong, "From Viral Videos to Fox News: How Rightwing Media Fueled the Critical Race Theory Panic," *The Guardian*, June 30, 2021.

6. *The ReidOut*, MSNBC, June 21, 2021.

7. "Marc Lamont Hill Interviews Key Opponent of Critical Race Theory—BNC News," *Bright News*, May 25, 2021, www.brightnews.com/marc-lamont-hill-interviews-key-opponent-of-critical-race-theory-bnc-news/.

8. Neli Esipova, Anita Pugliese, and Julie Ray, "More Than 750 Million Worldwide Would Migrate If They Could," *Gallup*, December 10, 2018.

9. *Ethnic Studies Model Curriculum, Chapter 5: Lesson Resources*, approved by the State Board of Education on March 18, 2021, www.cde.ca.gov/ci/cr/cf/documents/apr2021esmcch5.docx.

10. Tara Bahrampour, "Census Data Shows Widening Diversity: Number of White People Falls for First Time," *Washington Post*, August 12, 2021.

11. Joy Reid, *The ReidOut*, MSBNC, September 20, 2021.

12. Bari Weiss, "Whistleblower at Smith College Resigns Over Racism," Bari Weiss Substack, February 19, 2021, https://bariweiss.substack.com/p/whistleblower-at-smith-college-resigns.

13. Robin DiAngelo, *Nice Racism: How Progressive White People Perpetuate Racial Harm* (Boston: Beacon Press, 2021), p. 11.

14. Rosie Pentreath, "English Touring Opera Drops Half Its Orchestra in Controversial Move, Citing 'Increased Diversity,'" *Classic FM*, September 13, 2021.

15. "Is the West Fundamentally Racist?," www.youtube.com/watch?v=XNOlY DjbUqo.

16. Thomas Chatterton Williams, *Self-Portrait in Black and White: Family, Fatherhood, and Rethinking Race* (New York: W. W. Norton, 2020), p. 76.

17. Williams, pp. 122–24.

18. Williams, pp. 128–29.

19. Williams, pp. 137–38.

INDEX

A is for Activist (Nagara), 37
Abbott, Diane, 127, 219
Abu Dhabi, United Arab Emirates, 253
academia. *See* colleges/universities
Achebe, Chinua, 110
activism, racism and, 37–39
Adebajo, Adekeye, 105
African American spirituals, 242–44
age of atheism, 264–65
age of empire. *See also* colonialism
    assessing ethics of, 108, 109–10
    assessing legacy of, 108
    botanical gardens linked to, 229–30
    country independence success after, 80
    merits and demerits of, 111–12
    payment for reparations, 147
    reparations for descendant victims of, 139–40
    school curriculum on, 84–85
Albarn, Damon, 65–66
Aleksandrov, Grigori, 78
Alexander, Danny, 70
Alexandria, Virginia, 93, 200
Allard, Brave Bull, 163

Allen, Jim, 153
Allen, John, 14–15
America-China bilateral summit, 76–77
American Civil War, 169–70
American Medical Association (AMA), 61
Amritsar massacre of 1919, 109, 111–12
Andrews, Kehinde, 122, 123, 171, 270–71
Anselm, Saint, 187
antidiscrimination laws, 17
Antifa activists, 45–48
antiracism, 39–44, 55, 61, 155–56, 201
Antiracist Baby (Kendi), 38
anti-Semitism, 136–37, 177–78
anti-Westernism, 66, 78–79, 97
apologies, ethics of, 142–43
Appleyard, Bryan, 65–66
Appomattox statue, 93
Arab slave trade, 114–15. *See also* slavery
architecture, 246
Aristotle, 165
Arizona Department of Education, 38

Arom, Simha, 236
art/artists, 213–20, 244–46. *See also* Whistler's mural
Aschenbach, Gustav von, 251
associative guilt, 62, 224–25. *See also* guilt
Atlantic slave trade. *See* slavery
Austen, Jane, 102
Austen, Ralph, 114
Australia, 2
Aztec gods, 265

Bachelet, Michelle, 76–77
Bachelor, The (television show), 49–50
Baghdad, Iraq, 261–62
Balinese Ceremonial Music, 250
Baltimore Symphony Orchestra, 234
Bamuthi Joseph, Marc, 234
barbarism, 105, 106, 158–59, 204
Barbary pirates, 115
Bathilda, Saint, 187
Belgium, 138
Bell, Derrick, 16–17
belonging, forms of, 3–4
Bengal famine of 1943–44, 126
Bevan, Aneurin, 123
BHR Partners, 71
Bible burning, 154
Biden, Hunter, 71
Biden, Joe, 140–41
Biggar, Nigel, 107–10
bigotry, 26, 130, 136, 192, 210, 229
Birmingham, Alabama, 93
bitterness, 210–11
Black, Jeremy, 171–72
Black History Month, 149–50
Black Lives Matter movement, 44–48, 74, 130–31
"Black National Anthem," 266
black people, enacting whiteness, 25

Blackwell, Ken, 41
Blake, Jacob, 56
Blinken, Anthony, 76
Bonilla-Silva, Eduardo, 20
Bougainville, Louis Antoine de, 157
Brentwood, Los Angeles, 54–55
British Library, 224–26
British Museum, 133
Britten, Benjamin, 250
Brothers Karamazov, The (Dostoyevsky), 203–4
Buffalo public schools, 52
Bush, George W., 41
Butts, Gerald, 193

California State Board of Education, 265
Cambridge University, 132–33
Cameron, David, 71, 72
Canada
   church burnings in, 192–93
   decolonizing public lawns in, 230
   Indigenous populations, 192–93
   McPhee, Colin, 249–50
   migration challenges, 2
   statue toppling and/or defacement, 131–32
   Truth and Reconciliation Commission, 193
Canagarajah, Nishan, 221
cannibal tribes, 158–59
capitalism. *See* Western capitalism
CAREN Act, 150
Castro, Fidel, 138
Catholicism, 191–92
Centers for Disease Control and Prevention (CDC), 59–60
Chapelle, Dave, 147
Charles V, king of Spain, 113
Chaudhuri, Nirad C., 110–11
Chauvin, Derek, 24, 28

Chen Guangcheng, 68
Child of Our Time, A (Tippett),
   242–44
China. *See* People's Republic of
   China
Chinese Communist Party (CCP).
   See also People's Republic of
   China
   buying up influence, 68–71
   Cameron and, 71, 72
   as China's ruling party, 67
   Marx statue donation, 175–76
   one hundredth anniversary of,
      77
   reining in political liberalism,
      67
   weaponizing Western
      weaknesses, 78
Chinese culture, 262
Chinese racism, 73–74
Chomsky, Noam, 126
Christianity
   church burnings, 192–93
   Church of England, 134, 184–88
   churches' presumption of guilt,
      192–93
   churches shifting with cultural
      tides, 183–84
   cultural assimilation of
      churches, 186–87
   declining church attendance,
      155, 190
   Episcopal Church, 188–91
   opposition to slavery, 187
   Roman Catholic Church,
      191–92
   withdrawing of, 155
Church of England, 134, 184–88
Churchill, Winston
   on Amritsar massacre, 112
   anti-Churchill sentiment, 122
   as antifascist, 122
   attacks on reputation of, 122–29

Bengal famine of 1943–44 and,
   126
   defacing statues of, 124–25
   Hitler and, 122
   McDonnell's views on, 126–27
   panel discussion on racial
      consequences of, 122–23
   racial allegations against,
      122–24
   Tonypandy events and, 127
   white supremacism accusations,
      125–26
Cigna, 56
Circus (film), 78
Civil Rights Act, 17
Civilisation documentary series, 8
Clark, Kenneth, 8
Clegg, Nick, 70
Coates, Ta-Nehisi, 39, 139–40, 141
Coca-Cola, antiracism training at,
   56–57
Colbert, Stephen, 34–35
colleges/universities. *See also*
   schools; *universities by name*
   admissions systems for, 199–201
   critical race theory and. *See*
      critical race theory (CRT)
   criticizing the West, 160–61
   decolonizing curriculums,
      220–21, 237–38
   decolonizing Shakespeare,
      221–22
   racially charged panic at, 31–33
   racism and, 16–17, 31–33
   self-audits on level of benefit
      from slave trade, 132–33
   using non-Western natives,
      160–61
Collins, Alison, 199–200
colonialism. *See also* empire
   Kew Gardens linked to, 227
   legacy of, 110–11
   reevaluation of, 108–9

Colston, Edward, 129, 186
Columbus, Christopher, 93–94, 157
"The Commission for Diversity in
    the Public Realm," 129–30
Communist Party of Britain, 175
Confederate monuments, 93
Cook, James, 132
Coon Come, Matthew, 137–38
Cooper, Andrew, 165
coronavirus/COVID-19 crisis, 44,
    58–59, 149, 184, 215, 268
corporate racism, 55–58
Corredera, Vanessa, 222
Coughman, Edawn Louis, 33
Crenshaw, Kimberlé, 16, 256, 257
critical race theory (CRT)
    academics who created, 16–17
    activist dimension to, 19, 52
    attributing power based on skin
        color, 20
    criticism of, 257–59
    defining racism, 20
    Episcopalians defining, 188
    "generalizing" about people, 23
    invisible racism, 17
    learning curve, 255
    as a movement, 18–19
    proponents of, 256–57
    Reid's views on, 257–58
    rules of, 17–18
    school board meetings on, 256
    shifting to mainstream, 20–21
    teaching of. See schools
    on whiteness as contagious,
        25–26
Critical Race Theory (Delgado and
    Stefancic), 18–19
cross-racial friendships, 267–68
Crozet, Julien Marie, 160
cultural admiration, 241–44
cultural approbation, 244–50
cultural appropriation, 239–41,
    244, 252

cultural inheritance, 252
Culture Cult, The (Sandall), 161

Dai Bing, 75–76
Dallas Morning News, 29
d'Anghiera, Peter Martyr, 158
Darwin, Charles, 177
Davidson, George, 54
Davis, Angela, 37
Debussy, Claude, 247
Declaration of Independence, 89
decolonization, 98, 148, 238
deconstruction/descontructionists,
    207–8
Dehghani-Taft, Parisa, 150
Delacroix, Eugène, 244
Delgado, Richard, 18–19, 52
Desmond, Matthew, 89–90
Deutsche Bank, 71
Deverell, Richard, 227–28
DiAngelo, Robin, 21–23, 267–68
Dietsche, Andrew, 188–89
"Dirt on Our Hands" (podcast),
    228
"Discourse on Inequality" (Rousseau),
    159
Dismantling Racism (Jones and
    Okun), 196–97
Disney, 57–58
Disrupt and Dismantle campaign,
    52
diversity quotas, 185, 268
Donohue, Kelly, 50–51
Dostoyevsky, Fyodor, 203
Douglas, John, 230
Douglass, Frederick, 177
Durban, South Africa conference,
    136–38
Dyson, Michael Eric, 22

East Side Community School, New
    York, 52
Edinburgh University, 168–69

education. *See* colleges/universities; schools
elite capture, 70
empire. *See* age of empire
Empire (television show), 34
employment. *See* workplace
Engels, Friedrich, 175–77
English Touring Opera, 268
Enlightenment, 10–11, 166–68, 171–72, 174. *See also* Western philosophers
Episcopal Church, 188–91
equality, 206–7
Equiano, Olaudah, 114
equitable maths, development of, 196–98
equitable medicine, 60
equity. *See* racial equity
equity toolkit, 38–39
Ernst & Young, 56

Fallon, Jimmy, 14
Fanon, Frantz, 97–99
Fees Must Fall campaign, 113
feminists, 3–4
Fentanyl, 66
Ferdinand of Aragon, 113
Ferrar, Nicholas, 225
Floyd, George, 24, 26–30, 37–38, 66
Fonteyn, Margot, 215
forgiveness, 141–43
Foucault, Michel, 181–83
Fourteenth Amendment (USA), 150
"Fuck Gentrification" march, 47

gamelan music, 250, 251
Gandhi, 187
Gardener, The (Tagore), 248
gardens, as racist, 226–30
Gates, Henry Louis, Jr., 272
gays, 3
Gebreyohanes, Zewditu, 126

generalizations, 23, 101, 149
genocide, 21, 23, 75, 105, 117–18, 204
Gilley, Bruce, 108–9
Gladstone, William, 176
Globe Theatre, 221–22
Goldberg, Michelle, 256–57
Gopal, Priyamvada, 122–23
Grace Church School, 53–54, 256
Grainger, Percy, 249
Grant, Ulysses S., statue of, 94
gratitude, 204, 210–12
Great Britain
    British Library, 224–26
    historical illiteracy of people of, 80–81
    Kew Gardens, 226–30
    migration challenges, 2
    National Curriculum in England and Wales, 84
    "National Trust" in, 9–10
    slave trade, 120–21
    statue toppling and/or defacement, 129–32
    West Africa Squadron, 120–21
Grier, Kelly, 56
Grynszpan, Herschel, 241–42
Guardian, The, 59, 216, 226–30, 256–57
guilt, 20, 58, 108, 120, 149–50, 192. *See also* associative guilt

Halloween costumes, cultural appropriation and, 240–41
Hamilton, Clive, 71
Handel, George Frideric, 238
Hannah-Jones, Nikole, 86, 91–92
Hanson, Allan, 160–61
Harris, Cheryl, 63
Harris, Kamala, 34
Harrison, Chris, 49–50
Harvard-Westlake School, Los Angeles, 54

health care, racial equity in, 58–62, 194

Herzog, Katie, 83

Hidden Hand (Hamilton and Ohlberg), 71

Hitler, Adolf, 122

Hobsbawm, Eric, 166

Hofstra University, 94–95

Holocaust, 117

Holst, Gustav, 248–49

Holst, Imogen, 250

Homer, 223

hooks, bell, 16, 61

horticulture, 226–30

Household Cavalry, 131

How to Be an Antiracist (Kendi), 39–40, 116, 167, 188–89

How to Be an Antiracist Family (Sekkat), 43

Howard, John, 7–8

Huddleston, Trevor, 187

Hughes, Ted, 225

Huitzilopochtli (Aztec god), 265

Hume, David, 167–69, 173

Hutton, Lauren, 161

identity politics, 3–4

implicit bias, 54

"Improver of the Race" medals, 73–74

In Pursuit of Rare Meats. See Whistler's mural

inanimate objects, 133, 266. *See also* statues

Indian subcontinent, 5–6, 13, 63, 117–18, 236, 261

Indigenous populations, 9, 23, 117, 163–64, 192–93, 227–28

individualism, 23, 53, 196

Ingres, Jean-Auguste-Dominique, 244

Inside Higher Education (journal), 256

institutional racism, 184–85, 189–90. *See also* racism

institutional whiteness, 48. *See also* whiteness/white identity

intersectionalists, 18

invisible racism, 17

Islamic State, 14, 118

Israel, 136

Italy, 70

Jackson, Jesse, 7

Jacksonville, Florida, 93

Jacksonville Light Infantry, 93

Jacob, John, 111

James, Matt, 49

Japanese lithography, 246

Jebreal, Rula, 14–15

Jefferson, Thomas, 94–95, 172–73

Jeopardy (game show), 50–51

Jim Crow laws, 144

Johnson, James Weldon, 266

Jolly, Liz, 224

Jones, Kenneth, 196–97

Jones, William, 111

JP Morgan, 71

justice, 60, 74–75, 85, 150, 185–86, 205. *See also* revenge

Kang Youwei, 73–74

Kant, Immanuel, 164–65, 173

Kendi, Ibram X.
  Antiracist Baby, 38
  Coates compared to, 39
  on defining "civilization," 8
  defining racism, 40–41
  How to Be an Antiracist, 39–40, 116, 167, 188–89
  How to Be an Antiracist Family, 43
  on Hume, 167–68
  imposing race into every conversation, 42–44
  on Jefferson, Thomas, 172–73

as MacArthur "genius"
fellowship recipient, 267
opposed to certain forms of
racism, 41
political prejudices of, 41–42
on racist abuse, 40
on slavery, 115–16
Stamped from the Beginning,
54–55
on standardized testing in
schools, 200
on Thomas, Clarence, 41
Kew Gardens, 226–30
Key, Francis Scott, statue of,
94
Khan, Sadiq, 124, 129–30
Khilanani, Aruna, 63–64, 83
King, Martin Luther, Jr., 15
Kirkconnell, Rachael, 49
Klein, Naomi, 162–64
Knussen, Oliver, 251
Kraus, Dan, 230
Ku Klux Klan (KKK), 31
Kuya, Dorothy, 176

Lal, Deepak, 264
Lamont Hill, Marc, 258–59
Lancet, The, 194
Lasso, Orlando di, 246
Lawrence, John, 111
Lawrence, Stephen, 130
learning. *See* colleges/universities;
schools
Lévi-Strauss, Claude, 159–60
liberalism, 171
"Lift Every Voice and Sing"
(ballad), 266
Ligeti, György, 236
Listener, The, magazine, 215
literature, racism in, 220–26
London Virginia Company,
225
Los Angeles, California, 94

Macdonald, John, 131
Macron, Emmanuel, 124
Madness of Crowds, The (Murray),
3
Mahler, Gustav, 247–48
Mandela, Nelson, 103–4
Mandela Rhodes Scholarships, 104
Mansfield Park (Austen), 102
Mao Zedong, 127
Maori people, 160–61
Marion du Fresne, Marc-Joseph,
160
Martin, Michel, 23
Marx, Karl
as anti-black, 176–77
as anti-Indian, 178
anti-Semitism of, 177–78,
179
correspondence with Engels,
176–77
defense of, 179–81
gravesite as place of pilgrimage,
175
on slavery, 179
statue of, 175–76
Marxism and Literature (Williams),
221
Marxist ideology, 99
Masani, Zareer, 110–11
mass migration, 2–3
mathematics, as inherently racist,
196
Maylam, Paul, 105–6
McDonnell, John, 126–27
McGill, Anthony, 233
McIntosh, Peggy, 18
McPhee, Colin, 249–50
McWhorter, John, 155
medical community, 194. *See also*
health care, racial equity in
Messiaen, Olivier, 249
Michigan State University, 32–33
Middle East, 5

Midsummer Night's Dream, A (Shakespeare), 222
migration challenges, 2–3
Mill, John Stuart, 169–70
Milley, Mark, 255
Moloney, Daniel Patrick, 191
monogenesis, 172, 177
Montaigne, Michel de, 158–59
Moore, Michael, 21
Moorish traditions, 246
Moss, Donald, 64
Mount Rushmore, 95–96
Mugabe, Robert, 79, 147
Muhammad, Zarina, 216
Mukerjee, Madhusree, 122–23
multiracial whiteness, 25–26. *See also* whiteness/white identity
Murray, Charles, 165
Murray, Douglas, 2, 3, 14–15
music, racism and
    black composers and, 234
    blind auditions, 231–33
    Canadian composers, 249–50
    classical music, 231–33
    cultural approbation vs. appropriation, 247–51
    diverse orchestras and, 232
    English Touring Opera, 268
    European composers, 247–49
    gamelan music, 250, 251
    Holst, Gustav, 248–49
    Mahler, Gustav, 247–48
    minority underrepresentation in orchestras, 231–34
    music notation systems and, 235–37
    opera, 233
Muslim community, 154–55
Muslim Empire, 113

Nagara, Innosanto, 37
Napier, Charles, 111

National Alliance for Audition Support, 233
National Curriculum in England and Wale, 84
national identity, 3–4
Native Americans' philosophy, 164
Nature (magazine), 194–95
Nazir-Ali, Michael, 111, 187–88
N'Diaye, Tidiane, 114–15
Negro spirituals, 242–44
Nelson, Horatio, 121
New Left Review, 166
new racism, 51, 63. *See also* racism
New York Post, 92
New York Times, 85–92, 180, 233, 256–57
New Yorker, 140
New Zealand, 118
Ngoasheng, Asanda, 148
Nice Racism (DiAngelo), 267–68
Nietzsche, Friedrich, 205–6
1984 (Orwell), 199
No Is Not Enough (Klein), 162–63
non-Western cultures, 9, 99, 101, 156–58, 162
noose sightings, 32–33
Norrington, Roger, 243
North Korea, 139
Nubia, Onyeka, 122–23

Oakes, James, 91
Obama, Barack, 24–25
Oberlin College, Ohio, 31–32
objective truth, 173
Odyssey, The (Homer), 223
O'Grady, Jane, 168
Ohlberg, Mareike, 71
Okun, Tema, 196–97
Oluo, Ijeoma, 239
"On the Cannibals" (Montaigne), 158
"On the Manner and Spirit of Nations" (Voltaire), 157

opera, 233
opioid war on America, 65–67
Organisation of African Unity, 138
Oriel College, Oxford, 104–6, 112
Orientalism, 100–101, 209–10
Orientalism (Said), 100
Orwell, George, 199
Osundairo, Abimbola, 34
Osundairo, Olabinjo, 34
Ottoman Empire, 118, 148
overrepresentation, 269
Oxford University
  anti-Rhodes campaign, 103–8, 112–13
  decolonizing music curriculums, 237–38
  Oriel College, 104–6, 112
  racism at, 109–10

Page, Ellen, 34–35
Pelosi, Nancy, 27, 34
People's Republic of China. *See also* Chinese Communist Party (CCP)
  America-China bilateral summit, 76–77
  anti-Westernism and, 66
  Belt and Road Initiative, 69–70
  concentration camps in, 67–68
  elite capture and, 70
  forced abortions in, 68–69
  human rights' abuses, 67–68, 74
  music notation system and, 235–36
  one-child policy, 68–69
  opioid war on America, 65–67
  treated as normal, 4
  Uighur Muslim minority, 67–68
  United Kingdom's relation with, 71–72
  on West as unqualified to pass moral judgment, 78–79

Xi Jinping, 67, 77
Xinjiang camp system, 69
Petraeus, David, 154
philosophers. *See* Western philosophers
polygenesis, 172, 177
Portland, Oregon, 45–48, 94, 154
postcolonial thinkers/writers, 97–103
Prince of the Pagodas, The (Britten), 250–51
Princeton University, 95
Prinsep, James, 111
public health, 194
Puente, Gabrielle de la, 216

quotas, diversity, 185, 268
Quran burning, 153–54
Qwabe, Ntokozo, 104, 112–13

race relations, 17, 24–25, 35–36
race science, 165
race traitors, 4
racial equality, 4–5
racial equity, 38, 53, 57–62, 199–200
racism. *See also* antiracism; critical race theory (CRT); institutional racism; new racism; systemic racism
  definition of, 20
  DiAngelo's view of, 21–23
  dismissing people based on skin color, 14–15
  double standards over, 181–82
  equity toolkit, 38–39
  as invisible, 17
  Kendi's definition of, 40
  in non-Western countries, 5–6
  in popular entertainment, 49–51
racist microaggressions, 40
Ramdani, Nabila, 167

Ramsay Centre for Western
　　Civilisation, 7–8
Randall, Vernellia, 55
Rani, Anita, 50
Reid, Joy, 257–58, 266
religion. *See* Christianity
religion of antiracism, 155–57
reparations
　　in America, 140–41
　　Britain's Labour Party and, 140
　　British government on, 145–46
　　Coates's views on, 139–40
　　for descendants of slave trade,
　　　　139
　　Durban Conference, 136–38
　　Episcopal Church and, 190
　　ethics of apologies and, 142–43
　　forgiveness and, 141–42
　　how much is enough, 147–48
　　passing on to heirs, 149
　　as politically credible, 140
　　questions to answer surrounding,
　　　　135
　　slave trade, 139, 145–46
　　wealth transfer and, 141–45
resentment (ressentiment), 204–6,
　　210
revenge, 99, 103, 150–51, 205–6,
　　208, 212. *See also* justice
Rhodes, Cecil, 103
Rhodes Must Fall campaign,
　　103–8, 112–13
Richards, Sophie, 227
Richmond, Advolly, 228
Rickey, Branch, 272
Roberts, Andrew, 126
Roman Catholic Church, 191–92
Rosenthal, Caitlin, 90
Rossi, Paul, 53–54
Rousseau, Jean-Jacques, 159–60
Roy, Tirthankar, 126
Royal Academy of Music,
　　238

Rufo, Christopher F., 55, 257–59
Runcie, Robert, 134
Rutherford, Adam, 37
Rwanda, 138

Said, Edward, 100–103, 157, 181
Salford University, 175
Sandall, Roger, 161–62
San Francisco, California, 94, 150
Santiago, Leyla, 96
Sarpong, June, 149–50
Sartre, Jean-Paul, 97–98
Scheler, Max, 206
Schmidt, Harold, 59–60
Schoeck, Helmut, 206
School Library Journal, 223
schools. *See also* colleges/
　　universities; critical race
　　theory (CRT)
　　board meetings regarding critical
　　　　race theory, 256
　　in Church of England schools,
　　　　185
　　classical music aid in, 232
　　Ethnic Studies curriculum, 265
　　racism in mathematics
　　　　instruction, 197–99
　　on racism issues, 52–55
　　religious education, 185
　　on slavery, 84–85
　　standardized testing, 199–200
　　State Board of Education,
　　　　California, 265
Schreiner, Olive, 106
Schumer, Chuck, 27
scientific research, 194–99
Scotland, 67
Scruton, Roger, 212
Seattle, Washington, 44–45
secularism, 10
self-abuse, 65
Self-Portrait in Black and White
　　(Williams), 271

Sen, Amartya, 126
Sentamu, John, 184
"Sermon of the Fifty" (Voltaire),
　157
Serra, Junipero, statue of, 94
Shakespeare, William, 221–23
Shaw, George Bernard, 213
Shaw, Jodi, 267
Silverman, Sarah, 33
Silverstein, Jake, 86, 87
Simkov, Isidor, 78
1619 Project
　comparing modern corporations
　　to slave plantations, 89–90
　corrections to, 91
　critiques of, 91–92
　defining America's independence
　　from Britain, 88–89
　Desmond's essay on, 89–90
　Hannah-Jones's introductory
　　essay, 86, 88–89
　New York Times launch of,
　　85–92
　pushback on, 86–87
　Silverstein's introductory essay,
　　87
skin color, 13, 15, 20, 144, 259–60,
　267–68
slavery
　Africans selling other Africans
　　into, 114, 120
　Americans' ignorance of history,
　　84–85
　Arab slave trade, 114–15
　Barbary pirates and, 115
　in Brazil, 118
　Britain's fight against, 120–21
　Christian faith's opposition to,
　　187
　Church of England's slave trade
　　involvement, 186
　as genocide, 116
　Kendi's views on, 115–16

Milligan, Robert and, 129
modern slave trade, 118–19
Muslim Empire and, 113
Ottoman Empire and, 118
reparations and, 139, 145–46
schools on, 84–85
Voltaire on, 120
West Africa Squadron and,
　120–21
white European slaves, 119
Sloane, Hans, bust of, 133
Smollett, Jussie, 33–35
So You Want to Talk about Race
　(Oluo), 239
social justice movement, 156
Somerset vs. Stewart, 89
Sorman, Guy, 181–82
South Africa, 103–4, 112, 136,
　148–49, 187
Soviet Russia, 78
Sowell, Thomas, 21
Sprott, Weston, 232
St. Catherine's College, 133
Stamped from the Beginning (Kendi),
　54–55
Standing Rock Sioux tribal council,
　163–64
Stanford University, 7
state of nature, 159, 160–61
statues, toppling/defacing/removal
　of, 93–96, 124–25, 129–32,
　175
Stefancic, Jean, 18–19, 52
Steyn, Mark, 138
Strange Death of Europe, The
　(Murray), 2
Strictly Come Dancing (television
　show), 50
Stupid White Men (Moore), 21
Sunflower, The (Wiesenthal),
　141–42
systemic racism, 189–90, 194–95.
　See also racism

Tagore, Rabindranath, 248
Tan, Clarissa, 73
Tate Gallery. *See* Whistler's mural
techno-racism, 138
Tezkatlipoka (Aztec god), 265
There Was a Country (Achebe), 110
Thomas, Clarence, 41
Thomas Jefferson High School for Science and Technology, 200–201
Thomas-Greenfield, Linda, 74–75
Thompson, Ayanna, 223
Time magazine, 256
Timpa, Tony, 28–30
Tippett, Michael, 241–44
Toulouse-Lautrec, Henri de, 246
Trémaux, Pierre, 177
Trudeau, Justin, 132
Trump, Donald, 95–96
truth, verifiable vs. "my truth," 174
Tsipras, Alexis, 147
Turn of the Screw, The (Britten), 250
Two Bears, Cody, 163–64

Uganda, 79
Uighur Muslims, 67–68
UN General Assembly, 74–75
UN Human Rights Council, 75–77
United Daughters of the Confederacy, 93
United Kingdom. *See* Great Britain
United States
  America-China bilateral summit, 76–77
  census, 13–14
  Civil War, 169–70
  Declaration of Independence, 89
  Fourteenth Amendment, 150
  historical illiteracy of people of, 81

  migration challenges, 2
  opioid war on, 66–67
  race relations poll, 24–25
  racist policing in, 26–30
  reshaping foundation of. *See* 1619 Project
  statue toppling and/or defacement, 93–96, 124–25
  as white-supremacist society, 25
  at World Conference against Racism, 136
universities. *See* colleges/universities; *universities by name*
University of Alabama, 93
University of Cape Town, 103
University of Indiana, 31
University of Leicester, 221
University of Liverpool, 176
University of Maryland, 32
University of Missouri, 32
US Constitution, 92–93
US Military Academy at West Point, 255
US National Center for Health Statistics, 66
Uwagba, Otegha, 43–44, 63

Vincennes University, 33
Voltaire, 120, 157, 166–67, 173

Wang Xisha, 71
Washington, George, statue of, 94
Washington Post, 165, 233, 266
Weingarten, Randi, 200
West, Nan, 214
West Africa Squadron, 120–21
West Point Academy, 255
Western capitalism
  Desmond's attack on, 89–90
  feminists' attacks on, 3–4
  Klein's views on, 162–63
  lifting people out of extreme poverty, 261

Marxist critique of, 85
as racist enterprise, 138
Western civilization/culture. *See
also* anti-Westernism
accomplishments in, 260–62
Andrews's views on, 270–71
appeal of non-Western cultures
to, 161–63
Athens pillar of, 165–66
critics of, 9
cultural approbation, 244–50
encouraging dialogue against
itself, 263
governing class in, 263–64
Jerusalem pillar of, 165
Kant's views on, 164–65
openness to ideas/influences,
230–31
as opposition to itself, 265–66
overturning, 270–71
respect for other cultures, 252
teaching of, 7–8
as unqualified to pass moral
judgment, 78–79
Western debt, 2
Western philosophers, 120, 157,
164, 167–70, 173. *See also*
Enlightenment
Western tradition, 8–11, 151,
156–57, 166, 180–83, 194
Whistler, Rex, 213–15. *See also*
Whistler's mural
Whistler's mural
call for removal of, 217–19
museum's response to racist
comments, 216–18
In Pursuit of Rare Meats as title
of, 213
Tate closing restaurant over, 215
Tate Ethics Committee review
and recommendation on,
215–16, 218
Tate Gallery commission of, 213

Tate trustees on, 219–20
White Pube, The, Instagram
account reporting on, 216–17,
218
white children, 38–39
white culture, out of step with
nature, 161–62
White Fragility (DiAngelo), 21–23,
24
White Pube, The, Instagram
account, 216–17, 218
white rage, 62–63, 255, 266
white suffering, 83
white supremacy, 53, 56, 197
white Western peoples
acceptable bigotry of, 136
accomplishments by, 260–61
demonizing, 13
DiAngelo's view of, 22–23
dismissed based on skin color,
14–15
giving up racialized privileges, 63
pushing back on permissible
bigotry, 267
as racists, 22
whiteness/white identity
black people enacting, 20, 25
college campus ranking system
for, 55
as contagious, 25–26
cultural appropriation and, 240
DiAngelo's view of, 22
as a disease, 25
equity toolkit and, 38–39
health disparities and, 62
as inherently racist, 23
as institutionalized, 48
learning from non-Western
cultures, 261
multiracial whiteness, 25–26
music education and, 231
as open to all people, 260
as a pandemic, 62

whiteness/white identity – *cont.*
  as parasitic-like condition, 64
  parents' toolkit, 52
  positive, 258–60
  problematizing, 256
  racial health disparities blamed
    on, 61–62
  Shakespeare and, 222–23
  teachers' challenging literature
    of, 223
  Uwagba on, 63
  white people relinquishing, 63
Whites (Uwagba), 43–44
white-supremacist society, 25
Whole Foods, 44–45
Wiesenthal, Simon, 141–42
Wilberforce, William, 187
Williams, Raymond, 221
Williams, Thomas Chatterton, 271
Winter, Colin, 187
Wong, James, 228–29
Woodrow Wilson School of Public
    and International Affairs,
    Princeton, 95

workplace
  confronting racism training in,
    57–58
  corporate racism, 55–58
  equity vs. equality, 57–58
  in-house racism training,
    55–58
  intersectionality workshops,
    55–56
  white supremacy awareness
    training, 56
World Conference against Racism,
    Racial Discrimination,
    Xenophobia and Related
    Intolerance, 136–38
World Trade Organization, 69
Wu Bangguo, 71

Xi Jinping, 67, 77

Yang Jiechi, 76

Zemlinsky, Alexander von, 248
Zimbabwe, 79

ABOUT THE AUTHOR

Douglas Murray is a bestselling author and journalist. His books include the *Sunday Times* No.1 bestseller *The Strange Death of Europe: Immigration, Identity, Islam* and *The Madness of Crowds: Gender, Race and Identity*. He has been Associate Editor at the *Spectator* magazine since 2012 and has written regularly there, as well as for other publications including the *Wall Street Journal*, *The Times, Sunday Times, Sun, Mail on Sunday* and *National Review*. A regular guest on the BBC and other news channels, he has also spoken at numerous universities, parliaments, the O2 Arena and the White House.